INTERNATIONAL YEARBOOK COMMUNICATION DESIGN 2013/2014
[Edited by PETER ZEC]

VOL 2

INTERNATIONAL YEARBOOK COMMUNICATION DESIGN 2013/2014

[Edited by PETER ZEC]

VOL 2

INTERNATIONAL YEARBOOK COMMUNICATION DESIGN 2013/2014

MULTIMEDIA SPECIAL

CLIPS ON DVD
EVENT DESIGN, INFORMATION DESIGN & PUBLIC SPACE,
CORPORATE FILMS, TV, FILM, CINEMA & ANIMATION,
INTERFACE DESIGN, MOBILE & APPS, GAME DESIGN,
SOUND DESIGN, RED DOT: JUNIOR AWARD

VOL. 2

006–015	**RED DOT: CLIENT OF THE YEAR** AUDI
016–073	**EVENT DESIGN**
074–089	**INFORMATION DESIGN & PUBLIC SPACE**
090–111	**CORPORATE FILMS**
112–139	**TV, FILM, CINEMA & ANIMATION**
140–187	**ONLINE WORLD** ONLINE COMMUNICATION ONLINE ADVERTISING SOCIAL MEDIA
188–225	**INTERFACE DESIGN**
226–273	**MOBILE & APPS**
274–283	**GAME DESIGN**
284–291	**SOUND DESIGN**
292–391	**RED DOT: JUNIOR AWARD**
392–437	**DESIGNER PORTRAITS**
438–463	JUNIOR DESIGNER PORTRAITS
464–513	**JURY PORTRAITS**
514–523	**INDEX**
524–531	**RED DOT – WORLD OF DESIGN**

INTERNATIONAL YEARBOOK COMMUNICATION DESIGN 2013/2014

VOL. 2

RED DOT:
CLIENT OF
THE YEAR

Red Dot: Client of the Year

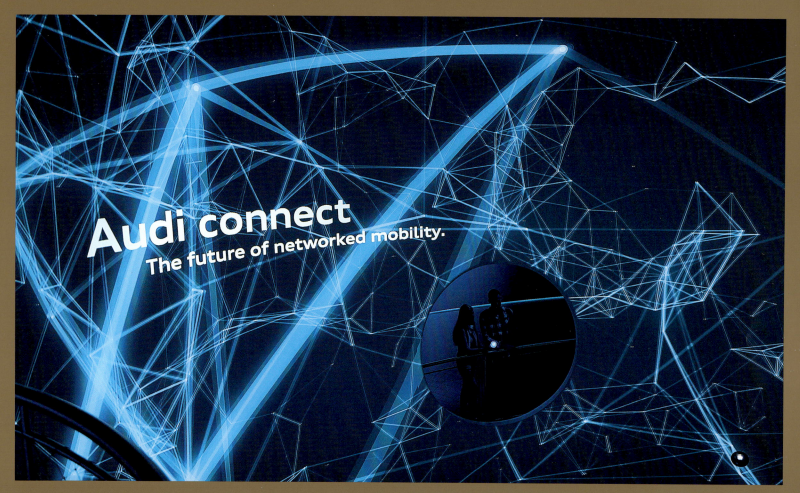

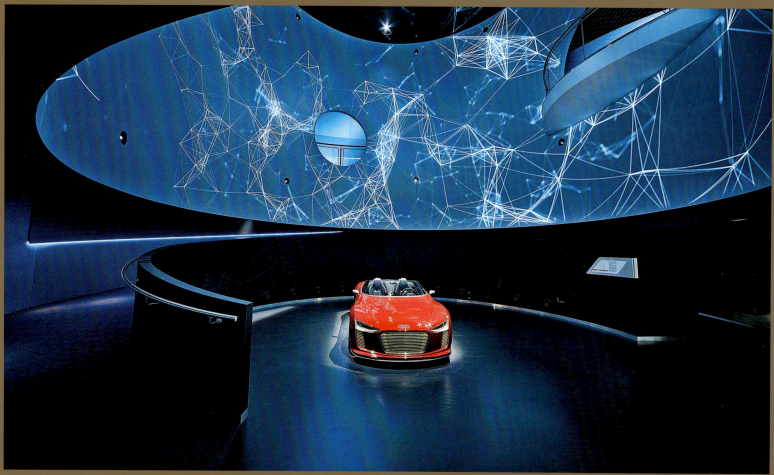

Red Dot: Client of the Year

THE AUDI UNIVERSE
DRIVE. MOVE. INSPIRE.

"A company is more than the sum of its products, and a car is more than the sum of its technical possibilities," says Luca de Meo, Member of the Board of Management for Marketing and Sales at AUDI AG. "To be successful, a brand has to fascinate. Primarily with quality, performance, service and sustainable stability of value."

At Audi, the direct driving experience is considered the key to captivating clients. Those who drive an Audi, regardless of the model, type of motor or build, will experience the superior quality, performance and efficiency of an Audi, and thereby be convinced of the brand's value.

To allow for this experience, Audi invests primarily in product design, complemented by communication and event design to further bolster the brand. Synonymous with premium quality and bold, progressive and dynamic design, the Audi brand is created and brought to life by various and diverse design firms. Together, the works of these firms are among the highlights of this year's Red Dot Award: Communication Design and earned Audi the title "Red Dot: Client of the Year" for the third time, following 2010 and 2011.

No other company was more successful in the year 2013. In all, the international jury awarded eight Red Dots to Audi. In addition, the jurors honoured Audi with the Red Dot: Best of the Best distinction for its presentation at the Consumer Electronics Show 2013 in Las Vegas.

We congratulate Audi for these exceptional achievements and hope to draw readers into the Audi universe with our feature of their awarded works on the following pages.

01 Audi Brand Pavilion, Wolfsburg
    Design by KMS BLACKSPACE, Munich
    Red Dot 2013, page 110–111

Red Dot: Client of the Year

02 AUDI AG Trade Fair Stand Consumer Electronics Show 2013
Design/concept by tisch13 GmbH, Munich
Red Dot: Best of the Best 2013, page 20–21

Red Dot: Client of the Year

Red Dot: Client of the Year

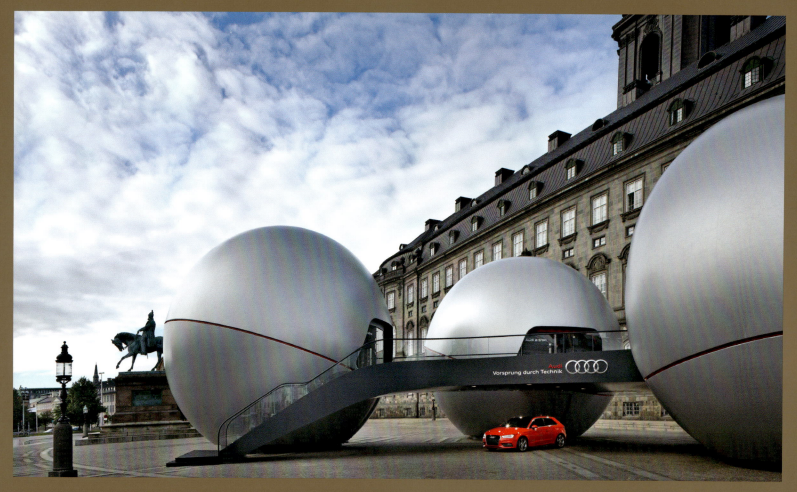
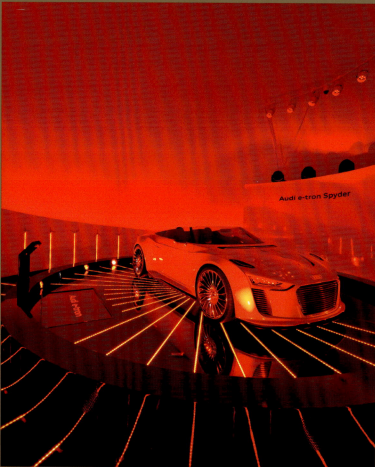

Red Dot: Client of the Year

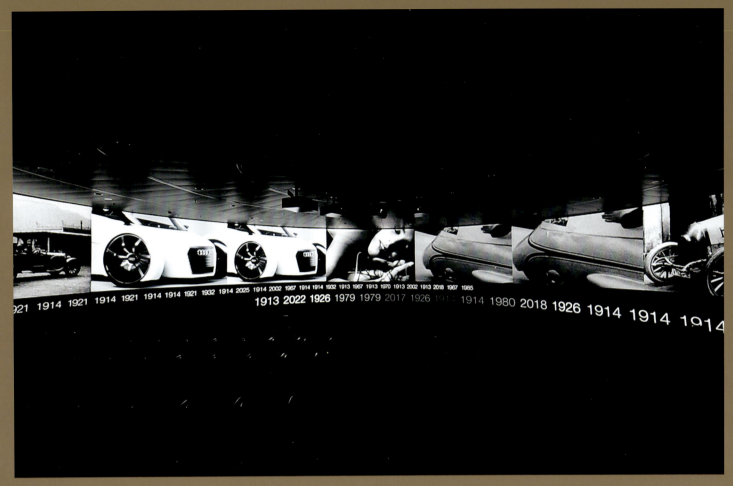

04

AUDI
Event Design

The successful positioning of the Audi brand requires a solid promise to deliver while also speaking to the emotions.

The company lives up to its famous promise "Vorsprung durch Technik", meaning the technical edge that leads to a leading position, through its three main brand values: exceptional quality, vitality and cutting-edge design. The manufacturing of the products as well as the communication about those products are oriented towards these values – everywhere and at all times. In its desire to fascinate clients, the company recognises the crucial importance of design. It implements event design, for example, to provide clients with lively and interactive experiences of the latest models.

Among these events were the Consumer Electronics Show 2013 in Las Vegas and the Audi Brand Pavilion in the Autostadt in Wolfsburg, where a sophisticated use of light and dark achieved a powerful effect. At this venue, the brand also proved its forerunner role with regard to its integration of LED light technology based on a concept that is as expressive as it is simple. In order to fascinate, Audi creates situations where clients can have positive experiences and impresses with high-quality exhibitions in Europe's major cities. In Copenhagen, for example, the temporary exhibition "Audi Sphere" gave a preview of the mobility of the future.

Interactive exhibits allowed visitors to experience the Audi themes in a playful way. Among others, for example, the "Audi e-tron" family was presented by means of a staged wind park and an "e-tron" vehicle placed in the centre of the space. And, to promote its new "Audi ultra" lightweight technology, a mobile negative scanner circulated around a space frame of a vehicle placed in the centre of the room and gradually completed the image until viewers saw the finished vehicle.

A further impressive video installation is situated at the Audi Museum in Ingolstadt. Visitors are taken on a remarkable journey through a historical time stream across a 180-degree panorama screen – 30 metres in length and 4 metres in height – and a 7.1 surround sound installation.

03 Audi Sphere, Copenhagen 2012
    Design by SCHMIDHUBER, Munich,
    KMS BLACKSPACE, Munich
    Red Dot 2013, page 26–27

04 Audi Tradition – Museum Mobile
    Design/concept by velvet mediendesign GmbH, Munich
    Red Dot 2013, page 108–109

AUDI
Digital & Mobile Media

With the Internet becoming ever more widespread as a means of communication, so are product apps for smartphones and tablet PCs. The most popular product apps are product catalogues in e-format, offering integrated product videos, individualised configuration options and connectivity to social media.

Audi seeks to provide existing and potential clients with an interactive experience of models and services, be it through tablet-optimised websites or individually programmed apps. Of course, smartphones and tablet computers cannot replace the real experience of driving. However, the new devices are getting better and better at offering virtual product experiences and complementary services.

In addition to the factual information they provide, these digital media are also designed to facilitate the purchase decision process. In fact, the main priority of the overall digital service offer is to support potential clients and to allow them to experience the products and the brand through their mobile devices.

Nowadays, companies like Audi maintain constant and consistent contact with their clients through a wide range of communication channels, ranging from company websites to social media offers and personalised customer service and support.

As new tools in the toolbox, smartphones and tablet computers have significantly accelerated that communication, be it at home or on the road. These tools are also widely used by the younger generation as a means to link to their social network and exchange with friends.

Designed to benefit from these developments in digital and mobile media, the "Audi car chat" invites Internet users to configure their preferred Audi model down to the smallest details and to invite their Facebook friends to chat about their choices.

05 Audi Le Mans Experience – Paris Motor Show 2012
    Design by KMS BLACKSPACE, Munich
    Red Dot 2013, page 185

Red Dot: Client of the Year

06 myAudi Mobile Assistant
    Design by Razorfish GmbH
    Red Dot 2013, page 240

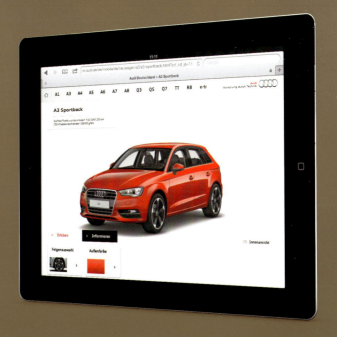

07 Audi car chat
    Design by Andreas Kraft, Das Büro am Draht, Berlin
    Red Dot 2013, page 184

08 Audi Website
    Design by SapientNitro, Cologne
    Red Dot 2013, page 241

INTERNATIONAL YEARBOOK COMMUNICATION DESIGN 2013/2014

VOL. 2

EVENT DESIGN

| Event Design | Information Design & Public Space | Corporate Films | TV, Film, Cinema & Animation | Online World |

Red Dot: Grand Prix

The Soul of Rubber
[Exhibition]

The exhibition "The Soul of Rubber" centres on rubber as a material and relates to its industrial uses as well as to Pirelli's research and development through clothing and advertising. From the beginning of the 20th century to the present day, it covers the entire history of the company in the field of fashion and the accompanied changes in Italian society. A virtual ball serves as the signifier of rubber's own essence and is reminiscent of the very ancient origins of its use. The design is conceived as a single video sculpture and features a ball that bounces in every direction, playing with perceptions and triggering events that animate the walls, floor and ceilings. The exhibition starts in a long corridor with extrusions that form a kind of playground for the virtual rubber ball. And it ends with an interactive installation where visitors can play with the ball, now projected onto the floor, until it is sucked back onto the wall to trigger images of a dreamlike world populated with characters to which it transmits its properties.

Statement by the jury

»The exhibition presents the heritage of Pirelli in an approach that is both entertaining and plain in its use of authentic images and posters from all decades. The key focus is a ball that keeps reappearing throughout the exhibition, inviting visitors to play. This interactive aspect is further underlined by the fact that all four dimensions are covered and that, alongside the floor and walls, the concept even includes the ceiling.«

Interface Design   Mobile & Apps   Game Design   Sound Design   Red Dot: Junior Award   Designer Portraits

client
Fondazione Pirelli,
Milan

design
N!03 srl,
Milan

graphic design
LeftLoft

exhibition stand construction
Allestimenti Benfenati

technical direction
Federico Colletta,
CO3 Progetti

→ clip on DVD
→ designer portrait: p. 423

reddot design award
grand prix 2013

| Event Design | Information Design & Public Space | Corporate Films | TV, Film, Cinema & Animation | Online World |

Red Dot: Best of the Best

AUDI AG Trade Fair Stand Consumer Electronics Show 2013

The idea of the Audi stand at CES 2013 in Las Vegas was to stage the premium car manufacturer as visionary in lighting technology, conveyed in a spatial experience that was defined by light. Experiencing light also means knowing darkness, as exemplified by driving at night when cones of light slice through the blackness. This notion gave birth to the basic architectural concept of a cubistic black box, cut into a dynamic light-space by tapering cones of light. Audi, a symbolic light source, presented a beaming space. A total of 2,600 fluorescent lights were mounted behind special wall and ceiling membranes, uniformly diffusing and distributing light without a recognisable indication of its source, an effect that pulled in visitors from afar. Spaces of complete darkness served to exhibit the revolutionary lighting technology, contrasting the main space. This exciting interplay of light and darkness made the stand become a visual experience, meant as a stage to express Audi's innovative strengths in a fascinating and engaging way.

Statement by the jury

»The work convinces with its simplicity of presenting the Audi models in a tunnel of black and white, light and darkness. Audi thus claims light, which always gives some kind of a positive attitude – light is about the future. It is daring to see a car manufacturing company at a consumer electronics fair, because such a fair is a different world.«

Interface Design   Mobile & Apps   Game Design   Sound Design   Red Dot: Junior Award   Designer Portraits

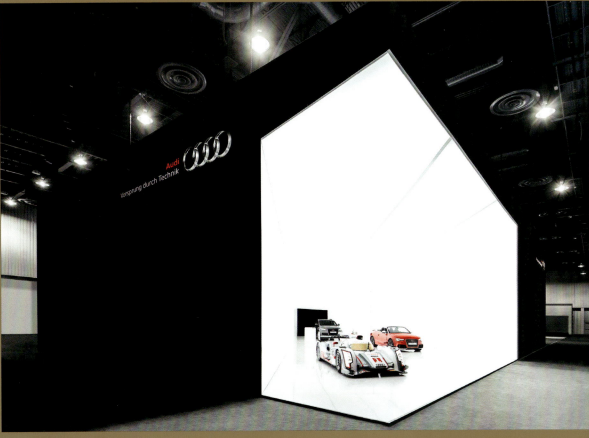

client
AUDI AG,
Ingolstadt

design/concept
tisch13 GmbH,
Munich

creative direction
Carsten Röhr

art direction
Melanie Molnar,
Claudius Gagalka

project management
Michaela Ganter

architecture
Bathke Geisel Architekten

→ designer portrait: p. 436

Red Dot: Best of the Best

Jordan Brand – Melo M8 Sneaker
[Pop-up Installation]

This interactive pop-up installation was created to launch the New York Knick's basketball star Carmelo Anthony's new M8 Jordan Brand sneaker. It was inspired by the star himself and fully immerses the visitor into his life. The exterior of the installation mimics Anthony's outstanding athletic talent and performance on court, displayed by the shattered and diverging basketball floorboards. Apparel and Melo M8 sneakers, specifically engineered to support his unique play, hang throughout the devastation of planks where its technological advancements are showcased alongside original quotes. Anthony's calm demeanour off the court can be experienced inside the installation where two concave white walls display digital footage speaking about what drives and inspires this athlete. The interactive experience thus conveys the artistry of the athlete and his on-court fiery range of motions, and in doing so, it conveys the potential of the new sneakers in a strong and convincing manner.

Statement by the jury

»This pop-up installation impresses with the simplicity in visualising the idea that it was the enormous energy of basketball player Carmelo Anthony that made the basketball court floorboards shatter. The athlete's talent and temperament are further elucidated on video walls on the inside of the installation, effectively rounding off the cleverly staged concept.«

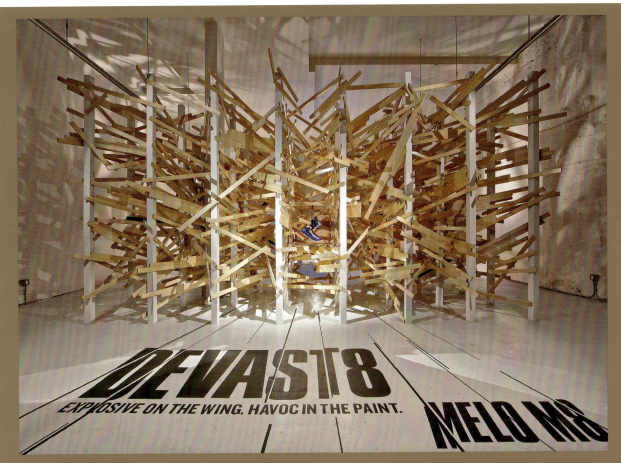

client
Nike Inc.,
Beaverton, Oregon

design
Eight Inc.

→ designer portrait: p. 404

Event Design | Information Design & Public Space | Corporate Films | TV, Film, Cinema & Animation | Online World

Porsche Pavilion
[Exhibition Pavilion]

The exhibition concept of the Porsche Pavilion in the Autostadt in Wolfsburg stages and combines the notions of evolutionary continuity, the art of car engineering and the fascination of sports cars into an impressive image and an immersive spatial experience. The Original Porsche is the starting point for a swarm of 25 silver-coloured vehicle models at a scale of 1:3. This swarm flows dynamically into the room and symbolically embodies the evolution of the Porsche car series and racing cars.

client
Dr. Ing. h.c. F. Porsche AG, Stuttgart

design
hg merz architekten museumsgestalter, Stuttgart
jangled nerves, Stuttgart

creative direction
Prof. HG Merz,
Prof. Thomas Hundt,
Ingo Zirngibl

graphic design
Heiko Geiger,
Christian Stindl

project management
Markus Betz,
Jochen Zink

film direction
Marc Schleiss

animation
Jörg Stierle,
Marcel Michalski

architecture
HENN Architekten

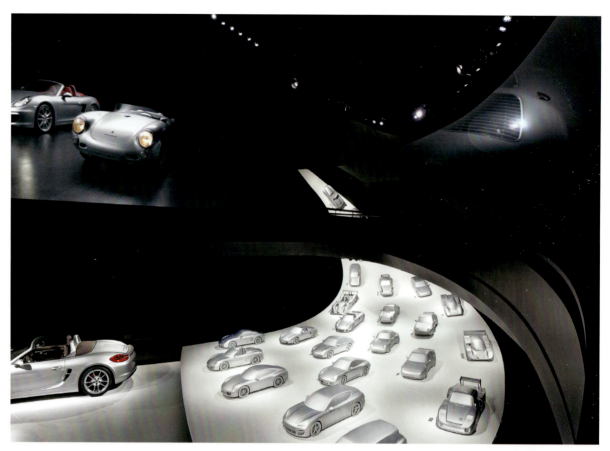
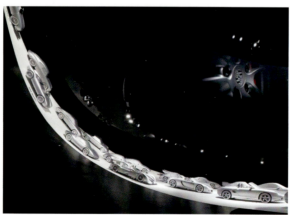

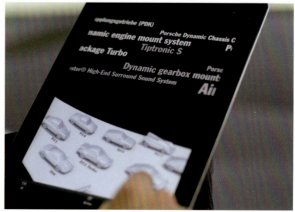

Mercedes-Benz Trade Fair Stand Detroit Auto Show 2013

At the Detroit Auto Show, Mercedes-Benz presented five models of the new E-Class. A central grandstand staged the entrance to the stand and allowed visitors an elevated view of this world premiere. The silver, polygonal "brand ribbon", typical of the trade fair architecture of Mercedes-Benz, formed a seamless transition into a ceiling-high LED display. A brand film transformed the stand into an external urban scene that captures the dynamics of driving. Time-lapse techniques, trick layering, music and lighting were combined to create an immersive brand experience.

client
Daimler AG, Stuttgart

design
jangled nerves, Stuttgart

creative direction
Prof. Thomas Hundt, Ingo Zirngibl

art direction
Jörg Stierle, Kristian Labusga, Heiko Geiger

graphic design
Gerd Häußler

project management
Jakob Eckert

film direction
Marc Schleiss

exhibition architecture
Sophia Maier, Thomas Sachs

Event Design | Information Design & Public Space | Corporate Films | TV, Film, Cinema & Animation | Online World

Audi Sphere, Copenhagen 2012

[Roadshow]

This roadshow crossover event visited several European cities with the aim of providing a broad public with answers to issues of sustainable mobility in the future and creating a special experience of the Audi brand core statement "Vorsprung durch Technik" (advancement through technology). Consisting of spatial presentations in connection with interactive exhibits, it brought the technologies developed by Audi to life. The theme of lightweight construction was embodied by three textile, air-filled globes that also served as walk-in exhibits.

client
AUDI AG,
Ingolstadt

design
SCHMIDHUBER,
Munich
KMS BLACKSPACE,
Munich

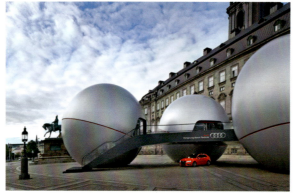

Audi Sphere, Copenhagen 2012
[Media Display]

The temporary exhibition "Audi Sphere" in Copenhagen provided insight into the sustainable mobility of the future, with interactive installations that allowed the Audi themes to be experienced playfully. The "Audi e-tron" was visualised through a wind power plant and an e-tron vehicle placed in the middle of the room. For "Audi ultra", a movable negative scanner revolved around a space frame at the centre of the room, completing the picture of the space frame to create an entire vehicle.

client
AUDI AG,
Ingolstadt

design
KMS BLACKSPACE,
Munich

→ designer portrait: p. 416

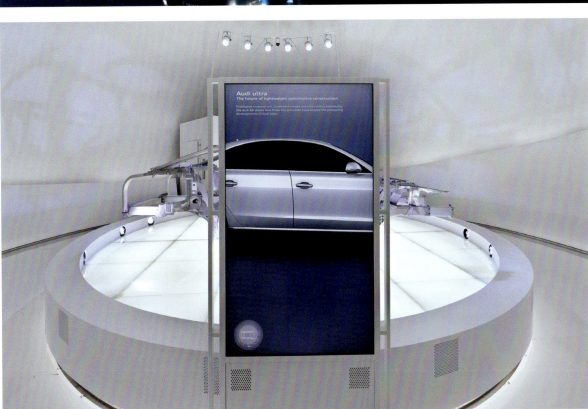

| Event Design | Information Design & Public Space | Corporate Films | TV, Film, Cinema & Animation | Online World |

BMW – The Target
[Trade Fair Presentation]

Taking the notion of a "target" as a metaphor, this trade fair stand aims to convey that the BMW 3 Series represents sportiness and holds the top position in its segment. The vehicle placement and stand architecture symbolise the BMW 3 Series Sedan "crossing a finishing line" within the context of other sports personalities and categories: different vehicle lines are positioned behind and above each other along three tracks and are aligned with a centred target projected in the stage background.

client
BMW AG,
Munich

marketing management
Manfred Pernitsch,
Wolfram Greiner,
Alexandra Karg,
Jörg Heine

design/lead agency
Mutabor Design GmbH,
Hamburg
gate.11 GmbH,
Munich

creative direction
Christian Dworak,
Christian Künstler,
Oliver Dering,
Conny Krause,
Arnd Buss von Kuk

art direction
Lennard Niemann

customer advisory service
Anne Wolkodaw,
Anja Neumann

architecture
Britta Henkel,
Anna-Liska Wallner

design team
Wanjo Koch,
Stefan Mückner,
Moritz Lenhart

Sympatex Trade Fair Stand ISPO 2013

The concept of this fair stand is to present the company SympaTex at the ISPO 2013 as open, communicative and transparent. The main element is the concave curved picture wall which communicates the core competence of SympaTex conveying the corporate design to architecture. The typical layer technology appears in all fields of the design. The shape chosen for the rear wall provides discreet storage space behind the curved side wings. As an add-on and special highlight the display "Target CO" emphasises the main issue of SympaTex focusing on carbon-free textile production.

client
Sympatex Technologies GmbH, Munich

head of marketing
Beate Hoerl

design
BUERO PHILIPP MOELLER, Munich

creative direction/photography
INK corporated GmbH & Co.KG, Munich

project management
Zweiplan GmbH, Munich

| Event Design | Information Design & Public Space | Corporate Films | TV, Film, Cinema & Animation | Online World |

Siemens Trade Fair Stand IFA 2012

The Siemens trade fair stand at the IFA 2012 in Berlin combined around 500 products into one brand universe. The central performance element consisted of a "ShowFrame" that structured the stand into distinctively themed zones, each presenting a different home appliance product. The exterior or front of this fair trade stand acted as an animated showcase, entertaining visitors with product-related pictures and presentations. Additional product experiences were offered by allowing visitors to virtually "clean stains" or "sort dishes" via a touchscreen.

client
BSH Bosch und Siemens Hausgeräte GmbH, Munich

design
SCHMIDHUBER, Munich
KMS BLACKSPACE, Munich

→ clip on DVD

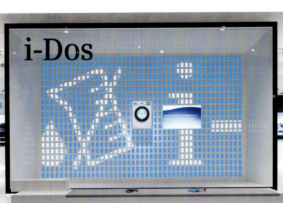

Siemens Home Appliances Trade Fair Stand IFA 2012
[Interactive Installations]

This trade fair stand at the IFA 2012 presented the topic of "integrated system intelligence" in a series of interactive installations. Oversized show frames staged one product each while the front of each frame served as an animated shop window to show off the product features. The "warmth" show frame, for example, revealed an amusing ballet of pots and pans that glided across the induction surfaces as if moved by magic. The interactive backside of the frames invited visitors to learn about the advantages of Siemens' system intelligence.

client
Siemens-Electrogeräte GmbH, Munich

design
KMS BLACKSPACE, Munich

creative direction
Nina Wiemer

graphic design
Cindy dos Santos

strategic planning
Christoph Rohrer
(Managing Partner)

project management
Christine Reitschuster

customer advisory service
Alrun Merkl

motion design
Börries Müller-Büsching, Gabriel Weiss

→ designer portrait: p. 416

Event Design | Information Design & Public Space | Corporate Films | TV, Film, Cinema & Animation | Online World

Janoschka Trade Fair Stand drupa 2012

The design of the trade fair stand by the janoschka company for drupa 2012 aimed to present a comprehensive spectrum of services and production competencies in the field of printing plates and reproduction. Special exhibits and communication areas convey the often quite abstract processes and services to the visitor in a lively and easy-to-understand manner. The stand design features a conscious play on extreme leaps in scale to make the world of printing-plate production and reproduction come to life for the visitor as an easily graspable, immersive experience.

client
Janoschka Holding GmbH, Kippenheim

design
Ippolito Fleitz Group GmbH, Stuttgart

graphic design
Axel Knapp,
Anna Maier

interior design
Peter Ippolito,
Gunter Fleitz,
Daniela Schröder

text
Skalecki
Marketing & Kommunikation

exhibition stand construction
Holzbau Harr GmbH

Armstrong Trade Fair Stand BAU 2013

The design of the Armstrong trade fair stand creates a multi-faceted image based on the idea of sensitising a younger target group of architects to the appeal of linoleum. The surfaces of the stand were covered by a geometric pattern consisting of different cuts of materials. A large rear wall, concealing several support rooms, carried a striking, abstract interplay of colours and shapes that fostered a sense of depth and perspective. From this starting point, the spatial graphics spread out across the entire floor and even covered the reception counter and conference tables.

client
Armstrong DLW GmbH, Bietigheim-Bissingen

design
Ippolito Fleitz Group GmbH, Stuttgart

interior design
Peter Ippolito,
Gunter Fleitz,
Tim Lessmann,
Tanja Ziegler,
Alexander Assmann,
Sungha Kim

| Event Design | Information Design & Public Space | Corporate Films | TV, Film, Cinema & Animation | Online World |

Calligaris Trade Fair Stand Salone Internazionale del Mobile 2013

The design of the Calligaris trade fair stand was previewed at the Salon del Mobile 2013, introducing a new corporate communication strategy based on modernity and innovation. Its appearance is characterised by an external monochrome-filled background in modular forex that creates an uneven see-through surface – a structure that enables an intense and progressive discovery of the product. The central part of the trade fair stand is devoted to the functional areas of reception and is distinguished by a suspended installation celebrating the history of the company.

client
Calligaris spa,
Manzano

design
Nascent Design,
Milan

creative direction
Massimiliano Bosio

art direction
Giacomo Vignoni

graphic design
Dalila Piccoli,
Chiara Valsecchi

**project management/
account management**
Penelope Sarrocco

Brazil Design Trade Fair Stand Cannes Lions 2012

The aim in designing this trade fair stand was to represent Brazilian design at the Cannes Lions International Festival of Creativity 2012 in an eye-catching and attention-grabbing manner. The theme "Brazil. Unique Blend. Unique Design" was translated into a large mosaic of postcards. Each postcard worked individually, though when displayed together they formed a unique visual image depicting the country in its cultural and visual diversity. Visitors were invited to interact with the panel and thus take a "piece of Brazil" with them when heading back home.

client
ABEDESIGN,
São Paulo

design
Greco Design,
Belo Horizonte

creative direction
Gustavo Greco

graphic design
Tidé,
João Corsino

strategic planning
Ellen Kiss,
Anna Carolina Maccarone

account management
Laura Scofield

motion design
Ricardo Donato

motto
Lorena Marinho,
Tathiana Machado

Event Design | Information Design & Public Space | Corporate Films | TV, Film, Cinema & Animation | Online World

iLux – Identities of Luxembourg
[Exhibition]

This exhibition visualises the results of a scientific study on the topic of "Identity Construction in Luxembourg". It centres on the basic idea that living in a relatively small country like Luxembourg – which entails "having to (and being willing to) tolerate and respect one another" – very much resembles the rules and expectations of everyday life in a student housing community. The results of the study are presented in the form of an abstract flat that manifests as a two-dimensional layout on the floor, with important objects and exhibits virtually "growing" out of it.

client
University of Luxembourg

design
krafthaus –
Das Atelier von facts and fiction, Cologne

The Culture of Smoking: From Taboo to Taboo
[Exhibition]

This exhibition in the Glyptotheque at the Croatian Academy of Sciences and Arts in Zagreb, Croatia follows a subtle approach to exploring the link between smoking, art and the related concept of taboo. The exhibition focuses on the role that smoking has played in Croatian artistic and popular culture over the last 150 years. Playing with the idea of taboo, the display hides the exhibits even from the museum itself: by concealing all of the existing elements of the gallery, the conventional exhibition space has disappeared.

client
Glyptotheque HAZU, Zagreb

curator
Fedja Vukić, Igor Zidić

design
Brigada, Zagreb
Bruketa&Žinić OM, Zagreb

creative direction
Damjan Geber, Brigada
Davor Bruketa, Nikola Žinić, Bruketa&Žinić OM

art direction
Ana Baletić, Bruketa&Žinić OM

project management
David Kabalin, Brigada

account management
Zrinka Jugec, Bruketa&Žinić OM

product design
Simon Morasi Piperčić, Brigada

architectural design
Marina Brletić, Kristina Jeren, Brigada

assistance
Lorenzo Cetina, Brigada

Event Design   Information Design & Public Space   Corporate Films   TV, Film, Cinema & Animation   Online World

ŠKODA MUZEUM
[Exhibition]

After complete refurbishment, the Czech Škoda Muzeum reopened its doors with an exhibition showcasing 46 highlights from the large collection of cars, thus taking its visitors on a fascinating journey through time. Instead of following a strict chronological order, the exhibits are divided into three main themes – Tradition, Evolution and Precision – implemented as distinctive and memorable narrative spaces. The section Tradition shows three pairs of cars from different eras that symbolise the company's three brand values of "pride, everyday life and challenge".

client
ŠKODA AUTO a.s.,
Mladá Boleslav

design
jangled nerves,
Stuttgart

creative direction
Prof. Thomas Hundt,
Ingo Zirngibl

media design
Marcel Michalski

interactive design
Tilman Faelker

graphic design
Stefka Simeonova

project management
Gesina Geiger

exhibition architecture
Lilian Fitch,
Sebastian Hirschfeld

technical direction
Hlaváček architekti

photography
Lukas Roth

Interface Design Mobile & Apps Game Design Sound Design Red Dot: Junior Award Designer Portraits

Waffen für die Götter
Weapons for the Gods
[Exhibition]

The Ferdinandeum in Innsbruck presented a unique selection of 800 pieces of armour and weaponry from the Stone, Bronze and Iron Ages and from Roman times. The special exhibition explored the complex subject of weapon consecration and offered visitors an impressive "layer by layer" experience of the chronologically arranged sacrified weapons, as well as the rituals and religious forms of expression reflected in them. The spatial layout concept of the exhibition was inspired by the principle of geological layering.

client
Tiroler Landesmuseen, Innsbruck

design
büro münzing,
3d kommunikation,
Stuttgart

art direction
Fabian Friedhoff,
Anne Sievers

graphic design
Linde Böhm

| Event Design | Information Design & Public Space | Corporate Films | TV, Film, Cinema & Animation | Online World |

Jenseits des Horizonts
Beyond the Horizon
[Exhibition]

client
Exzellenzcluster TOPOI
in cooperation with
Staatliche Museen zu Berlin –
Preußischer Kulturbesitz

design
res d
design und architektur,
Cologne

photography
Veit Landwehr

| Interface Design | Mobile & Apps | Game Design | Sound Design | Red Dot: Junior Award | Designer Portraits |

The Pergamon Museum's temporary exhibition "Jenseits des Horizonts" (Beyond the Horizon) deals with diverse questions about the knowledge of space in antique cultures. Visitors are guided through 16 exhibition spaces with the use of an artificial horizon. The overall design of the exhibition, transported by various communication media, gives way to a rich variety of individually styled exhibition spaces. A central theme of the exhibition deals with the mapping of the world. In this context, original maps are presented in parallel to a 20 metres long, audiovisual large-scale projection of our rotating planet, as it travels through the universe. More than 400 objects present a wide panorama of diverse findings including celestial observations and land surveys, the travels of the gods, rooms for body and soul, curses, oracles and acoustic chambers, drawing visitors into the antique world.

Event Design | Information Design & Public Space | Corporate Films | TV, Film, Cinema & Animation | Online World

dieForm, stilhaus Rothrist

[Exhibition]

client
stilhaus AG,
Rothrist

design/concept
Gessaga Hindermann GmbH,
Zurich

art direction
Jérôme Gessaga,
Christof Hindermann,
Reto Welz

photography
Tom Bisig

→ designer portrait: p. 406

Interface Design · Mobile & Apps · Game Design · Sound Design · Red Dot: Junior Award · Designer Portraits

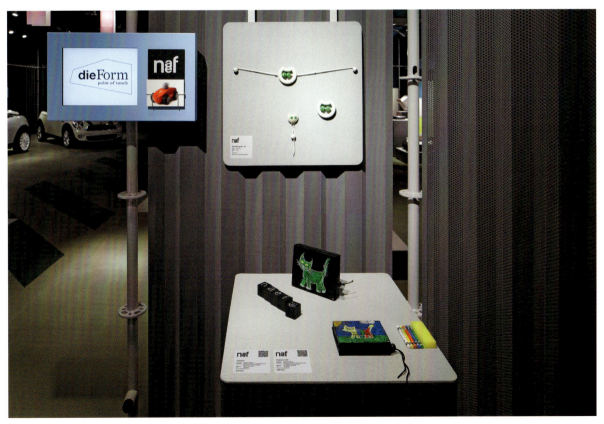

This design exhibition follows an exciting approach of combining the world of the oriental bazaar with modern design and innovative technologies. Since the stilhaus in the Swiss town of Rothrist is a showcase for brands and also a platform for small enterprises with well-designed products, the permanent exhibition features around 600 different objects from 70 exhibitors. Based on a well-thought-out concept and a clear layout, the exhibition manages to avoid the appearance of a trade exhibition by placing the products centre stage on illuminated, uniformly designed podiums. Additional information is offered by multimedia displays and in the virtual showroom via an app and a website that allow visitors to order the products directly.

| Event Design | Information Design & Public Space | Corporate Films | TV, Film, Cinema & Animation | Online World |

Choreography of the Masses – In Sport. In the Stadium. In a Frenzy.
[Exhibition]

The strong interactive effect of sports buildings and spectators was at the centre of this three-part exhibition. In the first section "Sport", six painted, larger-than-life protagonists were the human images that virtually guided visitors into the historic exhibition cycle. In the section "In the Stadium", large-format colour photographs conveyed a sense of the impressive dimensions found in the stadium building. In the third section, an emotionalising video/sound installation based on the musical principle of a chorus illustrated the theme "In a Frenzy".

client
Akademie der Künste Berlin
gmp Architekten von Gerkan, Marg und Partner, Hamburg

design
gmp Architekten von Gerkan, Marg und Partner, Hamburg

concept
Volkwin Marg,
Gert Kähler,
Michael Kuhn

exhibition design
Hanne Banduch,
Heidi Knaut

graphic design
Tom Wibberenz,
On Grafik,
Hamburg

Chung Guyon Archive
[Special Exhibition]

The National Museum of Contemporary Art in Korea has documented the life and work of architect Chung Guyon in this special exhibition. Selected drawings, writings and artefacts are presented in such a way that visitors can experience them as a journey of discovery. The exhibition arranges Chung's lifework into different sections, such as "Roots of Architecture" and "City and Architecture". Huge tables with pull-out drawers reveal interesting documentation, while framed wall openings lend the exhibition a sense of spatial openness.

client
National Museum of Modern and Contemporary Art, Korea

design
National Museum of Modern and Contemporary Art, Korea

creative direction
Kim Yong-Ju

graphic design
Song Hye-Min,
Kim Hyun-Sook,
Lee Yeon-Ock

photography
Jang Jun-Ho

→ designer portrait: p. 424

DARWINEUM
[Permanent Exhibition]

The Darwineum at the Rockstock Zoo is a combination of museum and living zoological collection, also serving as a new home for the zoo's apes. Designed as an attraction for the winter season, it offers visitors a new approach to the transfer of knowledge and presents its theme in an entertaining manner. A highly varied, interactive tour illustrates the evolution of life and the cultural evolution of human beings. The tour starts with Darwin's evolution theory and takes the visitor on a journey through millions of years of the earth's history.

client
Zoologischer Garten Rostock gGmbH, Rostock

design
ATELIER BRÜCKNER, Stuttgart

creative direction
Prof. Uwe R. Brückner

art direction
Monika Goebel,
Bernd Möller

graphic design
Sabine Loucka

media design
2av GmbH

lighting design
Licht Kunst Licht AG

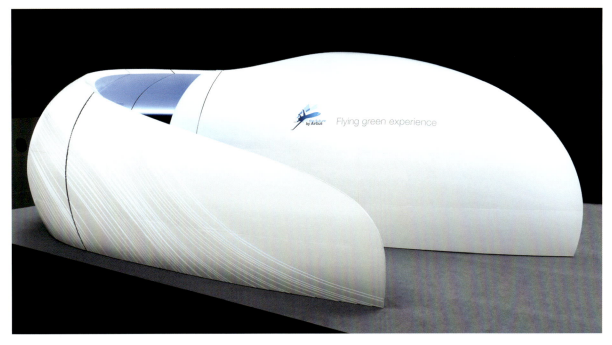
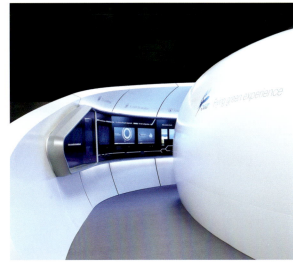
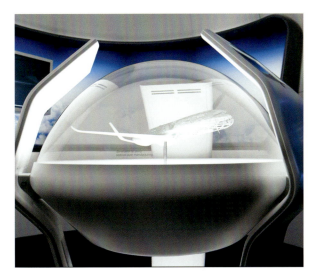

Airbus Flying Green Experience Showcase

The Airbus "Flying green experience" showcase aims to spread awareness of the current and future challenges in the aviation industry and conveys the Airbus vision of aviation in the year 2050. The highlight is an interactive scenario illustrating the Concept Plane and Concept Cabin. Visitors are invited to experience a flight in the Airbus Concept Plane, the centre of which is formed by a rotating, 3D-printed bionic model of the plane. Three interactive stations, which show a real-time 3D model synchronised to the airplane model, offer visitors more detailed information.

client
AIRBUS Operations GmbH,
Hamburg

marketing management
Axel Becker,
Tobias Mayer,
Susanne Rötzel,
Rainer Ristow,
Bastian Schäfer,
Nicolas Tschechne

design/lead agency
Mutabor Design GmbH,
Hamburg
VRPE GmbH,
Hohenbrunn

creative direction
Patrick Molinari,
Bernhard Wache

art direction
Neil Roth,
Michael Wagner,
Bernhard Wache

customer advisory service
Anne Wolkodaw

project management
Cordula Berchtold

design team
Lennard Niemann,
Frank Renner,
Florian Sattler,
Hamid Dulovic,
Max Toth

| Event Design | Information Design & Public Space | Corporate Films | TV, Film, Cinema & Animation | Online World |

Vision Hall, Hyundai Motor Group University, Mabuk Campus, South Korea
[Media Wall]

client
Hyundai Motor Group,
Seoul

design
Suh Architects,
Seoul
Do Ho Suh,
London

creative direction
Do Ho Suh,
London
Kia Design Center,
Frankfurt/Main

concept
Do Ho Suh,
London
Suh Architects,
Seoul
Kia Design Center,
Frankfurt/Main

project management
Innocean Worldwide,
Visual Communication Division,
Seoul

motion design
Do Ho Suh,
London
Universal Everything,
Sheffield
Imagebakery,
Seoul

exhibition stand construction
Suh Architects,
Seoul

photography
Kyungsub Shin,
Seoul
Nils Clauss,
Seoul

→ clip on DVD
→ designer portrait: p. 433

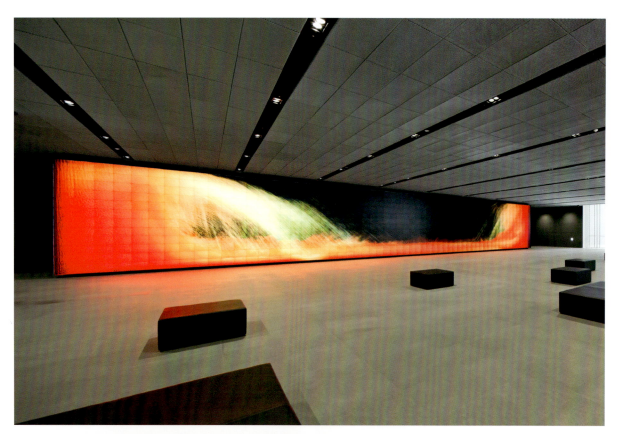

Interface Design Mobile & Apps Game Design Sound Design Red Dot: Junior Award Designer Portraits

Vision Hall, which belongs to a human resources development centre of Hyundai Motor Group, was designed for its employees to visually experience the company's philosophy. The hall uses state-of-the-art technology like a 3D sound system and a media wall (24 x 3.5 metres) to present interactive content of up to 48K resolution. The current multimedia exhibition of international artists was organised to stimulate an ongoing dialogue between the company and employees. Vision Hall and the selected artworks are meaningful, as they open up a space of dialogue and reflect on the company's willingness to communicate.

Event Design | Information Design & Public Space | Corporate Films | TV, Film, Cinema & Animation | Online World

FLUIDIC –
Sculpture in Motion
[Interactive Light Installation]

client
Hyundai Motor Company
Innocean Worldwide

design
WHITEvoid interactive
art & design /
Christopher Bauder,
Berlin

project management
Anna Pilarska

music/sound design
Daniel Teige,
Marian Mentrup,
Hammersnail

programming
Joreg,
Sebastian Gregor,
Checksum5

engineering
Steven Morgan,
Benedikt Frisse-Bremann

technical direction
Philipp Rasehorn,
Rob Feigel

laser technology
Michael Sollinger,
Laseranimation Sollinger

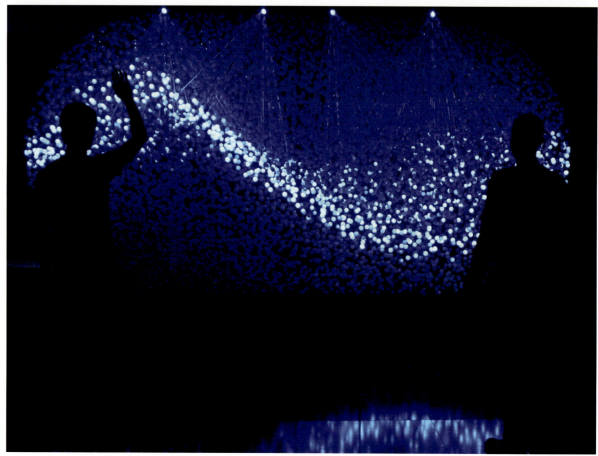

This installation involves a suspended point cloud formed by 12,000 small, translucent spheres, evoking the appearance of a poetic light sculpture. The organic and seemingly arbitrary arrangement of these spheres is actually based on a complex computer algorithm that calculated both the positioning and the projection angles of eight high-speed laser projectors placed around the installation. The lasers send dense beams of light into the point cloud arrangement, making it light up wherever the beam hits a sphere. The graphics and three-dimensional objects generated within the array come to life as dynamic, three-dimensional light sculptures.

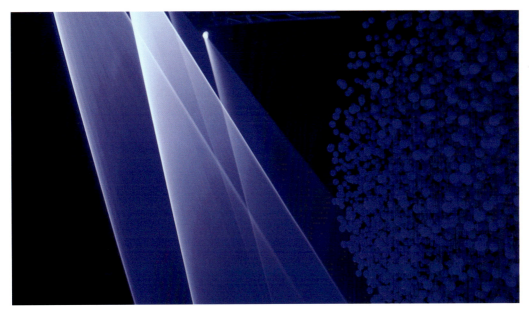

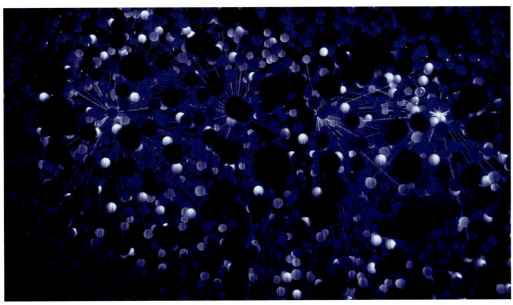

Event Design | Information Design & Public Space | Corporate Films | TV, Film, Cinema & Animation | Online World

Festival of Lights
[Projection Mapping]

As part of the Festival of Lights, the visual display for the Brandenburg Gate in Berlin communicated the themes of "communal living" and "Berlin's architectural history" in an entertaining presentation. Taking into account the particular challenges posed by the location and the expectations of visitors, a film collage was created that traces architectural styles in three stages: from pre-World War II building design through pre-fabricated housing to today's contemporary mix of styles.

client
Zander & Partner GmbH, Berlin

design
giraffentoast design gmbh

creative direction
Philip Braun, giraffentoast

animation
Björn Fiekert, Gabi Nagel, Bettina Gericke, giraffentoast

production/technical direction
Gunter Birnbaum, 1a Event Services GmbH

Tree Concert
[Interactive Installation]

With an unusual concept, this installation for Friends of the Earth Germany (BUND) set out to raise public awareness of the fact that Berlin loses thousands of city trees every year. A chestnut tree serves as a "musician" that "performs" an extraordinary charity concert, with each falling chestnut becoming part of an artistic composition of sound and light. Thus, the tree could "play" to promote the protection of its companions. The "Tree Concert" gained massive media coverage and led to a new donation record for the preservation of trees.

client
BUND Bund für Umwelt und Naturschutz Deutschland, Landesverband Berlin e.V., Berlin

design
BBDO Proximity Berlin GmbH
Gang of Berlin

creative direction
Jan Harbeck, David Mously

art direction
Daniel Schweinzer

text
Lukas Liske

account management
Dirk Spakowski, Sebastian Schlosser, Joris Jonker, Mia Lücker, Frank Hägele, Emily Dietzsch, Christof Biggeleben, Monika Groewe

production
Mat Neidhardt, Friederike Seifert, Gang of Berlin

design director
Steve Bergmann, Alexej Alschiz, Kamil Garbacz, Philipp Tögel, Sandra Glaser, Gang of Berlin

director of photography
Simon Baumann, Sebastian Lampe

→ clip on DVD
→ designer portrait: p. 396

| Event Design | Information Design & Public Space | Corporate Films | TV, Film, Cinema & Animation | Online World |

Royal Inauguration of King Willem-Alexander

[City Dressing, Event Identity]

The event identity for the Royal inauguration of King Willem-Alexander on 30 April 2013, the first King of the Netherlands in 122 years, fulfilled the demand of being both festive and regal. As the design could not include a crown, nor could it show text or images of the new monarch, the identity centred on the colour orange, the national colour of the Netherlands. With 1,100 flags, more than 500 posters, 30 decorated buildings and 140,000 paper crowns, Amsterdam put on its best face for the 1,100 press professionals from over 50 countries.

client
Municipality of Amsterdam

design
Koeweiden Postma, Amsterdam

creative direction
Eddy Wegman

concept
Jacques Koeweiden,
Eddy Wegman,
Jorn Dal,
Mark Holtmann

graphic design
Eddy Wegman,
Mark Holtmann

account management
Ermelinde van Reusel

pre-press
Ingmar Evers

production
Vollaerszwart,
Teepe Productions

Hyundai Department Store – Happy Gift
[Event Design]

Celebrating Children's Day in South Korea, the Hyundai Department Store organised a collaboration stage with the pop artist duo Friends With You. Both the Hyundai Department Store and Friends With You took the sky and sunlight as a motif to create the character Happy Gift, expressing the warmth of May, which is known as the "family month" in Korea. Happy Gift was used as the department store's mascot for the month. Characters designed by Friends With You decorated the entire inside and outside space of the department store and appeared on the building facade advertisement.

client
Hyundai Department Store Co., Ltd., Seoul

design
Idispartners, Seoul

creative direction
Hyosun Jung

graphic design
Hyosun Jung,
Hyeyun Choi,
Joohee Moon,
Sunhee Na

visual merchandising
Il Park

artist
Friends With You

| Event Design | Information Design & Public Space | Corporate Films | TV, Film, Cinema & Animation | Online World |

Hong Kong International Airport Master Plan 2030
[Exhibition]

client
Airport Authority Hong Kong

design
Oval Design Limited,
Hong Kong

The graphic symbol "2030 Our Airport Our Future" thematically informs this exhibition design by embracing the form of a tree. Partitioning structures resembling tree branches divide the exhibition into irregular-shaped thematic zones, while the shape of the entrance resembles both a tree trunk and a runway. To add a dose of fun and create instant association with the subject matter, the exhibition features enlarged versions of pictograms related to airport operations. Sophisticated interactive models illustrate the future development of the airport by projecting animations onto the models, such as planes taking off and landing on a third runway.

Event Design | Information Design & Public Space | Corporate Films | TV, Film, Cinema & Animation | Online World

2050 – Dein Klimamarkt
2050 – Your Climate Market
[Pop-up Store]

client
energiekonsens,
Bremen

design
GfG / Gruppe für Gestaltung,
Bremen

creative direction
Carsten Dempewolf,
Björn Voigt

graphic design/illustration
Asja Beckmann,
Lada Hendrichova

project management
Anne Götzel

production
Ulrike Rosemeier,
Carsten Koralewski

The concept of the pop-up store 2050 – Dein Klimamarkt (2050 – Your Climate Market) conveys to the people of Bremen that it is possible to shop and reduce CO_2 at the same time. Commissioned by the Bremen-based climate protection agency energiekonsens, consumers are targeted directly by taking the everyday shopping experience and putting a playful twist on showing people how they can reduce CO_2 themselves. All elements in the store, including sales stands, shelves, shopping baskets and the checkout area, are well designed and made from recyclable paper. Since the customers fill their shopping baskets with sample products, the idea of climate-friendly shopping is transformed into a sustainable and memorable experience.

WakuWaku Dammtor
[Interior Design]

The fast-food restaurant WakuWaku Dammtor in Hamburg organised a relaunch with the aim of also positioning itself as an organic food store. The design approach visualises this through an open façade providing an unrestricted view of space. Almost entirely encased in solid wood panelling, this space serves as a stage to display the products in the WakuWaku world. The rough wooden surfaces contrast with a canopy of fine wire lamps and intricate wall sketches created by the artist Chris Rehberger using taut strings.

client
WakuWaku,
Hamburg

design
Ippolito Fleitz Group GmbH,
Stuttgart

interior design
Peter Ippolito,
Gunter Fleitz,
Moritz Köhler,
Michael Bertram,
Markus Schmidt,
Timo Flott

artwork
Chris Rehberger

Interface Design   Mobile & Apps   Game Design   Sound Design   Red Dot: Junior Award   Designer Portraits

not guilty Zurich
[Interior Design]

The design concept for the Swiss restaurant chain "not guilty" aims to convey a philosophy of openness, harmony with nature and joy. A long, open space welcomes the guests with its inviting-looking, natural oak wood flooring combined with a mixture of delicate white and pastel tones. The focal points in the entrance area are formed by a colourful salad bar and a menu board designed in a kitchen hutch form. Even from outside, the eyes of the guests are immediately directed towards the tables in the rear part of the restaurant.

client
not guilty Management GmbH, Zurich

design
Ippolito Fleitz Group GmbH, Stuttgart

interior design
Peter Ippolito,
Gunter Fleitz,
Tanja Ziegler,
Alexander Fehre,
Katja Heinemann,
Felix Rabe

artwork
Sonja Schneider

BMW Brand Store Paris – Brand Showcase in the Room

The renovation and redesign of the BMW Brand Store in the city centre of Paris was completed as part of the new Future Retail concept. The store centres on the idea of providing spatial brand experiences and, going beyond pure sales, illustrates the themes of innovation and the continual pursuit of advancement. The BMW i brand is presented through a clear design concept with special focus on distinctive exhibits. The spatial brand communication concept aims to convey how innovative development must go hand in hand with functional practicality, also in the mobility of tomorrow.

client
BMW Group,
Munich

design
becc agency GmbH,
Munich
GMK Markenberatung,
Munich

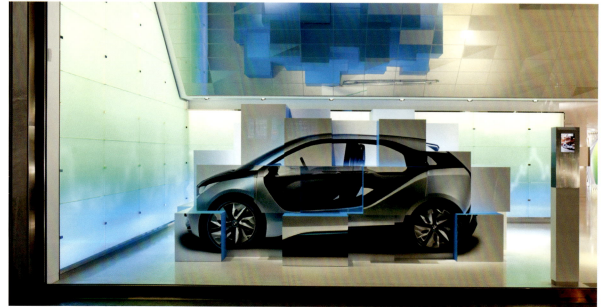

BMW Brand Experience Centre Shanghai
[Communication Concept, Architectural Design]

The BMW Brand Experience Centre in Shanghai presents itself with a formally reduced, transparent architecture. Local Chinese architecture is incorporated harmoniously into the concept by creating a reference in perspective with the adjacent Chinese pavilion. Inside the building, the major themes of "culture", "heritage", "future", "product", "technology" and "society" are staged across various spaces. Distinctive elements, including spiral stairs and an auditorium, create functional and visually impressive spatial relations.

client
BMW China,
Beijing

design
BMW China,
Beijing
becc agency GmbH,
Munich

design team
Alexander Schmidt,
Martin Oberpriller

| Event Design | Information Design & Public Space | Corporate Films | TV, Film, Cinema & Animation | Online World |

New Walk of Fame – A Journey to the Heart of the Brand

[Permanent Exhibition]

client
adidas AG, World of Sports, Herzogenaurach

design
simple GmbH, Cologne

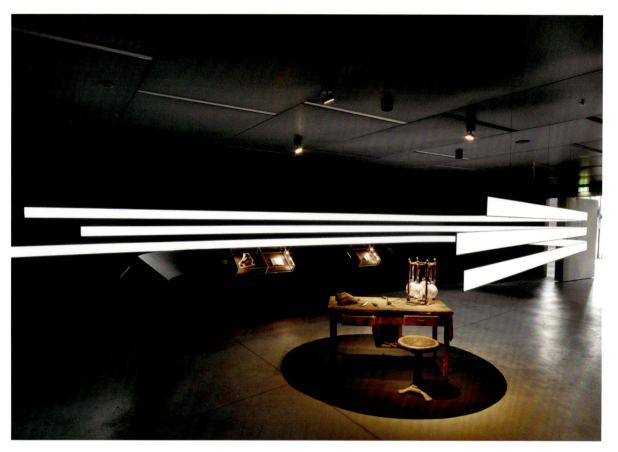

Interface Design   Mobile & Apps   Game Design   Sound Design   Red Dot: Junior Award   Designer Portraits

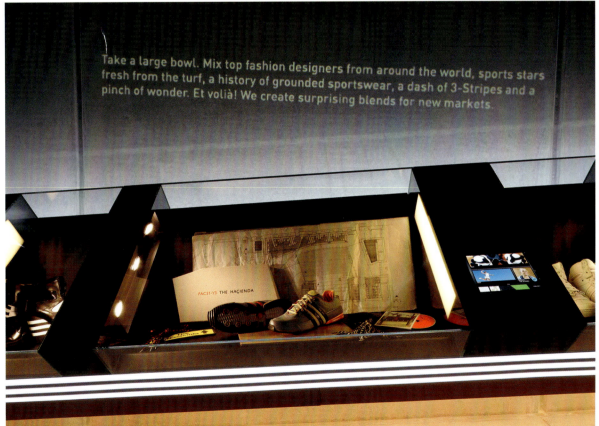

Designed as a journey to the "heart of the brand", the concept of this permanent exhibition puts the past, present and future of the adidas company into perspective. The design enters into dialogue with the sophisticated architecture of the building, while its spatial layout offers the dramaturgical opportunity to intensify the visitors' experience through narrow walkways following a six-level dramaturgy. The arrangement and content of the display cases and iPads with stories and interactive games can be changed with little effort.

KOKUYO FURNITURE Shanghai Flagship Showroom

client
KOKUYO FURNITURE Co., Ltd.

space design
Wataru Sato,
KOKUYO FURNITURE Co., Ltd.,
Tokyo
Naoki Sawada,
KOKUYO FURNITURE Commerce and Trading (Shanghai) Co., Ltd.,
Shanghai
Rui Ou,
UDS,
Beijing

planning/production
Tsuyoshi Wakahara,
Yojiro Kinoshita,
Yukiko Sugiyama,
KOKUYO FURNITURE Co., Ltd.,
Tokyo

lighting design
Masanobu Takeishi,
Toki Hirai,
ICE,
Tokyo

artwork
Mariko Hayahi,
A&M,
Tokyo

sign design
Aki Kanai,
KOKUYO FURNITURE Co., Ltd.,
Tokyo

structural design
Kiyotaka Nagai,
smart unit,
Osaka

camera
Keita Yamamoto,
Nacasa & Partners Inc,
Tokyo

→ designer portrait: p. 418

Interface Design   Mobile & Apps   Game Design   Sound Design   Red Dot: Junior Award   Designer Portraits

The design concept of KOKUYO's showroom space is defined by the principle of "Layers". The company's office furniture products are displayed on many different layers. Each layer conveys a specific message, illustrating the themes of "historical creativity", "advanced technology" and "preferences in manufacturing". This layer concept sets out to invite visitors to learn about the company's products, philosophy and creative activity from various perspectives. Consistent with the concept, the floors are of different heights as the most obvious feature of the showroom space, allowing the products and activities to be experienced from a 360-degree angle. This allows subtle details in the company's product manufacturing to be highlighted and brought to the fore. Without further explanation, yet at the same time attracting visitors, the showroom has been designed to express the charm of KOKUYO to be felt by five senses.

Event Design | Information Design & Public Space | Corporate Films | TV, Film, Cinema & Animation | Online World

The Social Kitchen 2012

[Trade Show]

This event at the Urbis Design Day aimed at communicating Fisher & Paykel's design philosophy to a design-minded audience. The key idea was to re-evaluate the kitchen, no longer conceiving it as just a room where food is prepared, but rather as a social hub in everyday life. A custom-designed, 65-metre-long kitchen in the cloud gave visitors an experience of moving along a journey of food. They could interact with Fisher & Paykel designers who wore T-shirts with questions about the experience to prompt conversations about the life lived around the product they designed.

client
Fisher & Paykel Appliances,
Auckland

design
Alt Group,
Auckland

creative direction
Dean Poole,
Mark Elmore

graphic design
Dean Poole,
Zoe Ikin,
Janson Chau,
Kate Cullinane,
Ben Corban,
Aaron Edwards,
Fisher & Paykel Design Team

text
Kate Cullinane,
Janson Chau,
Dean Poole

photography
Toaki Okano,
Garth Badger

Interface Design | Mobile & Apps | Game Design | Sound Design | Red Dot: Junior Award | Designer Portraits

Formex – Nordic Charm
[Graphic Identity]

In order to consolidate the position of the Scandinavian company Formex in the field of interior decoration and raise visitor interest in the trade fair stand and the latest trends shown there, this concept centres on the illustration of "Nordic Charm". It celebrates a "blonde, simple Nordic style" in combination with bold, colourful, graphic and playful patterns. Colourful 3D mobiles can be unfolded to become 2D surfaces, all done in various patterns, which allows for endless arrangement possibilities.

client
Stockholmsmässan AB, Stockholm

design
BVD, Stockholm

Aluminum Flower Garden

[Interior Design]

client
ronwit,
Tokyo

design
Moriyuki Ochiai Architects,
Tokyo

concept
Moriyuki Ochiai

art direction
Moriyuki Ochiai

construction
Aslego

→ designer portrait: p. 426

The interior design for the Flower bar/restaurant and dance hall was inspired by the Japanese art of origami. Aluminium – a recyclable material as thin and as flexible as paper – was used to create folded, three-dimensional flowers of organic appearance. These flowers were arranged across the ceiling to fill the space with their light and airy presence. Variations in the size and density of the flower petals impart both the function and the atmosphere suited to each area, such as lively and quiet zones that emerge through minute differences in the height and expanse of a given space. The visitors' position and angle of vision, as well as the reflection of images and lights from the mirrors on the walls, concur to perpetually redefine the appearance of the whole space.

| Event Design | Information Design & Public Space | Corporate Films | TV, Film, Cinema & Animation | Online World |

CIRCLE – PRIVATE HEALTH CLUB
Minimal space for maximal power

[Interior Design]

The interior design for the CIRCLE – PRIVATE HEALTH CLUB is based on pioneering knowledge of the interaction between architecture and performance. It follows the philosophy that an external concentration on essentials helps to focus internal attention on an individual training programme. The cardio, power and endurance areas are highlighted by special circular lighting that divides the different zones and is well integrated into the overall interior concept. The training conditions at the club are thus optimised for a target group with high demands.

client
CIRCLE –
PRIVATE HEALTH CLUB,
Munich

design
Brückner Innenarchitekten,
Munich

interior design
Susanne Brückner,
Mona Böttcher,
Carolin Köppel

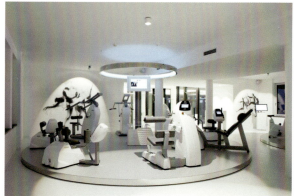

Interface Design | Mobile & Apps | Game Design | Sound Design | Red Dot: Junior Award | Designer Portraits

SYZYGY
Office Frankfurt

[Corporate Interior Design]

The interior architecture design for the Syzygy Office in Frankfurt creates distinctive spatial interactions based on the concept and idea of transformation. A 22-metre-long, curving envelope embraces the reception and the adjoining lounge zone, forming an atmospheric room-in-room situation. Wall openings of various sizes and subtle graphic perforations create visual connections to the surrounding conference areas and conduct daylight into the interior. Completely in white, the free-form structure is the visual and also the communicative heart of the agency.

client
SYZYGY Deutschland GmbH, Frankfurt/Main

design
3deluxe, Wiesbaden

photography
Sascha Jahnke

INTERNATIONAL YEARBOOK COMMUNICATION DESIGN 2013/2014

VOL. 2

INFORMATION
DESIGN &
PUBLIC SPACE

Red Dot: Best of the Best

When music flows into pictures
[Billboard]

In order to attract new visitors to the Philharmoniker Hamburg's upcoming concert "The Moldau" (Vltava) by Bedřich Smetana, an eye-catching work was created in a public space to arouse interest: a 16 by 2 metre billboard, on which artist Debbie Smyth visualised the storyline of this classical piece of music. Working for five days in a Hamburg shopping arcade in front of passers-by, she used 5,900 nails to make 1.2 km of string extend from the four strings of a real violin and flow into all the scenes that Smetana was picturing with his music: a hunting scene, a farmer's wedding, nymphs in the moonlight, the river growing into rapids and finally reaching the Charles' Bridge in Prague. Not only is the design concept of this accomplished piece of art – which afterwards was exhibited in front of Hamburg's music hall – based on an outstanding idea, the public was also included live in the realisation of this work of art. Furthermore, it invited beholders in a highly imaginative manner to contemplate the content of this classical composition.

Statement by the jury

»Visualising this musical composition, the mural-like artwork is based on the stories narrated in the music. The implementation is marked by a high design quality and artistic handicraft, as well as the purist appearance evoked by the black-on-white contrast. The thickness and structure of the string are informed by rhythmic expressivity, the main characteristic of all classical music.«

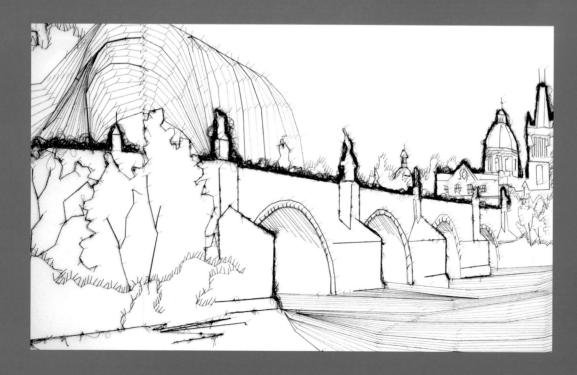

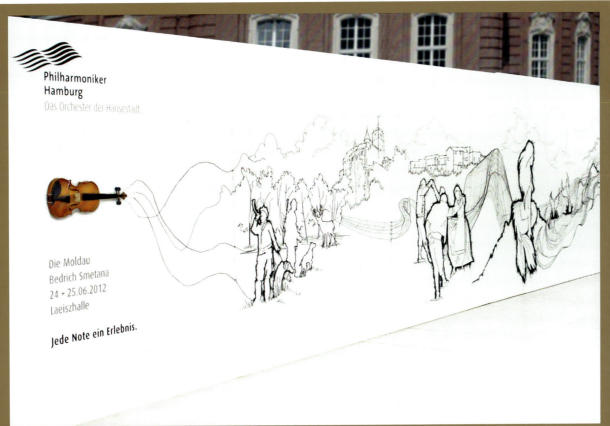

client
Philharmoniker Hamburg

artist
Debbie Smyth

design
Draftfcb Deutschland GmbH,
Hamburg

creative direction
Dirk Haeusermann,
Jessica Schneider,
Mario Anspach

art direction
Tim Lehnebach

text
Frederik Wetzel

account management
Guido Kirschner,
Sabine Classen,
Susanne Knauff,
Maik Schneider

art buying
Katja Nicklaus

→ designer portrait: p. 403

Event Design | **Information Design & Public Space** | Corporate Films | TV, Film, Cinema & Animation | Online World

Red Dot: Best of the Best

Klagemauern für mehr Gerechtigkeit
Wailing Walls against Injustice
[Ambient Installation]

Prison walls are a symbol of violence and oppression throughout the world. To denounce social ills and even abuses related to this, Amnesty International transformed walls in public spaces into "Wailing Walls against Injustice". Images of barred doors and windows were installed on these walls to create the impression of prison cell walls, behind which eight real destinies from eight different countries were concealed. People encountering this ambient installation could learn more about the persons behind bars via QR code or a URL, and were asked to leave their personal desires and hopes for justice on a virtual wailing wall. Passers-by thus became part of a large petition that was forwarded to the appropriate government officials at the end of the campaign. In addition, social media such as Twitter and Facebook also helped to promote the "Wailing Walls", so that this installation event managed to address people in their immediate environment and those beyond it, and thus, in a highly unusual way, succeeded in drawing attention to a human rights issue.

Statement by the jury

»This installation in the public space adopts an approach that is as impressive as it is haunting in its attempt to bring attention to the issue of violence behind bars. It affects recipients directly as they are confronted in their immediate environment. Not only is the design implementation outstanding, the possibility and focus on interacting and direct engagement are also excellently solved.«

client
Amnesty International,
Frankfurt/Main

design
Leo Burnett,
Frankfurt/Main

chief creative officer
Andreas Pauli

creative direction
Hans-Jürgen Kämmerer

art direction
Hugo Moura,
Dan Witz,
Hans-Jürgen Kämmerer

text
Benjamin Merkel,
Hans-Jürgen Kämmerer

programming
Marco Randi,
Axel Käser,
Björn Brockmann

account management
Katrin Kester

Event Design | **Information Design & Public Space** | Corporate Films | TV, Film, Cinema & Animation | Online World

Frozen Cinema
[Promotional Event]

The promotional event Frozen Cinema was conceived for people to experience how it feels to be homeless in winter. The air conditioning was reduced to an absolute minimum in the cinema during the screening of a short film featuring homeless people talking directly to the audience. Donations could be made instantly via a QR code on distributed blankets or after the movie. The results were immediate donations, newspaper coverage, TV and blog reports and YouTube viewings. Also, Düsseldorf's mayor became an active supporter of the fiftyfifty organisation for the homeless.

client
fiftyfifty,
Düsseldorf

design
Havas Worldwide Düsseldorf

creative direction
Felix Glauner,
Torsten Pollmann,
Patrick Ackmann

art direction
Annika Weber

production
Eva Peschkes,
Nadine Baltes,
Jan Behrens,
Michael Koch

film production
Jotz! Filmproduktion

post-production
nhb Postproduktion

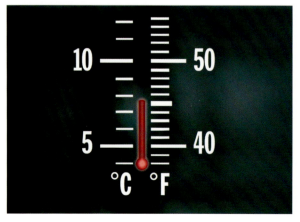

MuKK Children's Department Store

[Signage System]

Designed with child-appropriate wording, well-coordinated colouring and simplified information icons, the guidance system for the MuKK children's department store helps customers, especially children, find their way around the store quickly and easily. It takes into account their perceptual perspective while simultaneously providing parents with easy-to-grasp orientation at eye level. Consistently communicating on two levels, the colourful store guidance system encourages customers to discover the children's department store in a playful way.

client
MuKK GmbH,
Münster

design
cyclos design GmbH,
Münster

→ clip on DVD

Pentomino Signage System

The Pentomino signage system was created for SEBRAE-MG, an institution that offers a set of tools that can be combined in order to generate a broad range of different solutions for the development of small and micro businesses. The signage is based on a sophisticatedly designed puzzle consisting of pictograms and numerals, which facilitates a wide variety of combinations. In a light and playful manner, the Pentomino pictograms translate the entity's mission into a visual plan, expanding the brand personality to include new and unprecedented contact points.

client
SEBRAE-MG,
Belo Horizonte

design
Greco Design,
Belo Horizonte

creative direction
Gustavo Greco

graphic design/motion design
Zumberto

creative management
Tidé

account management
Victor Fernandes

production
Alexandre Fonseca,
João Corsino

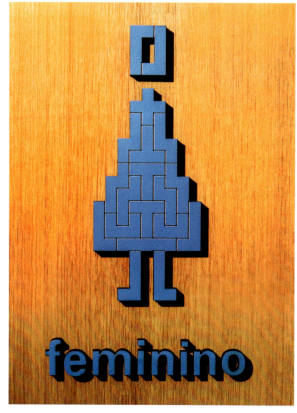

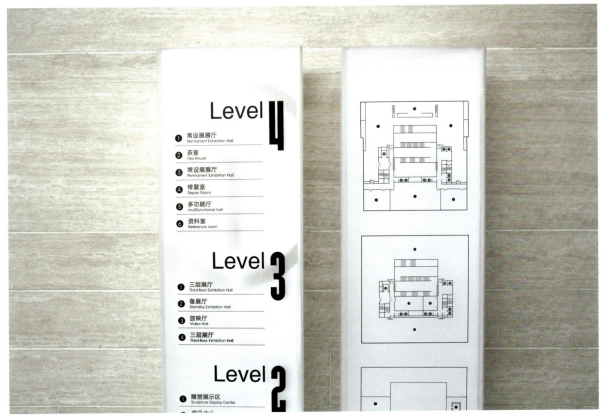

Tianjin Art Museum
[Signage System]

The Tianjin Art Museum, a landmark of the city of Tianjin, is one of the most modern museums in China. Stressing its architectural purism, the signage design uses simple boxes, with the idea of creating transparency and setting clear priorities in these public spaces. The special font used on the boxes fits well with the atmosphere of this modern art museum. For ecological purposes, the signage system was designed with a 3form Chroma renewable matte, as it helps reduce carbon consumption.

client
Tianjin Art Museum,
Tianjin

design
Dongdao Design Co.,
Ltd., Beijing

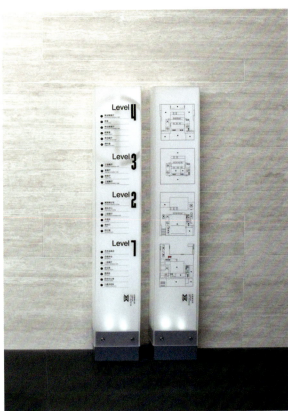

Event Design | **Information Design & Public Space** | Corporate Films | TV, Film, Cinema & Animation | Online World

University of Television and Film Munich
[Signage System]

client
Staatliches Bauamt München 2, Munich

design
Büro für Gestaltung Wangler & Abele, Munich

production
Conzept GmbH, Pößneck

photography
Jens Weber, Munich

The information and signage system for the new building of the University of Television and Film Munich is closely linked to the architecture and purpose of the building complex, which also encompasses public space. To ensure easy orientation, the university's logo and important information were applied, almost like projections, directly onto the concrete and glass facades for high visibility. More detailed information is contained on distinctively designed black signs that wrap around corners almost like shadows, so that they can be easily seen from the floors and the central staircase. The white typography, which is closely aligned to the black sign edges, creates an appealing interplay of juxtaposing light and shade.

Stadtwerke Essen

[Graphic Surface, Signage and Wayfinding System]

client
Stadtwerke Essen AG,
Essen

design
Dmitri Lavrow,
HardCase Design,
Berlin

architecture/interior design/ project management
Frithjof Eisenberg,
Eisenberg Architektur,
Essen
(formerly Eisenberg Hoffmann Architekten)

random generator
Dr. Mads Haahr,
random.org,
Trinity College,
Dublin

production coordination
Michael Debnar,
Kurt Munsteiner Werbetechnik,
Essen

photography
Markus Schwalenberg,
Dormagen

image editing
Dimitri Kireev,
Berlin

| Interface Design | Mobile & Apps | Game Design | Sound Design | Red Dot: Junior Award | Designer Portraits |

The geometrically clear, flowing architectural design of the new public-utilities administration building in Essen, Germany, has been harmoniously expanded by this integral graphic design interface concept. It provides a comprehensive, typography-centred coding, signage and wayfinding system for all building areas and outdoor facilities (including even the escape and rescue plans). The architectural principle of the edifice, which is monolithic yet pervious to light, is complemented in the interior by elaborate graphics applied to all glass wall surfaces. Semi-transparent stripe structures, based on a random mathematical algorithm, help provide both partial visibility and privacy, thus creating an impressively dense atmospheric effect.

Repsol – Meaningful Signage

[Environmental Design]

Against the backdrop of Madrid's comprehensive urban regulations concerning building signage, the environmental design for the new Repsol headquarters makes intelligent use of the building facade. The vertical panels of the facade were redefined as a narrative medium. A deconstructed wordmark was applied there, using anamorphic distortion. The environmental design has thus managed to both successfully deliver the message of the brand's leadership aspirations and lend it a modern, dynamic expression.

client
Repsol,
Madrid

design
Interbrand,
Madrid

creative direction
Borja Borrero
(Executive Creative Director)

art direction
Carlos Magro Mtnez-Illescas
(Design Director)

graphic design
David Angulo

retail design
Sergio Wullich
(Retail Director Latin America)

project management
Oliver Pacht
(Senior Project Manager)

production
Coro Iglesias
(Production Manager)

→ designer portrait: p. 412

Herdade do Esporão
[Signage]

The design of the Herdade do Esporão outdoor signage system integrates large rocks found in the area to convey information. They lend themselves well to the aim of harmoniously balancing man-made intervention and the natural feel of the area, without disturbing the landscape. These rocks were cut flush on one side to accommodate the lettering in white ink. This facilitates the necessary orientation and at the same time integrates the information into the surroundings in a natural way.

client
Esporão S.A.,
Lisbon

design
White Studio,
Porto

Red Dot: Best of the Best

Mobius Loop
[Film]

The Vision Hall at Hyundai Motor Group's Mabuk Campus is a symbolic space for presenting employees with the company's values, providing them with a sense of pride and allowing them to share its dreams. The films aim to simply inspire – allowing leaders, engineers, scientists, workers and designers to learn, re-think and collaborate in new ways. Building upon an artistic ethos of "maximum innovation", the films mix a myriad of animation styles and live action. With abstract visualisations, a huge target group is engaged while themes such as nature and technology, as well as man's relationship with them, feature heavily. The artwork composition shows various themes exploring the areas of the company's activities in hyper-real vision and audio – from steel creation and architecture to future technologies as well as the design and production of cars. The Mobius Loop, symbolising the infinite cycle of resource circulation, serves to connect all these activities of the Group into an organic whole.

Statement by the jury

»The way the Vision Hall integrates the employees into an interactive process is outstanding. This work does not only boast visually strong elements, the dynamics of which viewers can hardly resist, but also has the effect of making the employees feel more connected to the network and strengthened as individuals at the same time.«

Interface Design | Mobile & Apps | Game Design | Sound Design | Red Dot: Junior Award | Designer Portraits

client
Hyundai Motor Group,
Seoul

design
Universal Everything,
Sheffield

creative direction
Universal Everything,
Sheffield
Kia Design Center,
Frankfurt/Main
Do Ho Suh,
London

project management
Innocean Worldwide,
Visual Communication Division,
Seoul
Kia Design Center,
Frankfurt/Main

music/sound design
Freefarm,
Brighton

motion design
Universal Everything,
Sheffield

exhibition stand construction
Suh Architects,
Seoul

photography
Nils Clauss,
Seoul

→ clip on DVD
→ designer portrait: p. 414

Red Dot: Best of the Best

Mahou – Living Life to the Fullest
[Video]

To achieve greater visibility in a little differentiated advertising segment, beer manufacturer Mahou decided to generate branded content for special events such as the Madrid Fashion Week. A video was produced which conveys the characteristics of their latest premium product, "original, daring and related to night life", and which was shown in a continuous loop in a space that was open to the public during the various events. Limiting the narrative elements to just the logo and label design, the story delivers an unexpected and surprising audiovisual experience, underlining the manufacturer's expertise. Different elements of the logotype and the label were used in a deconstructive mobile installation, rotating and superimposing them on top of the bottle to convey the high quality of this beer. This approach resulted in the illusion of an endless ballet that would revolve or dance around the bottle. Filmed in 360 degrees against a black background, a work was thus generated that took a different path to convey its message.

Statement by the jury

»This video manages to break loose from the familiar advertising aesthetics in this branch by creating an entirely new style. The various elements such as animation, typography and, above all, the sound design are interwoven in a highly elegant manner in order to create an engaging and lasting impression. The video thus gives convincing proof that beer can also be envisioned differently.«

Interface Design Mobile & Apps Game Design Sound Design Red Dot: Junior Award Designer Portraits

client
Mahou,
Madrid

design
Interbrand,
Madrid

creative direction
Borja Borrero
(Executive Creative Director)

art direction
Carlos Magro Mtnez-Illescas
(Design Director)

film direction
Enrique Rodríguez
(external film director)

→ clip on DVD
→ designer portrait: p. 412

Red Dot: Best of the Best

denkwerk Social Media Guidelines
[Video]

The agency denkwerk employs web professionals, social media enthusiasts and newcomers. To meet the demands of modern online communication and to ensure that its employees behave appropriately when using the social web, fundamental social media guidelines were staged in the form of an amusing cartoon video. Each of these guideline directives is presented on a sophisticatedly designed book page and, thus, a story begins that draws attention by illustrating the subject. The aim of this lovingly designed production was to arouse the interest of the employees and show them how important this subject is for the agency. The video deals with the behaviour among employees, the question of how to deal with so-called "trolls" – that is, grumblers and troublemakers – as well as the communication of sensitive content and corporate affiliation. Employees thus become familiar with the codes and rules of behaviour within just three minutes, enabling them to use social networks with a clear conscience.

Statement by the jury

»This video impresses in particular with its charming, high-quality appearance and strong love for detail, two characteristics that are highly unusual and surprising as the work is meant only for in-house use at the agency. Also remarkable, alongside the aesthetic implementation, is the fact that these guidelines are conveyed not by force-feeding information but rather in a tongue-in-cheek way.«

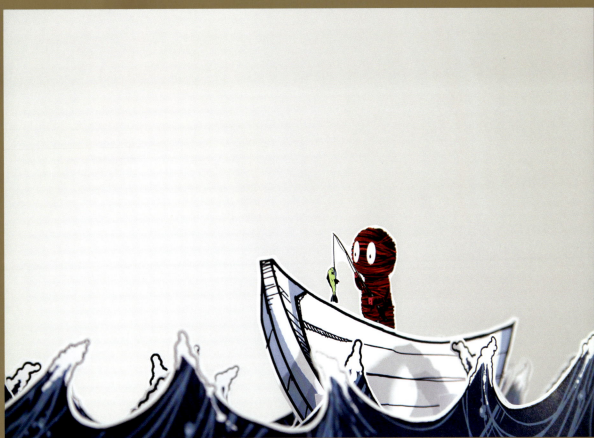

client
denkwerk GmbH, Cologne

design
denkwerk GmbH, Cologne

illustration/animation
Christian Warstat

motion design
Gregor Kuschmirz

→ clip on DVD
→ designer portrait: p. 401

Bergfürst

[Image Film]

In order to introduce and illustrate the topic of crowd funding – a business model in which members of a "crowd" can participate in innovative companies during their growth phase – this image film teases viewers with seemingly contradictory visual ideas. In a way that is rather untypical for the financial world, the film features a collage style of imagery and mixes stop motion with 3D animation, as well as photographs with illustrations. Due to many positive reviews, this film about the phenomenon of crowd investing thus became a phenomenon itself.

client
Bergfürst AG,
Berlin

design
Realgestalt GmbH,
Berlin

art direction
Anne Kohlermann,
Cornelius Mangold

animation
Susan Kreher,
Luisa Le van,
Felix Kumpfe,
Atelier Hurra,
Berlin

→ clip on DVD

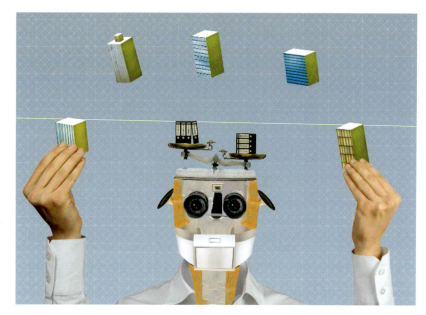

PREONmarine
[Exhibition Video, Event Opener]

A camera diving into the sea demonstrates how much noise and threat to marine life is caused by common anchoring systems. An innovative offshore wind tower anchoring system drastically reduces the noise, which is exemplified in this video. It visualises the advantages and illustrates the contrast it creates to the environment. Based on construction plans only, the conceptual design was defined without having a physical prototype at hand. Finding triangle forms in these plans, a key visual was developed, which is used throughout the stylised 3D animation film. It points out the construction method of this invention by "translating" the abstract idea into clear geometric forms.

client
Vallourec & Mannesmann Tubes, Düsseldorf

design
Quadrolux –
Agentur für Bewegtbild,
Mainz

creative direction
Marcus Stiehl

art direction
Melanie Schmidt

motion design
Bianca Schaurer-Spieß

→ clip on DVD

Event Design | Information Design & Public Space | **Corporate Films** | TV, Film, Cinema & Animation | Online World

One for All
[Image Film]

The manifold activities and international significance of TÜV Rheinland, a German technical services provider that goes far beyond simply checking the safety of cars, is visualised in this film by means of simple and easy-to-understand imagery. In conveying the new image, the commercial mainly addresses certification managers at TÜV's clients. More than 5,000 DVDs were mailed to key account clients worldwide. In addition, the film is also featured on TÜV Rheinland's website and at trade fairs.

client
TÜV Rheinland AG,
Cologne

design
Benjamin Kempf,
Cologne

film production
FRISCHE BRISE FILM,
Cologne

film direction
Roman Stricker,
Benjamin Kempf

music/sound design
Ilja Pollach

agency executive producer
Roy Sämerow,
alle freiheit werbeagentur GmbH,
Cologne

→ clip on DVD

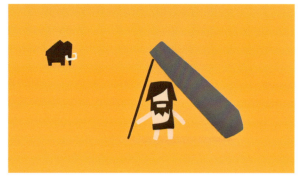

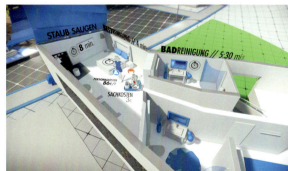

Kerkhoff Cost Engineering
[Animation Film]

With the objective of making the complicated topic of "service cost analysis" accessible to a broad audience, this animation film reduces the subject matter to a small cosmos. It features sophisticated motion graphics showing a detailed and lovingly crafted "service city" that visualises the variety of services in which Kerkhoff Cost Engineering specialises. The existing corporate design has been completely reinterpreted in the process and optimised for this motion picture.

client
Kerkhoff Cost Engineering GmbH, Düsseldorf

design/animation
Martin Jendrusch, Hagen

art direction/ graphic design
Marc Schultes

text
Felix Rodenjohann

project management
Martin Jendrusch

film production
tremoniamedia Filmproduktion GmbH, Dortmund

→ clip on DVD

40 Years of Illuminating Design

[Image Film]

Using the notion of "illumination", this image film illustrates the design philosophy that has driven Porsche Design Group for 40 years. The image is conveyed in a narrative approach so that the designed products "light up" the lives of the people using them. The film features dark backgrounds, whereas the products themselves are illuminated using strong lighting. The keywords "puristic", "innovative" and "engineered" serve as chapter headings that aid in chronologically imparting the history of the Porsche Design Group.

client
Porsche Design Gesellschaft mbH, Zell am See

design
Schober Design, London

concept
Damian Schober, Denis Kovac

project management
Arifa Sheikh, Lucy Martens

film production
Arifa Sheikh

film direction
Damian Schober

music/sound design
Ours

fashion styling
Florentine Pabst

→ clip on DVD

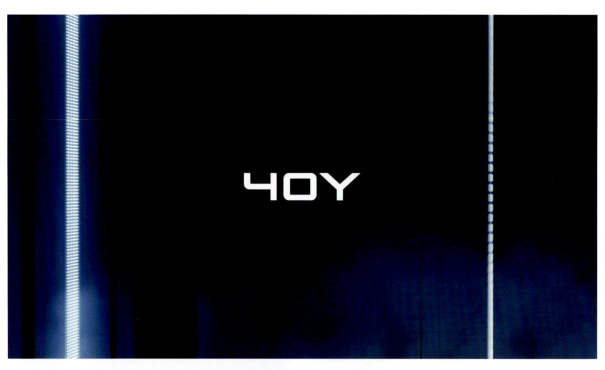

Sampo – 25 years as a listed company
[Corporate Video]

This corporate video was produced in order to celebrate the 25th anniversary of Sampo's listing on the Helsinki Stock Exchange. The goal was to provide an authentic portrait of the company's image and current values and to accurately reflect each period of its development from 1988 to 2013. The video combines old photos from various archives and new footage. In addition, different post-production effects and methods were employed to complete the final look and feel.

client
Sampo Group,
Helsinki

**design/
art direction**
YellowBlack,
Anima Boutique Oy,
Helsinki

**concept/
project management**
Sampo Group,
Anima Boutique Oy

film production
Anima Boutique Oy

live action sequences
Cocoa Mediaproductions Oy

**music/
sound design**
Humina Oy

animation
Anima Boutique Oy

Zumtobel Lighting
[Image Film]

client
Zumtobel Lighting GmbH,
Dornbirn

head of marketing
Stefan von Terzi

design/lead agency
BOROS GmbH,
Wuppertal/Berlin

creative direction
Christian Boros,
BOROS GmbH
Oriol Puig,
Trizz

account management
Martina Schiffer-Gottfried,
BOROS GmbH

production
Selim Sevinc,
ZEITSPRUNG COMMERCIAL GmbH

film direction
Oriol Puig,
Trizz
Reto Caffi,
ZEITSPRUNG COMMERCIAL GmbH

3D animation
Oriol Puig,
Christopher Vulpi,
Trizz

→ clip on DVD

Interface Design   Mobile & Apps   Game Design   Sound Design   Red Dot: Junior Award   Designer Portraits

The plot of this image film revolves around modern urban individuals of the twenty-first century and the role light plays in their everyday lives. Through a clever combination of live footage and 3D animation, the film shows how lighting solutions adjust to the respective situation and needs of people in a world of constant change. The audience follows a man on his way through everyday life, witnessing how light makes living and working easier for an enhanced sense of well-being, while increasing buildings' energy efficiency. The goal of the client Zumtobel to provide optimum lighting quality for people while protecting the environment is thus conveyed through an impressive and emotional story.

WDC 2016
Taipei Bid Video

client
Department of Cultural Affairs,
Taipei City Government,
Taipei

design
Grass Jelly Studio,
Taipei

film production
Yi-Chien Lee,
Grass Jelly Studio

film direction
Muh Chen,
Grass Jelly Studio

music/sound design
Tzu-Chieh Wen,
Taipei

camera
Jing Ping Yu,
Taipei
Dantol Peng,
Taipei

animation
Ming-Yuan Chuan,
Hsiao-Han Tseng,
Kang Li,
E.T. Liu,
Shu-Min Wu,
Chia-Hua Yu,
Pony Liu,
Chia-Hao Zhuo,
Winson Chao,
Weiting Chen,
Sheng Yang,
Grass Jelly Studio

→ clip on DVD
→ designer portrait: p. 407

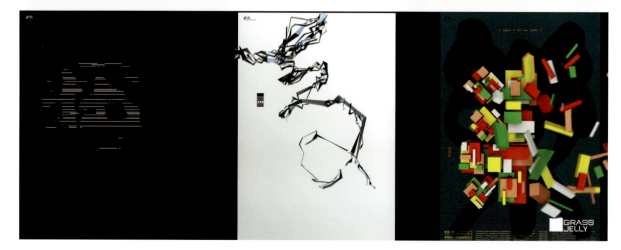

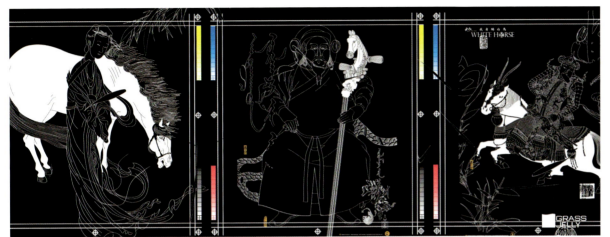

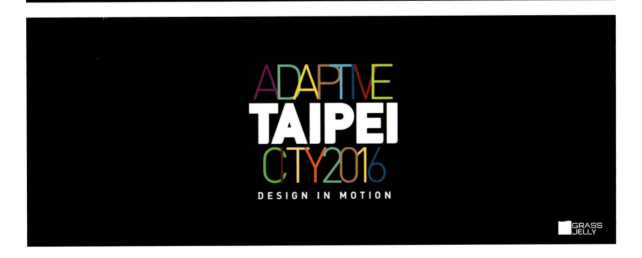

At the centre of the WDC 2016 Taipei Bid video is a highly expressive visualisation of the topics of "Taipei as an adaptive city" and "Design in motion". The video starts with a historic flashback of the city, complemented by short statements by renowned personalities in art, culture, design and philosophy in order to positively foster their subconscious awareness. The film thus underlines the city of Taipei's commitment to culture and also its representative significance for the entire country of Taiwan. Finally, a smoothly flowing sequence of images illustrates what significance the topic of design holds for this city and the related role of younger generations in particular.

Audi Tradition – Museum Mobile

[Video Installation]

client
Audi Tradition –
Museum Mobile,
Ingolstadt

design/concept
velvet mediendesign GmbH,
Munich

creative direction
Thomas Wernbacher

project management
Dieter-Ludwig Karg

editor-in-chief
Jochen Kraus

film direction
Matthias Zentner

music/sound design
Toni M. Mir,
Trafalgar

→ clip on DVD

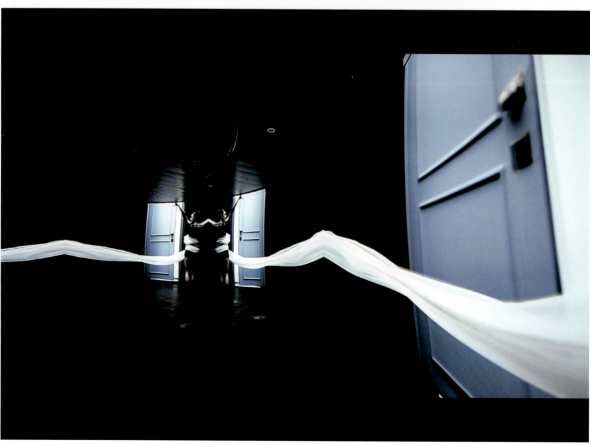

| Interface Design | Mobile & Apps | Game Design | Sound Design | Red Dot: Junior Award | Designer Portraits |

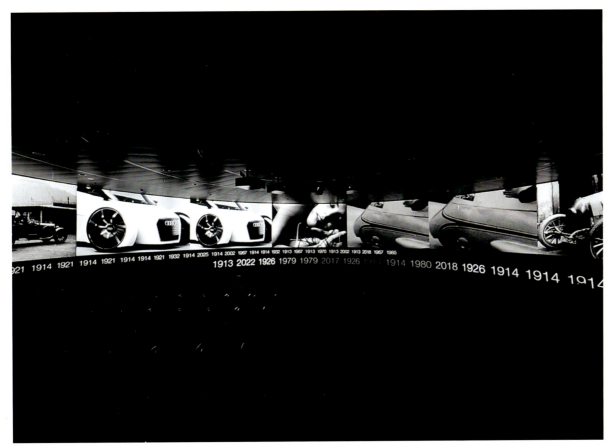

This video installation at the Audi Museum in Ingolstadt stretches across a 180-degree panorama screen and has a monumental size of 30 metres in length and 4 metres in height. It impressively visualises the "Mobility of Change" in a historical time stream. In close cooperation with the Audi Tradition's archive, footage from moving-picture landmarks were chosen and arranged in the film's narrative in parallel to the history of Audi. The voice-over of the installation was conceived as a solemn stream of thoughts in the sense of an internal monologue that merges to form the musical sound journey within the 7.1 surround sound installation.

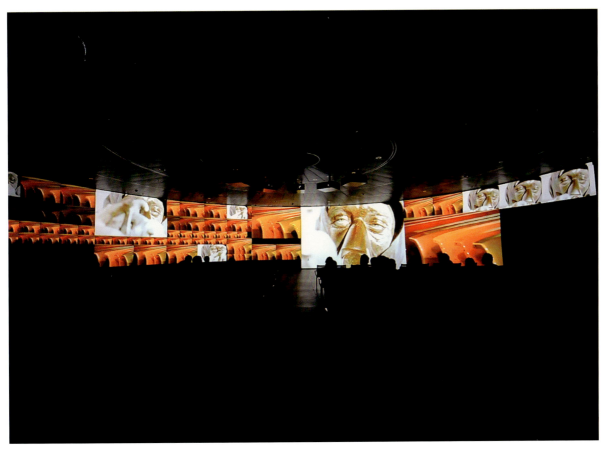

Audi Brand Pavilion, Wolfsburg

[360-Degree Media Display]

client
AUDI AG,
Ingolstadt

design
KMS BLACKSPACE,
Munich

→ clip on DVD
→ designer portrait: p. 416

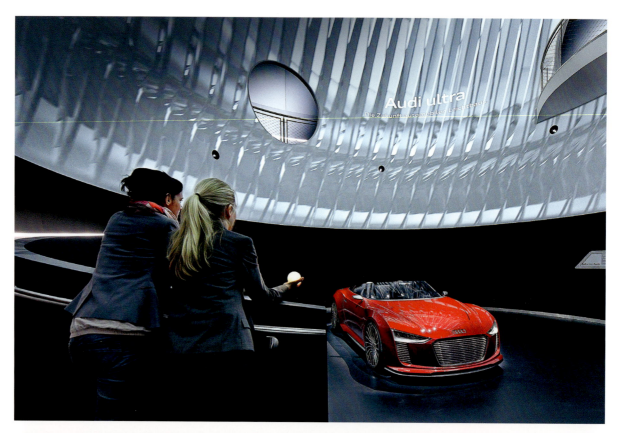

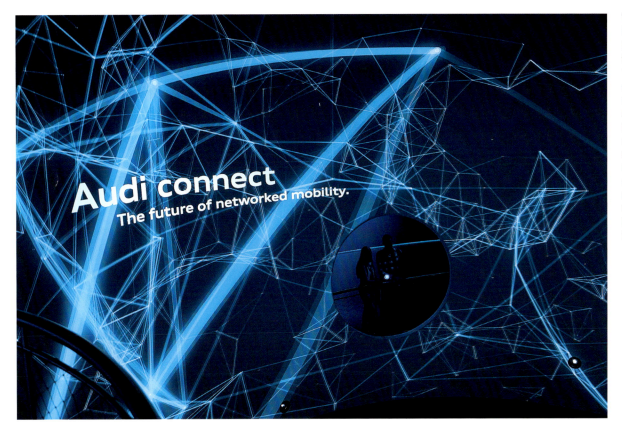

The highlight of this interactive brand installation at the Audi Brand Pavilion in Wolfsburg is the massive rotunda, which spans 12 metres in diameter and is 7.5 metres high. The corresponding media displays communicate Audi's latest technologies and innovations, accompanied by a world of fascinating images. The main themes of the brand – Audi ultra, Audi e-tron, Audi connect and Audi design – slowly rotate around the Audi e-tron Spyder in the centre of the room, while the lighting changes with each topic to create a different mood.

INTERNATIONAL YEARBOOK COMMUNICATION DESIGN 2013/2014

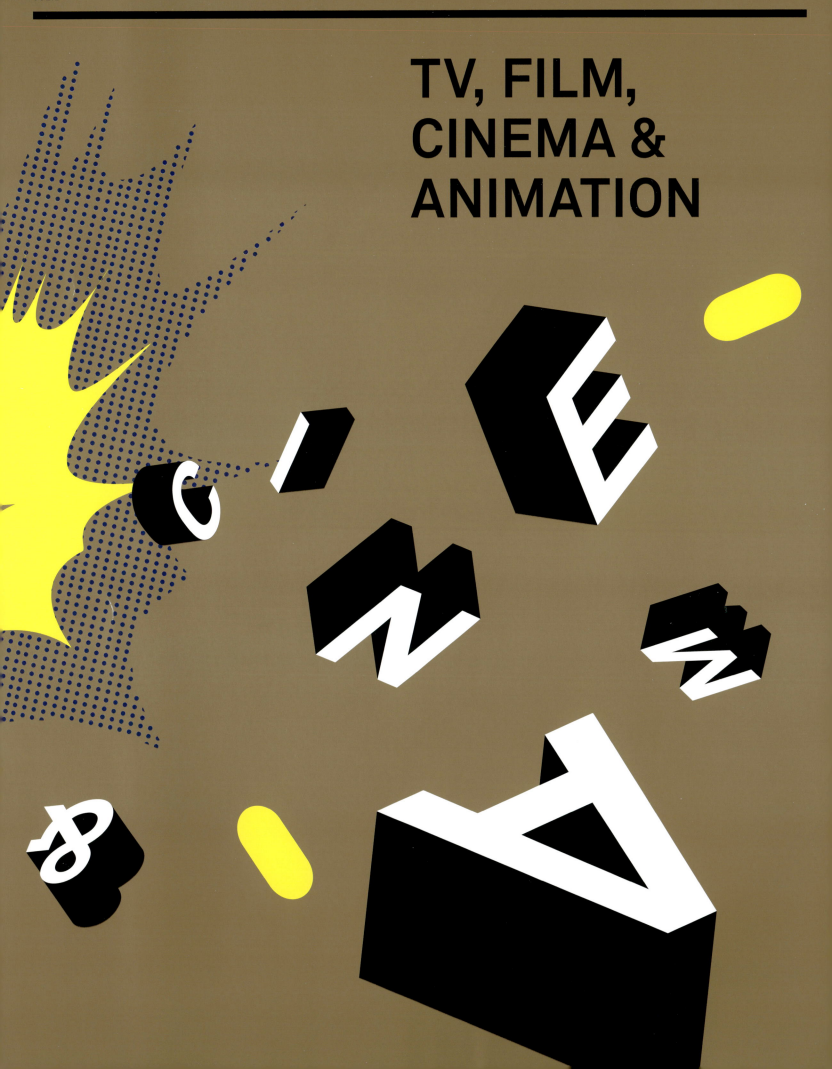

| Event Design | Information Design & Public Space | Corporate Films | TV, Film, Cinema & Animation | Online World |

Red Dot: Best of the Best

Who Am We?
[Interactive Film]

"Who Am We?" is an interactive film by a London-based Korean artist who, in an open letter, invited 218,000 employees at Hyundai Motor Group to participate in an exhibition which will be part of a permanent display at HMG's human resources development centre. The journey of the work began with the employees submitting their portraits, which were then assembled on a video wall. From a distance, these photographs appear as tiny dots that, in the course of the animation, constitute sentences. Participants can see their faces enlarge in the centre of the screen only when they log in to a smartphone application. This aesthetically outstanding, innovative work also examines the subtle boundaries between the individual and a group by demonstrating how the identities of individuals are minimised or neglected in a crowd for greater value. By utilising digital interaction and inviting employees as active participants, the clearly designed project opens up a new space of dialogue, and the employees are naturally led to explore their identity and develop a sense of belonging in their communities.

Statement by the jury

»The highly interactive installation embodies a wonderful integration of the employees into the company's media processes and thus strengthens both their identities and the corporate identity. "Who Am We?" is marked by a highly interesting design solution and a technically complex implementation.«

Interface Design   Mobile & Apps   Game Design   Sound Design   Red Dot: Junior Award   Designer Portraits

client
Hyundai Motor Group,
Seoul

design
Do Ho Suh,
London

creative direction
Do Ho Suh,
London

project management
Innocean Worldwide,
Visual Communication Division,
Seoul

motion design
Do Ho Suh,
London
Imagebakery,
Seoul

exhibition stand construction
Suh Architects,
Seoul

music/sound design
Cravesound,
Bucheon

photography
Kisu Park,
Seoul
Nils Clauss,
Seoul

→ clip on DVD
→ designer portrait: p. 434

Red Dot: Best of the Best

Playfield
[Cinema Spot]

This cinema commercial promotes the transitional stage "Playfield" at the Hamburg theatre Deutsches Schauspielhaus, as the big stage was being renovated and performances were held on this temporary stage in the middle of the auditorium. The effect of an even more intense theatrical experience as the audience was now even closer to the actors was picked up as the main idea in this commercial for the temporary stage. Focusing on the essentials, namely accompanying the heroes of the plays through the ups and downs of their lives, the spot resorts to a reduced style of illustration to show highly emotional moments in a man's life. The tension between the shown extremes touches the viewer thanks to the almost papercut-like minimalism of the illustrations, yet also irritates and piques curiosity about the temporary stage in the middle of Germany's largest auditorium space. The overall simple dramaturgy and staging of the spot makes the great emotions that theatre is all about come to life in a highly engaging and immersive manner.

Statement by the jury

»With its two-dimensional design, the cinema spot "Playfield" represents an aesthetic approach that is rarely seen today in the field of animation. It is integrated into the environment, structure and the design in a highly sophisticated manner so that the story is told efficiently and the message becomes clear and convincing.«

client
Deutsches Schauspielhaus in Hamburg

design
Pixelbutik by Deli Pictures, Hamburg
thjnk, Hamburg

creative direction
Patricia Pätzold, Patricia Wetzel

art direction
Patricia Wetzel, Juliane Lange

film direction
Jan Richter

animation
Pascal Reitz

music/sound design
Stephan Radom

production
Martin Klauder

→ clip on DVD
→ designer portrait: p. 427

Red Dot: Best of the Best

Offroad
[TV Spot]

Accompanied by heavy metal music, this TV spot shows a smart fortwo that drives around in a rough, off-road environment without any tracks or paths. In this rough terrain, the car tries to climb up a steep hill, cross a river and pass over large rocks, miserably failing every challenge. With these absurd images, the presumed weakness of the smart is turned into a strength, as the subsequent images of the spot demonstrate: just as SUVs are not made for the city, the smart fortwo is not made for off-road driving. Evoking a reversal conclusion, the subsequent images of the spot celebrate the urban environment. Unlike an SUV that is forced to circle around to find a parking spot, for the smart this is not a problem. On the contrary: the smart fortwo is perfect for the city. Realised in quick cuts, viewers follow this fast-paced ride that links the wit of the spot with coolness and the joy of driving.

Statement by the jury

»The humorously narrated story of the spot "Offroad" invests a lot of work into self-irony that is then turned around and projected positively onto the smart. This idea is conveyed convincingly through a series of highly sophisticated images full of wit and surprises.«

Interface Design | Mobile & Apps | Game Design | Sound Design | Red Dot: Junior Award | Designer Portraits

>> So gut im Gelände
wie ein Geländewagen in der Stadt.

client
Daimler AG,
Böblingen

design
BBDO Proximity Berlin GmbH

creative managing director
Jan Harbeck,
David Mously

creative direction
David Mously,
Ton Hollander,
Jens Ringena

art direction
Daniel Schweinzer

text
Lukas Liske,
Momme Clausen

account management
Dirk Spakowski,
Sebastian Schlosser,
Jan Hendrik Oelckers,
Joris Jonker,
Mia Lücker

film production
Bigfish Filmproduktion GmbH

film direction
Daniel Warwick

music/sound design
Eardrum Music & Sound Design

→ clip on DVD
→ designer portrait: p. 395

Red Dot: Best of the Best

BVB Bakery
[TV Spot]

Evonik Industries is not only BVB's biggest sponsor, but also its most loyal fan. This message was the inspiration behind the advert for the 2012/2013 season, which communicates the specialty chemicals company's deep passion for the football club Borussia Dortmund (BVB) and has been broadcast in commercial breaks during the German sports programme Sportschau. In the clip, the whole of Dortmund has lost its voice except for one man. The spot shows a group of customers at a bakery merrily chatting along with severely hoarse voices so that the words are utterly incomprehensible. Suddenly the man walks into the bakery, says a cheery "Good morning" and is met with hoarse but hearty laughter as everybody is aware there can only be one explanation for healthy vocal chords on this day in Dortmund: "If you still have your voice on Monday, you must have missed the match!" Staged in a familiar authentic bakery, this spot conveys its message in an unerring manner – without and especially beyond words.

Statement by the jury

»This spot stands out for its direct surprise effect: the hoarse voices make it clear what the spot is driving at. The story and with it the sense of fan culture are conveyed immediately. Plot, structure and sound design are consistently matched, forming a perfect unity.«

client
Evonik Industries AG,
Essen

design
KNSK Werbeagentur GmbH,
Hamburg

head of advertising
Werner Knopf

creative direction
Vera Hampe,
Olaf Hörning

art direction
Martin Augner,
Caroline Labitzke

text
Dirk Junski,
Jeanette Lindner

account management
Verena Gillwald

film production
Tony Petersen Film

→ clip on DVD
→ designer portrait: p. 417

Event Design | Information Design & Public Space | Corporate Films | **TV, Film, Cinema & Animation** | Online World

Red Dot: Best of the Best

Shaving
[TV Spot]

Be it a lumberjack in the woods, a horse guard in a castle or an ice hockey player – they are all men and therefore have a beard to shave. In short sequences, this TV spot shows several men in clothing typical of their profession and work environment, all of them in the same pose with their beards covered in shaving gel. Using a typical work tool – an axe, a sword or the blade of a skate – they start to shave in the next scene, which makes the key message of this commercial clear: shaving does not require a special blade. On the contrary, almost any blade can do the job. Instead, what matters is the right gel, namely the shaving gel by NIVEA MEN promoted in this commercial. The end of the commercial shows the different men proudly stroking their cleanly shaven faces, a final scene that summarises the message that this result is exclusively owed to the right shaving gel in a highly entertaining and humorous manner.

Statement by the jury

»The story of "Shaving" sharply gets its message across: the shaving gel is more important than the blade. Staging an old-fashioned image of men – a highly unusual approach for commercials in the field of cosmetic products – and twisting that image around is the outstanding quality of this work.«

client
Beiersdorf AG,
Hamburg

design
Draftfcb Deutschland GmbH,
Hamburg

creative direction
Dirk Haeusermann

text
Mathias Müller

account management
Thorsten Stoll,
Christin Ritter,
Jörg Hoppenstedt,
Olga Sow

film production
Jule Everts,
Ariane Müller,
Bigfish Filmproduktion GmbH

film direction
Daniel Warwick

post-production
Deli Pictures

→ clip on DVD
→ designer portrait: p. 403

Policeman
[Video Ad]

In order to illustrate how people can do fitness anytime and anywhere without having to join a fitness club, this TV video ad shows a traffic policeman at work. Walking along a road in uniform, he encounters a car coming around the corner. The policeman directs the car to keep moving and continues to stay in motion. He even starts moving and spinning his left hand, then does the same with his right hand and even starts jumping. All in all, it looks as if the policeman were exercising by following his very own personal fitness programme.

client
Russian fitness-aerobics Federation,
Moscow

design
e:mg,
Moscow

executive director
Tatiana Tarmogina

creative direction
Anton Melnikov,
Maxim Kolyshev

art direction
Maxim Kolyshev

photography
Vladimir Bashta,
Sergey Kirichenko

music/sound design
Vadim Kolosov

production
Anna Medvedeva,
Olga Yankevich,
Yulia Nikitina,
Yulia Samoilova,
Dmitry Makarov

→ clip on DVD

Security Guard
[Video Ad]

Following a humorous approach, this TV video ad aims to motivate people to work out and stay fit by being imaginative. It shows a security guard who, while working on a night shift in a large shopping mall, works out by running on an escalator in the opposite direction. The storyline of the video ad demonstrates that in order to keep fit it is not necessary to have membership in a fitness club or special clothes for working out.

client
Russian fitness-aerobics Federation,
Moscow

design
e:mg,
Moscow

executive director
Tatiana Tarmogina

creative direction
Anton Melnikov,
Maxim Kolyshev

art direction
Maxim Kolyshev

photography
Vladimir Bashta,
Sergey Kirichenko

music/sound design
Vadim Kolosov

production
Anna Medvedeva,
Olga Yankevich,
Yulia Nikitina,
Yulia Samoilova,
Dmitry Makarov

→ clip on DVD

Discovery Channel – Second World War

[TV Promotion]

This trailer for the Discovery Channel Germany advertised a special programme commemorating D-Day and the Second World War by following a novel approach. Instead of working with widespread real historical images, the clip showcased an entire theatre of war reconstructed in miniature. The camera movement was particularly serene, hovering over the non-action of the static backdrop. The rather sad and bleak atmosphere was supported by an intense audio composition that contributed to bringing the fate of the individuals involved to the fore.

client
Discovery Communications Deutschland GmbH & Co. KG, Munich

design
DMC Design for Media and Communication GmbH, Munich

art direction/camera
Aitor Benavent Cabanas

concept
Javier Collantes Rodriguez

film direction/editor
Javier Collantes Rodriguez

project management
Tilo Fischer

→ clip on DVD

Interface Design Mobile & Apps Game Design Sound Design Red Dot: Junior Award Designer Portraits

Take care …
[Internet Commercial]

In a spectacularly rapid sequence of images, this Internet commercial evokes the notion that we have to take care of a myriad of different things in our lives while simultaneously being bombarded with fragmented impressions. The narrative of the clip builds up and culminates with the claim that the chair sliders of the brand QuickClick are equipped with clickable, floor-protecting slide inserts that cause no noise, no stress and no damage. The commercial thus wants to communicate how very easy it can be to "take care".

client
Wagner System GmbH, Lahr

design
Bar Vinya Film, Ohlsbach

→ clip on DVD

Save the Ingots – use Crypton

[3D Animation Movie]

The 3D animation movie "Save the Ingots – use Crypton" promotes the advantages of a new material called crypton for the production of dental superstructures. Since the production thereof has previously involved difficult work for the dental technician in casting so-called ingots, the film features eponymous animated characters. Shown doing hard and risky work, the Ingots are saved by other characters representing the material of crypton. In a funny style, the movie promotes the advantages of working with this new and clean non-precious alloy.

client
DeguDent GmbH,
Hanau

design
KINOBLAU,
Büro für Kommunikationsdesign,
Düsseldorf

→ clip on DVD

Diamante Concept Car

[3D Animation]

The eco-friendly characteristics of the Diamante Concept Car are visualised in this 3D animation film through the diamond, from which the car's name is derived. Just as the diamond is the most valuable mineral in the world, this sports car is promoted as "the dream car with the white collar", not least because it features a similar silhouette and appears unpolished and rough. The film describes the genesis of the octahedron-shaped crystal in an abstract way, from its formation to its eventual journey to different places.

client/automotive design
Thomas Granjard Design,
Tourrettes-sur-Loup

design/production
Lean Design GmbH,
Cologne

creative direction/art direction
Tom Nowak,
Christoph Große Hovest

concept
Tom Nowak,
Christoph Große Hovest

music/sound design
Tom Nowak

motion design
Christoph Große Hovest

→ clip on DVD

Acousticons
[Cinema Spot]

client
Philharmoniker Hamburg

design
Draftfcb Deutschland GmbH,
Hamburg

creative direction
Dirk Haeusermann,
Patrik Hartmann,
Michael Okun

art direction
Vitali Nazarenus,
Markus Schmidt,
Semjon Janzen,
Elena Balzer

text
Saemi Sebastian Bouchareb,
Verena Kessler,
Elena Praetze

film production
Estelle Bolin,
Holger Siegle,
onehousemedia,
Optix Digital Pictures

music/sound design
Loft Tonstudios Hamburg

programming
Akryl Digital Agency

→ clip on DVD
→ designer portrait: p. 403

| Interface Design | Mobile & Apps | Game Design | Sound Design | Red Dot: Junior Award | Designer Portraits |

The Acousticons campaign was created with the aim of bringing the Hamburg Philharmonic Orchestra and classical music in general back into the lives of youth. A messenger app lets users feel the emotional power of classical music by sending text messages that are enhanced by the philharmonic's full orchestral accompaniment. In the cinema commercial accompanying the campaign, the Acousticons represent charmingly animated, emoticon-like note icons, different musical tempi and also the emotions associated with them.

| Event Design | Information Design & Public Space | Corporate Films | TV, Film, Cinema & Animation | Online World |

Cheers
[Music Video]

This video uses flashbacks to trace the entire life of a person with black humour from impending death to childhood. The protagonist in the film watches the events in his life through a kind of window showing familiar faces happily raising their glasses in salute. At the end of the video, the dying person has said farewell and opens a door that leads into a soft carpet of clouds. The six-minute film wants to convey that life does not have to be serious but can be delightful and simple, thus presenting an alternative life philosophy.

client
Bin Music,
Taipei

design
Grass Jelly Studio,
Taipei

film production
Yi-Chien Lee,
Grass Jelly Studio

film direction
Muh Chen,
Grass Jelly Studio

music/sound design
Bin Music

camera
Jing Ping Yu,
Taipei

lighting design
Pony Ma,
Taipei

post-production
Ming-Yuan Chuan,
Roland Yang,
Hsiao Han Tseng,
Kang Li,
Hao Xiang Lin,
Grass Jelly Studio

→ clip on DVD
→ designer portrait: p. 407

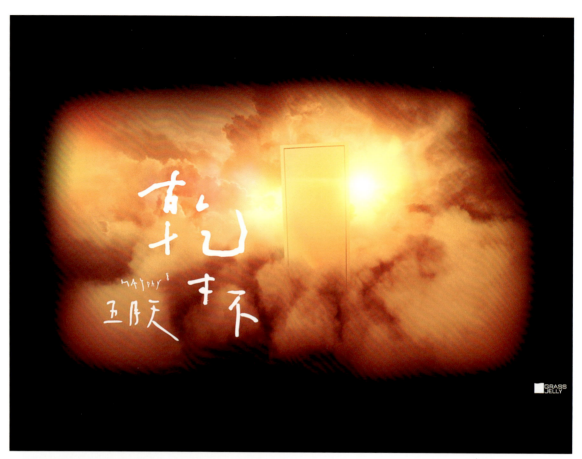

Interface Design | Mobile & Apps | Game Design | Sound Design | Red Dot: Junior Award | Designer Portraits

DER GROSSE AMEISENBÄR

AB SOMMER LIVE IM

KÖLNER ZOO

WWW.KOELNERZOO.DE

Kölsch beer glass
[TV Spot]

This TV spot announces the arrival of the newest addition to the Cologne Zoo, the giant anteater, by visualising the animal's main pastime of "licking up ants". It starts by showing an empty glass of Kölsch beer with an ant crawling around in it and a second ant that is on its way there. The meaning of the scene immediately becomes clear when the ants are licked up by the anteater. Employing simple means, this TV spot attracts the viewers' attention and invites them to come to the zoo to see the anteater live.

client
Aktiengesellschaft Zoologischer Garten Köln, Cologne

design
Preuss und Preuss GmbH, Berlin

creative direction
Michael Preuss

art direction
Felicitas Haas

concept
Felicitas Haas, Enno Wöhler

music/sound design
The Shack Berlin

production
The Shack Berlin

→ clip on DVD

Deckel auf und los!
Remove lid and go!
[Animation Clip]

This non-profit short animation clip aims to raise awareness of how important immediate help is for people who suffer sudden cardiac arrest. The clip demonstrates how to use an AED (automated external defibrillator), which recently have been installed in many public spaces. A key visual in the form of a balloon illustrates the first aid instructions and simplicity of use. The first deterrent effect on sudden cardiac death is communicated in a consistently positive and simple way through typography, illustration and language.

client
hillus Engineering KG, Krefeld

design
hillus Engineering KG, Krefeld

art direction/graphic design
Christoph Hillus

editor
Kamil Zaleski

animation
David Inhoven

voice
Lars Schmidtke

→ clip on DVD

Your Club. Your Shop.
[Animation]

The animation "Your Club. Your Shop." for eckball.de, an online shop for team sports equipment, sports accessories and retro jerseys, specifically appeals to the emotions of a sports-oriented target group. The aim is to promote the shop by strengthening positive perception among potential customers. A harmonious balance of club colours, stadium sound and typography that is typical of banners found in stadiums was employed to evoke the desired atmosphere and thematic proximity.

client
eckball.de,
Hannover

design
beierarbeit GmbH,
Bielefeld

creative direction/graphic design
Christoph Beier

music/sound design
Christoph Beier,
Rainer Falkenroth

animation
Christoph Beier,
Rainer Falkenroth

→ clip on DVD

Qualcomm
[Animations]

The animations for the International Consumer Electronics Show 2013 keynote presentation by the mobile chip giant Qualcomm were created to support and document the engineering expertise behind the inventions of the company. Inspired by technical drawings, a system of diagrams with a symbolic character was developed. These diagrams move and interact with each other on the digital screen in such a way that beholders are given the impression they are being taken on a visual journey inside the minds of the engineers.

client
Qualcomm,
San Diego

design
Interbrand,
New York

creative direction
Chris Campbell

art direction
Jeremy Grimes

concept
Fell Gray

graphic design
Ronan Tiongson

animation
David Hong

consultancy
Claire Falloon

→ clip on DVD

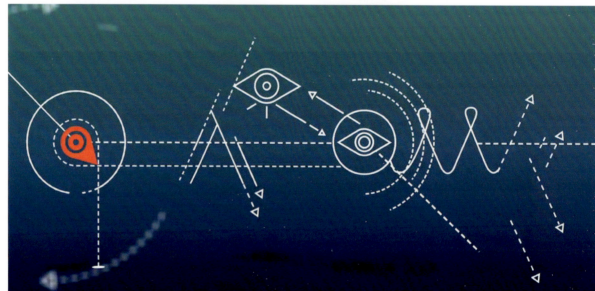

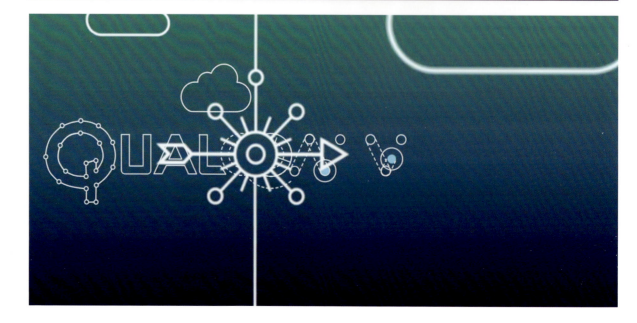

THE REVOLUTION OF CINEMA
DER BESTE SOUND IM CINEPLEX

The Evolution of Sound – The Revolution of Cinema
[Cinema Spot]

As part of a nationwide change-over from 5.1 to 7.1 surround sound in a major German cinema chain, this cinema spot campaign introduces new vistas of sound and imagery to viewers. It stages and makes audible otherwise unremarkable things and processes. The implementation has consciously avoided the imagery typical of movies shown in multiplex theatres. Instead, it has combined reduced and clear visual compositions with exceptional new sound worlds.

client
Cineplex Deutschland GmbH & Co. KG, Wuppertal

design
GUCC GmbH, Münster

art direction
Carsten Christochowitz, Christian Hund

graphic design
Jessica Comes

music/sound design
Thomas Bücker

camera
Karsten Jäger

editor
Christian Hund

→ clip on DVD

Event Design · Information Design & Public Space · Corporate Films · TV, Film, Cinema & Animation · Online World

Dandelion Mirror
[Interaction Design, Data Visualisation]

client
Chung Hua University,
Hsinchu

design
Scottie Chih-Chieh Huang &
BIO Lab + SDAID,
Chung Hua University,
Hsinchu

direction
Prof. Scottie Chih-Chieh Huang

graphic design
Jyun-Yan Chen

research assistance
Ji-Wei Jang,
Pai-Hsien Liao,
Wei-Hsiang Huang,
Chun-Mao Tseng,
Pi-Chu Chuang,
Yu-Shan Jeng,
Chuan-Bin Juang

text
Yu-Chun Huang,
Tatung University,
Taipei

→ clip on DVD
→ designer portrait: p. 410

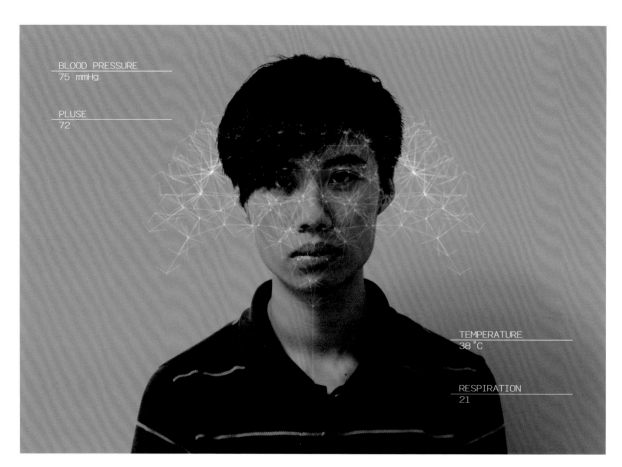

| Interface Design | Mobile & Apps | Game Design | Sound Design | Red Dot: Junior Award | Designer Portraits |

The Dandelion Mirror is a physiological measurement device featuring non-contact sensor technology. The biosensor-based unit is able to measure a person's temperature, pulse, respiration and blood pressure through a webcam and thus check on their current state of health. The health results are then presented on the surface of the mirror. Based on a complex fractal and recursive algorithm, the measured data are visualised in the shape of a "growing" virtual plant that mirrors each user's health. The morphological plant image transforms itself according to the individual physiological data, thus assuming a different shape for each person.

INTERNATIONAL YEARBOOK COMMUNICATION DESIGN 2013/2014

Red Dot: Grand Prix

Speel je toekomst
Play your future
[Website]

The online platform speeljetoekomst.nu was the heart of a campaign to create more awareness of the fact that the leading provider of life insurance and investment products makes people financially knowledgeable. It gives users a playful insight into the future by demonstrating how certain events might affect their lives. An advanced calculator application allows users to literally look into their future and get a realistic idea of their financial situation in future, and to subsequently play around with it by changing parameters. For a personal forecast, users only have to submit a few simple details such as age, family status, as well as expenses and details about living and leisure. A cheerful character guides users through the process and gives tips and badges for reaching milestones. The clear arrangement and comic-like design of the platform not only facilitates users to precisely overview their future financial possibilities, it also presents a supposedly dry subject in such a way that it becomes fun and arouses interest.

Statement by the jury

»The online platform manages to tell stories by following a highly interesting approach. Thanks to its interactive features, it allows users to change the story and thus decide on the best personal solution. By making optimal use of the digital medium, the complex topic is visualised in a clear and easy-to-understand manner and thus becomes more transparent.«

Interface Design | Mobile & Apps | Game Design | Sound Design | Red Dot: Junior Award | Designer Portraits

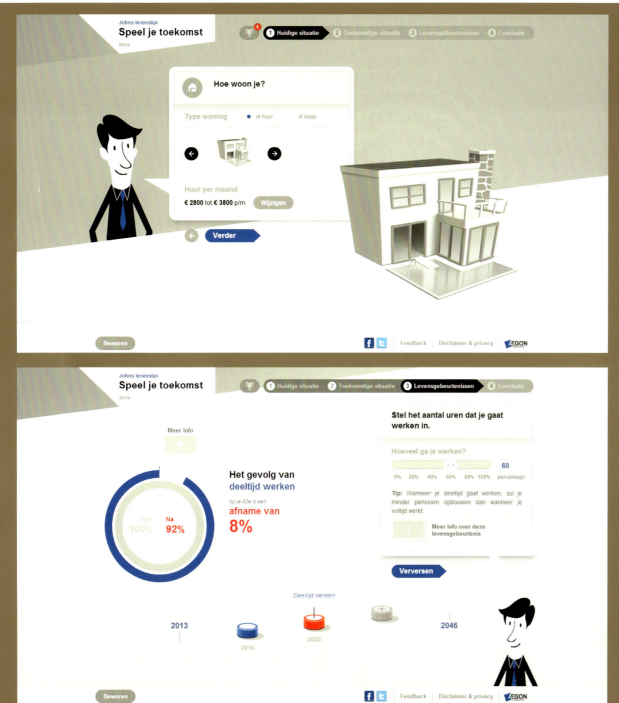

client
Aegon

concept
THEY
Momkai

design/realisation
Momkai

calculations
EPG

character animation
Comic House

game design
Subatomic

→ designer portrait: p. 422

reddot design award
grand prix 2013

Red Dot: Best of the Best

A. Lange & Söhne
[Corporate Website]

The task of the new corporate website of Saxon-based watch manufacturer A. Lange & Söhne was to create a digital stage for the drive for precision in analogue watch design. The guiding principle in the design was that nothing whatsoever should distract from the sole focus of attention, timepieces, which are among the best in the world. The minimalist impression of the home page is characteristic of the aesthetic standards displayed by the entire website. The spacious design and well-balanced interaction not only make the watches take centre stage, they also facilitate the introduction of the inside of the watches and follow up on the stories of their manufacturing. Be it on a desktop PC, tablet or smartphone, the featured images, photos and short video clips always take up the whole browser window. Complemented by text set underneath them and backed up by an overall clear and elegant design, they present a distinctive narrative of the history and quality of these timepieces.

Statement by the jury

»To make something complicated look simple and appealing is a high art. The website of A. Lange & Söhne is outstanding as it succeeds in doing exactly this. The statement of the highest quality that the watch manufacturer strives for is epitomised in the very reduction and concentration of the design and thus communicates the expression of elegance and perfection in the products.«

| Interface Design | Mobile & Apps | Game Design | Sound Design | Red Dot: Junior Award | Designer Portraits |

client
A. Lange & Söhne, Glashütte

design
Scholz & Volkmer GmbH, Berlin

creative direction
Larissa Honsek,
Judith Schütz

art direction
Mauricio Franicevich Garcia,
Sebastian Zirfas

project lead/concept
Stefan Ulfert,
Oliver Kunzmann

development
Florian Finke

account direction
Sabine Lee

project management
Sarah-Lu Bernhard

→ designer portrait: p. 430

Red Dot: Best of the Best

Arco – Table Manners
[Website]

Family business Arco has been making high-quality furniture for more than 100 years, focusing on providing technical innovation and design at a high level. Not being distant and elitist, its creations are made for use on a very human scale. Celebrating the enjoyment of this use with the theme "table manners", the website shows people who are working hard, fighting, polishing, doing arts and crafts or making love on tables. With a big dose of humour, these split-screen interactive video clips invite website users to control the course of events. Seriously, and yet tongue-in-cheek, the website stages apparent contradictions, yet also invokes that the quality of the Arco products pays off "seriously". To underline this, the furniture is displayed as appropriate for design products: cleanly and statically. By clicking on the heart, users can easily create their own collection of favourite products. Presented in an entertaining, diversified manner, the website possesses a surprising and discrete design.

Statement by the jury

»The website of Arco features a highly self-contained appearance. The layout and the choice of colours as well as picture motifs make a perfect match. Another feature, which is quite unusual for a furniture manufacturer, are the humorous film sequences that users can control and even develop further. This piques the interest in and the desire to possess these products.«

Interface Design   Mobile & Apps   Game Design   Sound Design   Red Dot: Junior Award   Designer Portraits

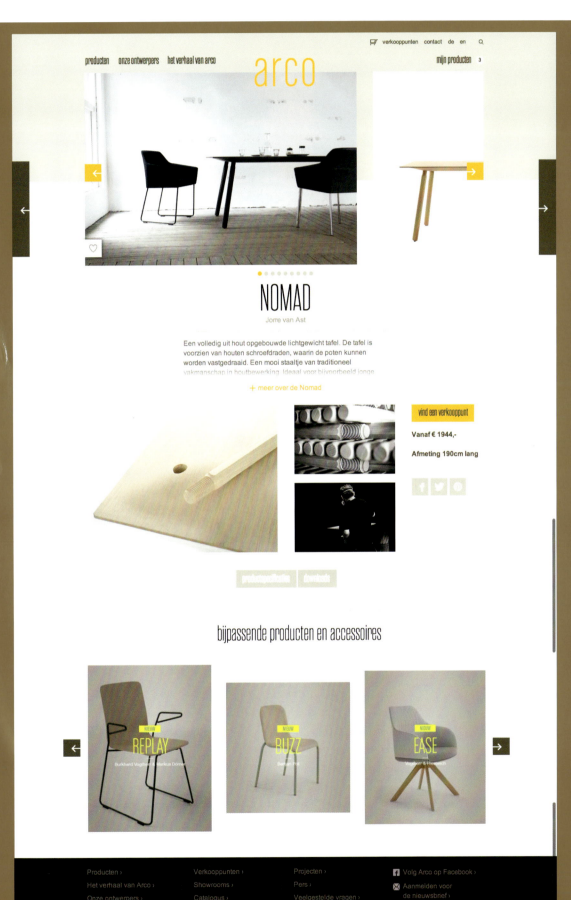

client
Arco,
Winterswijk

design
Fabrique
[brands, design & interaction],
Delft

art direction
Sanne Wijbenga

concept
Ronnie Besseling

project management
Ebelien Pondaag

photography
Maurice Heessen

animation
Marko Kruijer

interaction design
Rose-Anne Dotinga

→ designer portrait: p. 405

HOERBIGER

[Corporate Website]

client
HOERBIGER Holding AG,
Zug

design
GAXWEB GmbH,
Karlsruhe

art direction/concept
Tobias Holl

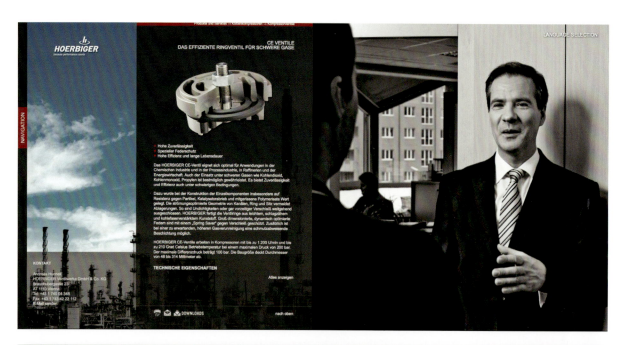

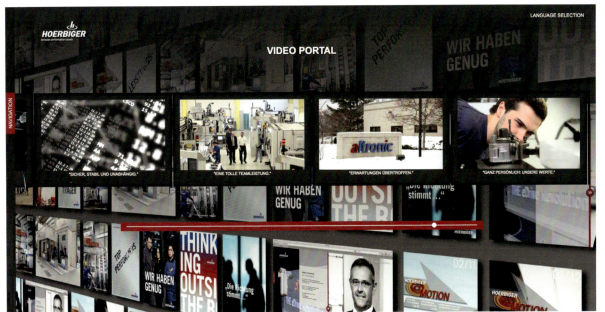

The key idea in designing this corporate website was to underscore the unique selling propositions of the commissioning client. With the help of strong imagery, it creates service and product worlds that aim to provide site visitors with a concrete overview of the benefits and added value provided by Hoerbiger technology. The primary navigation delivers a comprehensive first view of the website and fast access to relevant additional information. A highlight of the employed web technology is to put out visitor-targeted content, as the website detects the region from which a page is accessed, based on the transmitted IP address. The system then automatically supplies the user with content that is relevant to his or her location.

Event Design | Information Design & Public Space | Corporate Films | TV, Film, Cinema & Animation | **Online World** Online Communication

wagner-architecture.de
[Website]

In order to promote the advantages of Wagner office chairs for healthy sitting, the website wagner-architecture.de presents them in a spaciously dimensioned architectural setting. The brand's product portfolio is staged in an appealing and neatly arranged form. Alongside reduced product pictures, numerous illustrations and detailed information on all product dimensions provide a clear overview of the spatial planning. The multifarious design variations and options for use of the office chairs are presented through detailed explanations.

client
Topstar GmbH,
Langenneufnach

design
Martin et Karczinski,
Munich

creative direction
Peter Martin,
Birte Helms

art direction
Simon Maier-Rahmer

graphic design
Harun Oezduener

motion design
Björn Matthes

final artwork
Christian Gieb,
Martin Todt

technical direction
Christian Waldmann

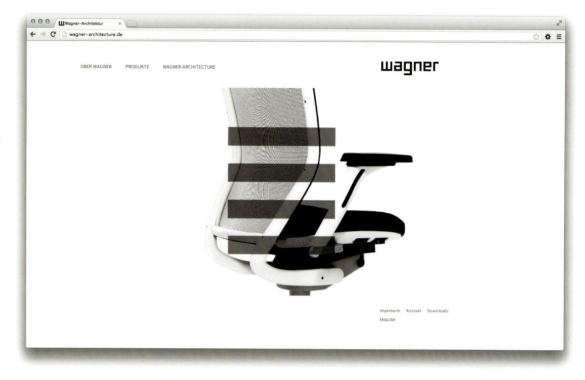

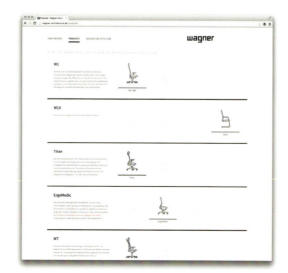

FSB
[Website Relaunch, Digital Catalogue]

With its reduced design approach, the new FSB website builds on the visual identity created by Otl Aicher and translates it into a contemporary design in both form and function. Aiming to provide information for the main target groups, architects and specialist planners, the website is supported by a responsive design optimised for touchscreen use. Lavish high-resolution images deliver a tangible experience of the FSB product worlds, while the simple navigational structure provides direct access to the desired content.

client
Franz Schneider Brakel GmbH, Brakel

design
salient doremus, Frankfurt/Main

| Event Design | Information Design & Public Space | Corporate Films | TV, Film, Cinema & Animation | **Online World** Online Communication |

ames culture of diversity

[Website]

This corporate website was developed to promote the new communication concept of a "culture of diversity" by the furniture company ames GmbH. The central hub is formed by an innovative homepage that dynamically fades in impressions from the four main sections of the website: Design, Culture, News and Space. In a kaleidoscopic manner, the ames corporate culture is thus visualised through constantly changing images, with each company product simultaneously mirroring the contemporary crossover of cultures.

client
ames GmbH,
Plaidt

design
achta design,
Dortmund

creative direction
Sara Böhmer,
Achim Böhmer

photography
Lea Lin Böhmer,
Michael Schmidtchen

→ designer portrait: p. 394

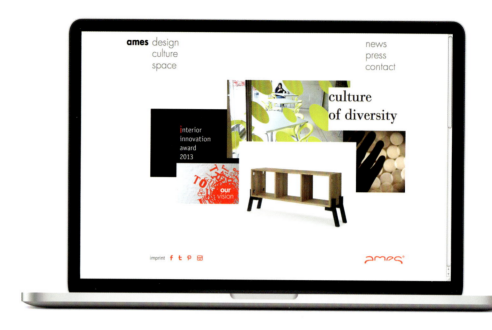

Echter Obstbrand
Real Fruit Spirits
[Microsite]

This microsite illustrates how Echte Obstbrand fruit spirits are a high-quality natural product, with all taste and alcohol content derived exclusively from the fruit itself. Reflecting this quality claim, the microsite was designed with clarity and a self-confident reserve, both expressed through generous, atmospheric images. Typography of functional, elegant appeal in combination with an intuitive, single-page layout has been employed with the aim of inviting users to discover the distilling process and the unique characteristics of this alcoholic beverage.

client
Bundesverband der Obstverschlussbrenner e.V., Freiburg

design
designconcepts GmbH, Furtwangen

→ designer portrait: p. 402

Lowdi

[Website]

The objective in designing this website for Lowdi, a new portable wireless speaker with high sound quality, was to visualise and impart the most important product details and to ensure an ordering process that is as simple as possible. The website is characterised by a subtle colour palette and strong illustration style, while a video towards the top of the homepage sets the overall mood, aiming to attune users to the product. Since Lowdi is a mobile speaker, the designers took great care to make all content available on a wide variety of devices.

design
Momkai

music/sound design
Audentity

animation
CRCR

→ designer portrait: p. 422

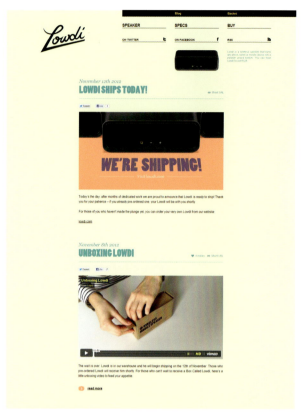

Interface Design   Mobile & Apps   Game Design   Sound Design   Red Dot: Junior Award   Designer Portraits

Canvasco
[Online Shop]

The redesign of the Canvasco online store is precisely honed to fit to the clearly defined target group of the "non-conformist urban cowboy". The design features eye-catching photomontages that are emblematic of the materials used in the production process, including canvas, cowhide, deerskin and Swiss army blankets, with the aim of delivering a virtual experience of the bags in their "natural environment". Additional customer-attractors are the style finder and the customisation tool for independently designing your own bag.

client
Canvasco GmbH,
Bremen

design
incorporate berlin GmbH
& Co. KG, Berlin

Event Design | Information Design & Public Space | Corporate Films | TV, Film, Cinema & Animation | **Online World** Online Communication

Das Auto. Magazine
[E-Magazine]

client
Volkswagen AG,
Wolfsburg

design
KircherBurkhardt GmbH,
Berlin

→ designer portrait: p. 415

Interface Design　　　Mobile & Apps　　　Game Design　　　Sound Design　　　Red Dot: Junior Award　　　Designer Portraits

Conceived as a cross-media brand magazine, "Das Auto. Magazine" is published online in six languages and targets seven countries. Based on a responsive design, the web magazine can be accessed equally well from all end-user devices, offering optimal readability. With a format that adapts from one column to four, it is suitable for all screens and smartphones. For iPad users there is a special issue every three months with exclusive audiovisual and interactive content that follows an explicitly journalistic approach in its storytelling.

Event Design | Information Design & Public Space | Corporate Films | TV, Film, Cinema & Animation | **Online World** Online Communication

The new Porsche Panamera. Thrilling contradictions.

[Web Special]

This web special underscores the characteristic traits of the Porsche Panamera by offering a visualisation of thrilling contradictions, or "Kraft der Gegensätze". Following the design of an online magazine, it stages an exciting yet contemplative journey through a world full of contradictions. Users are invited to experience these contradictions, which are aimed at promoting the Porsche Panamera by pushing the limits. Browsing through the web special, users are encouraged to discover interesting regions and people.

client
Dr. Ing. h.c. F. Porsche AG, Stuttgart

design
Bassier, Bergmann & Kindler, Ludwigsburg

creative direction
Martin Spies,
Jörg Heidrich

concept
Florian Stein

graphic design
Cindy Heller

project management
Stefan Weil

programming
Johannes Weil,
Jens Heidl,
Alessandro Scalisi,
Linus Fütterer

motion design
Carina Stöwe,
Patrick Eppler

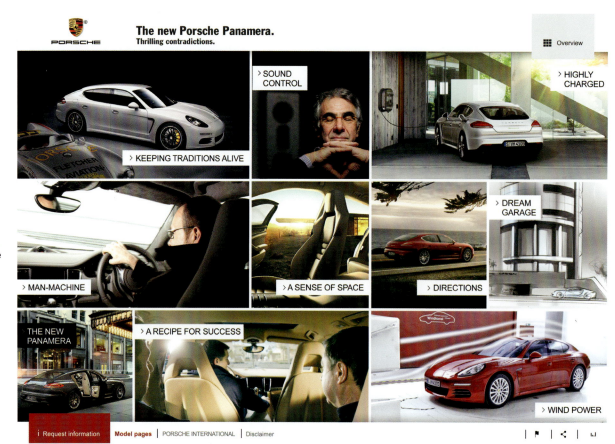

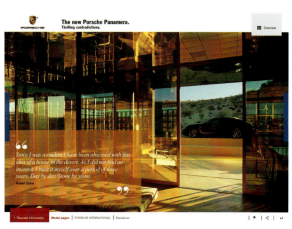

fiat500.de

[Website]

With the aim of advertising the Fiat 500 as a smart and contemporary mobility concept, this website takes a new navigation approach. Users can intuitively browse through the website with simple swipe movements of the mouse, which conveys an iPad-like feel, and thus experience the manifold configuration possibilities offered by this car. Since the website was developed using HTML5 technology, its stop-motion animations are also accessible from other mobile web devices, so that users may experience and spontaneously configure their individual Fiat 500 anywhere and anytime.

client
Fiat Group Automobiles Germany AG,
Frankfurt/Main

design
Leo Burnett,
Frankfurt/Main

creative direction
Andreas Pauli

art direction
Ronald Kraft,
Marcel Günthel

text
Axel Tischer,
Christian Vonscheidt

strategic planning
Björn Brockmann

project management
Axel Käser,
Christiane Fritsch

programming
Marco Randi,
Sergio Georgalli,
Oliver Goertz

Event Design | Information Design & Public Space | Corporate Films | TV, Film, Cinema & Animation | **Online World** Online Communication

PROJECT M Online
[E-Magazine]

PROJECT M is an executive and finance magazine published by the Allianz Group insurance company. It targets retirement planning experts, financial consultants, staff at international organisations, analysts, regulatory agency officials, journalists and Allianz Group employees. The online edition provides extensive information on long-term trends and developments related to retirement planning and the associated financial investment packages. It supplements the print version by adding features like charts, photo galleries and videos.

client
Allianz SE, Munich

publisher
HOFFMANN UND CAMPE
Corporate Publishing,
Hamburg

project management
Antonina Rudkowski

design
Robinizer Design Studio GmbH
& Co. KG, Hamburg

programming
neveling.net GmbH,
Hamburg

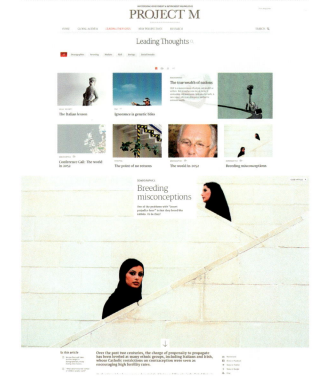

Interface Design   Mobile & Apps   Game Design   Sound Design   Red Dot: Junior Award   Designer Portraits

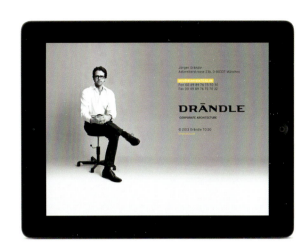

Drändle 70|30 Corporate Architecture
[Website]

The goal in designing this microsite was to convey, in next to no time, a characteristic image of the multifaceted work of the corporate architecture firm Drändle. It is reduced to key statements, consciously uses bold, full-screen images and focuses on the three visual theme levels of inspiration, information and contact. In addition, the page features a self-generating PDF updating process, as well as a random function on the information level that newly prioritises the theme areas at regular intervals.

client
Drändle,
Munich

design
Martin et Karczinski,
Munich

creative direction
Peter Martin

art direction
Ulrike Gottschild

graphic design
Daniela Fritzsch,
Björn Matthes,
Caroline Hüttinger

| Event Design | Information Design & Public Space | Corporate Films | TV, Film, Cinema & Animation | **Online World** Online Communication |

KircherBurkhardt
[Website]

The website of the media services company KircherBurkhardt was designed with a focus on multimedia features, including engaging videos and animations. Based on a responsive design, the content is meant to foster an inspiring user experience. The website also features the digital magazine "The Narrative", a compendium of news and views encompassing the worlds of content marketing, corporate communication, editorial design, visual journalism and technology. Composed in Wordpress, the website can be updated in real time.

client
KircherBurkhardt GmbH, Berlin

design
KircherBurkhardt GmbH, Berlin

programming
Digitalwerk GmbH

Interface Design Mobile & Apps Game Design Sound Design Red Dot: Junior Award Designer Portraits

serien.lighting
[Website]

The goal in designing this website for the company serien.lighting was to convey core characteristics and topics related to a fascination with design, technology and light. It provides retailers with simple and clear access while also making the site interesting for visitors. Since what is special about every luminaire is also reflected in its name, each lighting unit is staged together with its name, thus forming an entity and becoming a single mini-brand. The website is one of the first noticeable signs in a series of restructuring and optimisation measures.

client
serien.lighting,
Rodgau

design
hauser lacour
kommunikationsgestaltung
gmbh, Frankfurt/Main

creative direction
Laurent Lacour,
Bianca Elmer,
Felix Damerius

art direction
Bianca Elmer

strategic planning
Laurent Lacour

project management
Felix Damerius

programming
BlueMars,
Frankfurt/Main

NEXT AIA
[Website]

As part of a recruiting campaign, the Next AIA microsite aspires to make young people want to start a career with the company. The site design is therefore focused on a clear structure that facilitates an easy and direct approach to applying to the company. Thanks to responsive web design, the site will adapt to any user device for enhanced accessibility. The homepage features a single-page layout, so that the user can access all information at once. The content is presented using a friendly approach with a mentoring touch.

client
AIA Korea,
Seoul

head of marketing
Jong-Hun Heo

design
designfever,
Seoul

creative direction
Julie Lee

art direction
Hyun-Ju Cho

graphic design
Jaeho Song

strategic planning
Minkyoung Kim,
Jeong Hwangbo

Babiel GmbH

[Corporate Website]

For the repositioning of Babiel GmbH from a classic IT company to a one-stop consulting agency for customer-oriented communication, the new website aims to underscore the company's core competencies. Alongside a clearly structured overall impression, the website features elegant user guidance that provides customers with quick access to all relevant detailed information after only the second click. Consciously following a no-frills approach, the design is emotionally appealing and easy to navigate.

client
Babiel GmbH,
Düsseldorf

design
Babiel GmbH,
Düsseldorf

**head of marketing/
creative direction**
Dr. Rainer Babiel

art direction/illustration
Robin-Savas Savvidis

**strategic planning/
project management**
Dr. Rainer Babiel

| Event Design | Information Design & Public Space | Corporate Films | TV, Film, Cinema & Animation | **Online World** Online Communication |

Ottobock.
Living with
Michelangelo.
[Microsite]

The microsite "Living with Michelangelo" stages an explorative world revolving around the prosthesis of the same name. It presents consumer benefits in a clear and objective manner, instantaneously linking them to the respective technical feature. The site intercorrelates the visual and contextual perspectives so that users may experience how technology meets the challenges presented by everyday situations. The quality of the prosthesis is thus made accessible for patients, technicians and therapists.

client
Otto Bock HealthCare GmbH, Duderstadt

design
pilot Hamburg GmbH & Co. KG, Hamburg

creative direction
Daniel Richau
(Executive Creative Director),
Jörg Westpfahl
(Creative Director Art)

art direction
Liz Sanchez

concept
Michael Uhlemayr

project management
Pascal Kompalla

account management
Tobias Gärtner
(Managing Director)

programming
Matthias Brock

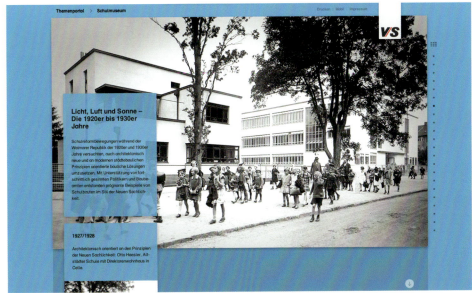

VS –
Das Klassenzimmer (Schulmuseum)
VS –
The Classroom (School Museum)

[Microsite]

Accompanying the permanent exhibition at the VS School Museum in Tauberbischofsheim, Germany, this microsite presents the "digital classroom" as cultural history. Historical photographs, drawings and film documents explain the development of the classroom from the end of the nineteenth century to the present day. Users discover innovations within the school system and gain insight into the collaborations of pioneering designers over the last 100 years. Individual exhibits and architectural models are visualised from a 360-degree view.

client
VS Vereinigte Spezialmöbelfabriken GmbH & Co. KG, Tauberbischofsheim

design
Zum Kuckuck /
Büro für digitale Medien,
Würzburg

text
Josef Mang

consulting on design history
Dr. René Spitz

Event Design | Information Design & Public Space | Corporate Films | TV, Film, Cinema & Animation | **Online World** Online Communication

KfW Foundation – Storytelling is the new way to inform
[Website]

Pursuing a concept of vivid storytelling, this website aims to leave a lasting impression on a broad target audience. Accompanied by atmospheric sounds and related through the words of a participant, the stories of the various KfW Foundation projects are documented in evocative images so as to establish an emotional connection. Users can thus directly experience not only the projects but also the people behind them. A navigation menu that is reduced to essentials, along with the dynamic appeal of the site layout, allows the project presentations to take centre stage.

client
KfW Stiftung,
Frankfurt/Main

design
SYZYGY Deutschland GmbH,
Frankfurt/Main

creative direction
Dominik Lammer

art direction
Peter Sellinger

text
Christiene Hock

project management
Max Boost

account management
Hideki Kose

programming
Michael Sattler

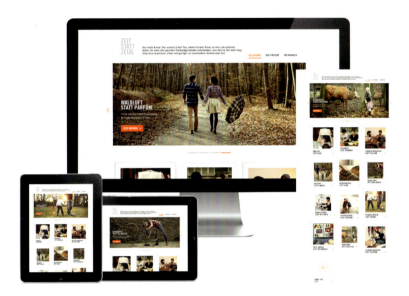

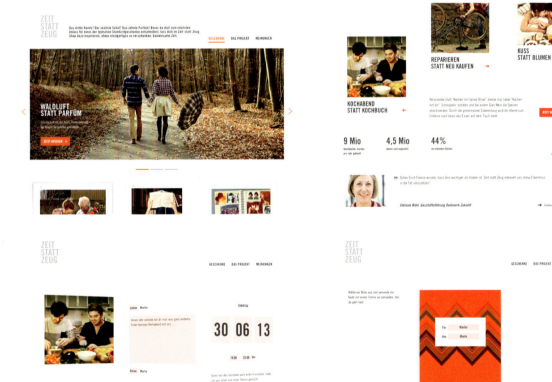

Zeit statt Zeug
Time rather than stuff
[Microsite]

The campaign Zeit statt Zeug (Time rather than stuff) aims to show alternatives to the familiar ways of presenting gifts and thus contributes to transforming the trend towards growing consumption into a new contemporary way of gift-giving. Real-life examples demonstrate that, instead of the "fourth mobile phone" or "seventh perfume", it makes more sense to give a more valuable present: time spent together. Showing such possibilities, the shop was launched four weeks before Christmas as a product of Scholz & Volkmer.

client
Scholz & Volkmer GmbH, Wiesbaden

design
Scholz & Volkmer GmbH, Wiesbaden

creative direction design
Jörg Waldschütz,
Michael Volkmer

creative direction text
Marco Obermann

art direction
Ann-Kristin Heier

concept/csr
Nanna Beyer

account management
Annika Firlus

programming front end
Christian Schweinhardt,
Martin Becher

technical direction
Andreas Klinger

The Bridge of Life
[Website]

The Bridge of Life website is at the centre of a campaign that wants to prevent people in Korea from committing suicide by jumping off the Mapo Bridge. Sensors installed on the bridge guard rails react to the movements of people walking by and turn on lights along the rails where short messages appear as if the bridge were speaking directly to the passers-by. Users of the website can experience the installation virtually via an "Experiencing the Bridge of Life" tab. If users leave a message full of hope or pictures online, they automatically elongate the "Lifeline Korea".

client
Samsung Life Insurance, Seoul

design
Cheil Worldwide, Seoul
ONCE

creative direction
Eunjung Ahn

concept
Hyojin Lee,
Seeun Lee

editor-in-chief
Yuri Lee

editor
Hyunsuk Jang

animation
Jonghoon Tak

motion design
Seonghun Kim

Froli
[Website Relaunch]

The reduced and clearly designed relaunch of the Froli.com website highlights the stylistic approach of an innovative premium brand. It focuses on the objective of conveying the core competencies of the company. Thanks to the use of a fully flexible framing grid, this website possesses a highly engaging and vividly structured appearance. A large font type provides high readability, while the attractive menu makes the site easy to navigate. An innovative element is the horizontal slide-in menu on the left side that stays in place across all subpages.

client
Froli Kunststoffwerk GmbH & Co. KG, Schloß Holte-Stukenbrock

design
Steuer Marketing & Kommunikation GmbH, Bielefeld

| Event Design | Information Design & Public Space | Corporate Films | TV, Film, Cinema & Animation | **Online World** Online Communication |

Namentliche Abstimmungen
Roll-Call Votes

[Website Module]

This visualisation of roll-call votes at the German Parliament aims to represent and document a striving towards transparency in politics. The website module allows citizens to become informed about the results of any roll-cast vote in Parliament, and to see how many parliamentary representatives from which party voted yes or no on the issue discussed. It combines the representatives' voting behaviour with auxiliary information, such as party affiliation, constituency or postal code. Users can choose which particular roll-cast vote they want to have visualised.

client
Deutscher Bundestag, Berlin

design
Babiel GmbH, Düsseldorf

creative direction
Georg Babiel

art direction
Robin-Savas Savvidis

strategic planning/ project management
Georg Babiel

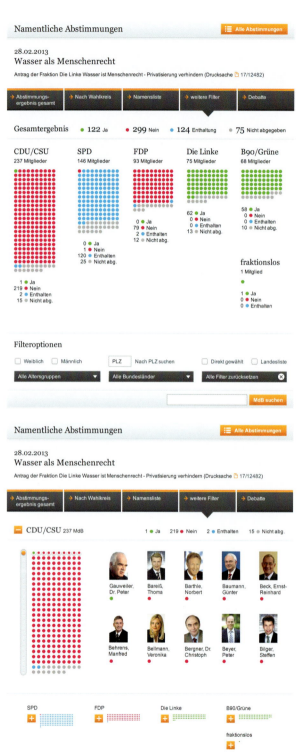
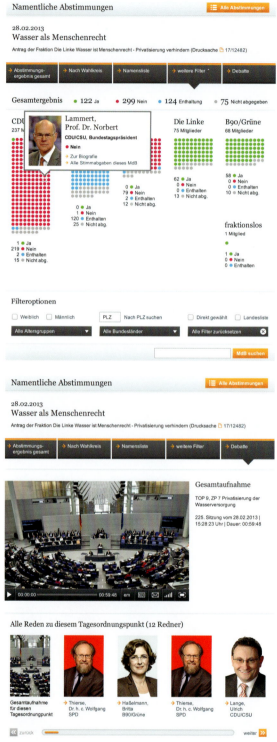

Visualisation of the German Federal Budget
[Website]

The German federal budget involves an enormous amount of money – over 300 billion euros. The budget plan covers more than 2,700 pages. In collaboration with the Bundesministerium der Finanzen (German Federal Ministry of Finance), Pixelpark has succeeded in making this data volume accessible to everyone. All revenue and expenditure can now be found in an easily accessible data visualisation that can also be viewed on smartphones and tablets. This makes the budget understandable – even for non-specialists.

client
Bundesministerium der Finanzen, Berlin
Dominik Grobien, Udo Fenchel (Referat Öffentlichkeitsarbeit)

design
Pixelpark/Elephant Seven, Berlin

concept
Christoph Krebs

graphic design
Michael Ledwig

account management
Stefan Schopp

project management
Nikola Kinsler

programming
Heiko Hardt

→ designer portrait: p. 428

| Event Design | Information Design & Public Space | Corporate Films | TV, Film, Cinema & Animation | **Online World** Online Communication |

hwdesign.de
[Corporate Website]

The starting point for the redesign of this corporate website was the relaunch of the agency häfelinger + wagner design. The new website was conceived to consistently reflect and promote the repositioning of the agency as it expanded from being a graphic and design studio that specialises in several disciplines towards a broadly positioned, full-service creative design and branding agency. The website uses subtle colouring and typography to dynamically convey a broad range of content.

client
hw.design GmbH,
Munich

design
hw.design GmbH,
Munich

creative direction
Frank Wagner,
Benjamin Klöck

graphic design
Veronika Kinczli,
Dirk Habenschaden

text
Angelika Schröger

Interface Design | Mobile & Apps | Game Design | Sound Design | Red Dot: Junior Award | Designer Portraits

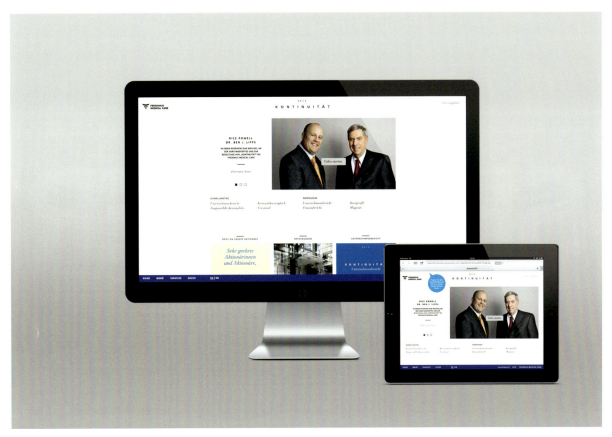

Kontinuität
Continuity
[Corporate Website]

Under the motto of "Continuity", the company Fresenius Medical Care published a new annual report trilogy in 2012 that adhered to the layout style of a magazine. In terms of content and design, the print version of the annual report also served as a model for the concept of the website. The design focused on a reduced online implementation optimised according to the highest usability requirements, while also lending it the stylistic look of a magazine. Users were to be guided through the complex topics to help them gain a good overview of FMC's financial year 2012.

client
Fresenius Medical Care AG & Co. KGaA, Bad Homburg

design
hw.design GmbH, Munich

creative direction
Frank Wagner, Dirk Habenschaden

art direction
Sandra Gieseler

graphic design
Manuel Rigel

project management
Sandra Loebich

photography
Matthias Ziegler, Matthias Haslauer, Ellen Callaway, Christian Lietzmann

programming
Ralf Flak, EQS

SHOOTER
[Branded Content Website]

The objective of the "Shootter" campaign was to raise awareness of adidas skincare protection through digital media. It consists of a simple-to-play football game that invites Twitter users to select any other Twitter user as an opponent and to battle for the best shot. The branded content website allows users to play not only against friends, but also against celebrities like Lady Gaga and Christiano Ronaldo. Great care was taken in developing the game visuals in order to deliver an authentic sporting experience.

client
Kose Corporation,
Tokyo

design
Hakuhodo,
Tokyo

creative direction
Kentaro Masamura

art direction
Jeong-Ho Im,
Kazumasa Teshigawara

planning
Kentaro Masamura,
Jeong-Ho Im,
Takeshiro Umetsu,
Kazumasa Teshigawara

music/sound design
Zin Yoshida

artwork
Koya Okada

technical direction
Hidekazu Hayashi

Interface Design   Mobile & Apps   Game Design   Sound Design   Red Dot: Junior Award   Designer Portraits

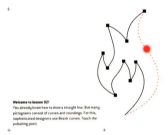

Lingua Digitalis
[Web Special]

The concept of Lingua Digitalis provides multimedia documentation of the international development of pictograms and their subsequent changes. The web portal offers an overview of all Lingua Digitalis books, the related app and the royalty-free icon sets. Thanks to its adaptive layout, the site is displayed optimally on all kinds of end-user devices, ensuring simple and intuitive navigation. Moreover, the Lingua Icon Designer system allows users to create their own personal pictogram from over 600 individual elements.

client
Die Gestalten Verlag GmbH & Co. KG, Berlin

design
Mutabor Design GmbH, Hamburg

creative direction
Patrick Molinari

art direction
Steffen Granz

design team
Florian Sattler,
Patricia Sutor,
Cynthia Waeyusoh,
Julia Görlitz,
Florian Hechinger,
Stefan Mückner

project management
Birte Schumacher

digital concept
David Gilbert

web design
Tom Schallberger

Treezer – Planting a tree with an iPhone
[iPhone App]

The Treezer iPhone app enables its users to demonstrate their green consciousness by taking a very direct approach. The app is available in the iTunes Store, and to take part in the campaign, users simply need an iPhone with a camera and an Internet connection. The task is to take a picture, virtually place a tree in the picture and then share it on Facebook. For every posted picture, a real tree is later planted. Participation in this project is thus very easy and has resulted in the planting of thousands of trees.

client
Stiftung Unternehmen Wald, Hamburg

design
Pixelpark/Elephant Seven, Berlin

creative direction
Udo Hoffmann

art direction
Faden Lidzba

concept
Dirk Kedrowitsch

programming
Sebastian Grimm,
Bastian Nuss,
Christian Koop

media
Matthias Mühlenhoff

public relations
Viviane Kruggel

→ designer portrait: p. 428

Interface Design   Mobile & Apps   Game Design   Sound Design   Red Dot: Junior Award   Designer Portraits

NAVER APPisode
[Website]

This website was the hub of a campaign with which the Korean Internet portal Naver wanted to address an especially young target group. In addition to two TV spots, the campagin site releases "Relay webtoon" and "Undisclosed Appisode", created by popular authors that users can enjoy and write a short comment. The user interface was designed in such a way that users could intensively experience the flickering motion on their mobile phones.

client
NHN CORP.,
Seongnam City,
Gyeonggi Province

design
NHN CORP.,
Seongnam City,
Gyeonggi Province

head of marketing
Kim Seung Eon

creative direction
Yang Sung Yul

graphic design
Ryu Seung Sook,
Kim Haeng Seon

motion design
Youn Moo Young,
Lee Sang Min

Event Design | Information Design & Public Space | Corporate Films | TV, Film, Cinema & Animation | **Online World** Online Communication

dryKorn.com
[Corporate Website]

This corporate website was realised as part of a relaunch, implementing a comprehensive concept that is reflected by the unity of e-commerce, magazine, product and brand presentation. The screen was meant to serve as a canvas and provide space for showing impressive cinematic image worlds and video content. All content pages and products on this website can be shared on social networks and are structured to be located easily via a store finder that leads to 900 "entrances" of the DRYKORN brand environment worldwide.

client
DRYKORN Modevertriebs GmbH & Co. KG, Kitzingen

design
Zum Kuckuck / Büro für digitale Medien, Würzburg

programming website
Zum Kuckuck / Büro für digitale Medien

programming online shop
ZYRES digital media systems GmbH, Frankfurt/Main

Viktor&Rolf – The World Round Web
[Website]

Under the motto "The circle is the new square", this website for the fashion house Viktor&Rolf places the design element of the circle at centre stage. Continuing the tradition of this brand, which operates at the intersection between art and fashion, the introductory film promotes the idea of redesigning the World Wide Web, where everything is made of square pixels, and basing it on circles instead, so that it becomes the "World Round Web". The clearly structured website displays news, collections, portraits and a historic overview of 20 years of Viktor&Rolf.

client
Viktor&Rolf,
Amsterdam

design
Fabrique
[brands, design & interaction],
Delft

creative direction
Lernert & Sander
Fabrique
[brands, design & interaction]

art direction
Ronnie Besseling,
Fabrique

project management
Kate Walsh,
Viktor&Rolf
Kay Timmers,
Fabrique

animation
Joost Korngold,
ReNascent

→ designer portrait: p. 405

Mercedes-Benz Night View Assist

[iPad Ad]

client
Daimler AG,
Stuttgart

design
Scholz & Volkmer GmbH,
Wiesbaden

creative direction design
Anne Wichmann

art direction
Kathleen Sterzel,
Martina Camps y Espinoza

concept
Andreas Daum,
Christian Daul

project lead
Linda Rau

text
Uwe Todoroff

programming front end
Julia Niemeyer

The aim in designing the Mercedes-Benz iPad advertisement for Night View Assist was to bridge the gap between the typical flow of reading digital content and the effectiveness of advertisements. It was conceived as a double-layer version, which relies on the iPad's normal swiping action to open as the user turns the page. The advertisement thus communicates the function of Night View Assist in a simple manner, demonstrating that it is possible to detect dangers early on when driving through a seemingly harmless night landscape.

| Event Design | Information Design & Public Space | Corporate Films | TV, Film, Cinema & Animation | Online World Social Media |

Audi car chat
[Social Media App]

Users like to talk about their new car with friends and family. The Audi car chat is a web application that facilitates the communication between automotive customers and their peer group. It uses the options that the Audi configurator provides, with the selected model, colours and technical details being displayed. After logging in via Facebook, users invite their social network friends to join a discussion about their configuration. They can vote for their favourite equipment, or add to the discussion by attaching images to comments.

client
AUDI AG

strategic planning
Tobias Knebel,
Kai Poborski,
Maria Nißl

concept
Fabian Hahn,
Peter Kubin,
Das Büro am Draht,
Berlin

design
Andreas Kraft,
Das Büro am Draht,
Berlin

programming
Lukas Hartmann,
Mark Müller,
Gerhard Lehmann,
Das Büro am Draht,
Berlin

| Interface Design | Mobile & Apps | Game Design | Sound Design | Red Dot: Junior Award | Designer Portraits |

Audi Le Mans Experience – Paris Motor Show 2012
[Film]

Visitors to the Audi Le Mans Experience theme lounge were able to become the Audi team drivers in the famous 24-hour race. Each participant's photo and name were integrated into a fast-paced film showing the event from the start preparations and the race to the finish line. Visitors were then presented with their personal Le Mans film on a big screen, starring themselves as the main actor in the cockpit. The films also could be shared online.

client
AUDI AG,
Ingolstadt

design
KMS BLACKSPACE,
Munich

→ designer portrait: p. 416

Treezer – Planting a tree with an iPhone

[iPhone App]

client
Stiftung Unternehmen Wald, Hamburg

design
Pixelpark/Elephant Seven, Berlin

creative direction
Udo Hoffmann

art direction
Faden Lidzba

concept
Dirk Kedrowitsch

programming
Sebastian Grimm,
Bastian Nuss,
Christian Koop

media
Matthias Mühlenhoff

public relations
Viviane Kruggel

→ designer portrait: p. 428

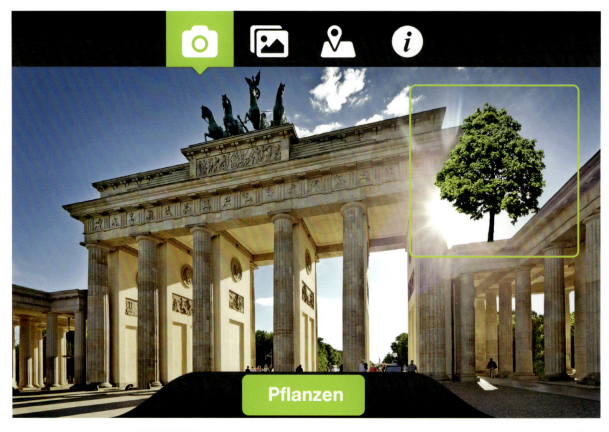

Interface Design · Mobile & Apps · Game Design · Sound Design · Red Dot: Junior Award · Designer Portraits

„Sobald uns aber ein »Ungeil« entgegenkommt, wird die Lage ernst und du solltest überlegen, ob du nicht noch ein paar belastbare Argumente aus dem Hut zaubern kannst: »Mein Freund, die Nummer sieht so unglaublich

Gefällt mir · Kommentieren · Hervorheben · Teilen   👍 2

 Udo Hoffmann
10. Juli 2012 via Treezer

Jeder Baum zählt! Er hilft bei der Vermehrung des Waldes, reichert die biologische Vielfalt an und sorgt für frische Luft! Hilf mit! Lade den Treezer und pflanze kostenlos Bäume! Denn jedes mit dem Treezer bei Facebook veröffentlichte Bild bedeutet einen real gepflanzten Baum. Mehr Informationen unter www.treezer.de

Gefällt mir · Kommentieren · Hervorheben · Teilen

Gefällt mir

Ud
8.
in memor

Gefällt mir

Ud
18.

Gefällt mir

Ud
16.
Jeder Bau

The Treezer iPhone app is at the centre of a campaign that allows people to directly show their environmental awareness. The app invites users to take a photo and to virtually place a tree in it before uploading it to Facebook. A real tree is then planted for every posted picture. This easy way to participate in the project has resulted in the planting of thousands of trees. The commissioning foundation, Stiftung Unternehmen Wald, has thus managed to raise public awareness for their cause and the "tree sponsors" are presented with each Facebook post.

INTERNATIONAL YEARBOOK COMMUNICATION DESIGN 2013/2014

Event Design | Information Design & Public Space | Corporate Films | TV, Film, Cinema & Animation | Online World

Red Dot: Grand Prix

MobiGlobe – A Production by Autostadt in Wolfsburg
[Interactive Stations]

The demand for mobility is increasing dramatically. At the same time, population growth, climate change and the scarcity of resources reveal our planet's limitations. MobiGlobe gives insights into such complex systems and functions as a visual databank covering 48 themes ranging from "space" to "resources". It can be experienced on interactive stations in various locations throughout the Autostadt in Wolfsburg, or on a gesture-controlled media wall. Its core application architecture, using the Unity Game Engine, allows for parametrically visualising, managing and renewing data, and is complemented with an interaction and display application layer specific to several installation formats. The media wall allows users to effortlessly navigate with a few intuitive gestures and body movements, enhanced by rich sound design, through a large and complex set of data visualisations.

Statement by the jury

»MobiGlobe compiles an enormous amount of complex data on the topic of worldwide mobility and makes them accessible on media walls and on interactive stations in such a way that the content is very easy to understand. Users navigate either by touching or through gestures and thus are able to gain insights into top issues of our times presented in an exciting and impressively visualised approach.«

Interface Design   Mobile & Apps   Game Design   Sound Design   Red Dot: Junior Award   Designer Portraits

client
Autostadt GmbH,
Wolfsburg

design
Hosoya Schaefer Architects AG,
Zurich

concept
Hosoya Schaefer Architects AG
Autostadt GmbH

creative direction
Markus Schaefer

art direction
Isabelle Bentz

graphic design
CHKY,
Bern
Büro Destruct,
Bern

interaction design
Jørgen Skogmo

music/sound design
Idee & Klang,
Basel

programming
Unity Studios,
Aarhus
base.io,
Aarhus

→ clip on DVD
→ designer portrait: p. 409

reddot design award
grand prix 2013

Red Dot: Best of the Best

Telstra
[Interactive Showroom]

How will people communicate in the future? What possibilities will telecommunication tools have to offer? And how can these topics be displayed in an impressive manner? To represent this topic of future communication, an interactive installation including the entire storyboard for the content was designed and produced for the new showroom of Australian telecommunication company Telstra, staging the topic in four thematic clusters: health, business, living and learning. For each area a scenario with a story was created that would illustrate, via voice-overs and special graphic and sound effects, how communication could possibly work in the future. In order to create a multimedia surrounding that visitors find themselves immersed in, the room featured 45 seamless plasma screens from the ceiling almost to the floor. Visitors were invited to retrieve information by interacting either via a centrally placed holo terminal or directly via the multi-touch functionality of the 270-degree plasma-wall.

Statement by the jury

»This multimedia showroom, tiled with seamless plasma screens, invites visitors to immerse themselves and explore various future communication scenarios with all their senses. Allowing even several users to change parameters simultaneously, thanks to multi-user functionality, enhances the fun aspect and further piques curiosity concerning the various simulation scenarios, thus rendering a vivid impression of dynamic communication processes.«

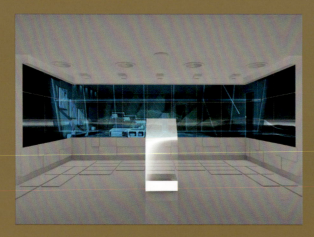
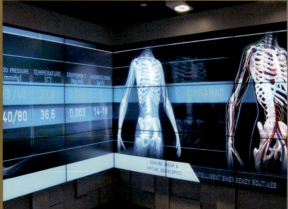

| Interface Design | Mobile & Apps | Game Design | Sound Design | Red Dot: Junior Award | Designer Portraits |

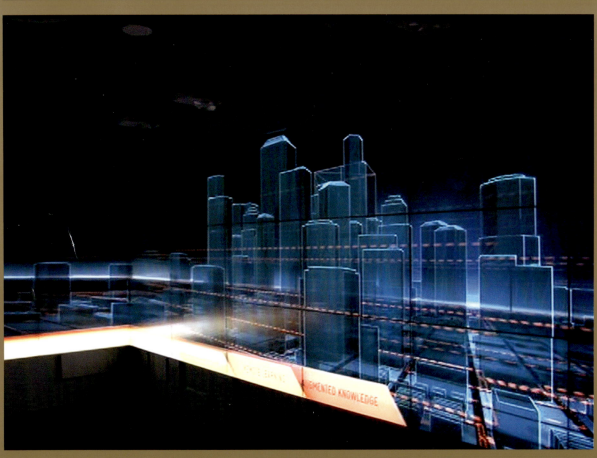

client
Telstra,
Melbourne

design
stereolize. GmbH,
Munich

→ designer portrait: p. 432

Event Design | Information Design & Public Space | Corporate Films | TV, Film, Cinema & Animation | Online World

Red Dot: Best of the Best

Speel je toekomst
Play your future

[Website]

In 2012, Aegon introduced the online platform speeljetoekomst.nu to give its users and clients a playful insight into their future and how certain life events may affect it. Based on advanced calculation algorithms, it is possible to literally foresee the future, provide a reliable projection of the user's financial life path and to alter it in a playful manner by changing parameters. The main goal of the campaign was to contribute to Aegon's brand recognition by promoting Aegon as a provider of life insurance and investment products who makes people financially aware. Only a few simple questions and personal details, including age, family status and living and leisure expenses, need to be answered and provided by users to get a fully informed overview of their financial future. Featuring a striking interface design with a subtle and uniform colour scheme, the entire user guidance is fully animated using JavaScript to offer an engaging experience across all platforms. In addition, a set of custom illustrations was created to portray transportation, housing and leisure.

Statement by the jury

»The platform simulates the lives of customers, who want to take control of their future financial situation, via a simple application that calculates the data and outputs an easy-to-understand projection. An otherwise rather dull topic is thus illustrated in an approach that makes it fun for users to interact with.«

Interface Design | Mobile & Apps | Game Design | Sound Design | Red Dot: Junior Award | Designer Portraits

client
Aegon

concept
THEY
Momkai

design/realisation
Momkai

calculations
EPG

character animation
Comic House

game design
Subatomic

→ designer portrait: p. 422

Red Dot: Best of the Best

TEGRIS
[Operating Room Control System]

The touch-based user interface facilitates central control of the diverse range of devices used during surgery in operating rooms: OR table, surgical lights, monitors, cameras, room lights, air-conditioning, music and more. In addition, the interface allows to access and to document all patient data at any time. The user guidance reflects the typical surgical workflow and is intuitive to use, requiring minimal training. The interface features a clean design and integrates a surgical safety checklist for maximum patient safety. Live video previews ensure efficient control of cameras, recording of still images and videos is another example of the system's many features. Implementing high-contrast interactive controls as well as icons representing the OR environment, the device ensures high operator safety.

Statement by the jury

»The TEGRIS user interface fulfils the high demands towards the procedures in modern hospitals. It can be configured quickly and adapted flexibly according to user needs and the workflow. The clear and sophisticated design concept makes controlling several devices an intuitive and easy-to-perform task.«

Interface Design Mobile & Apps Game Design Sound Design Red Dot: Junior Award Designer Portraits

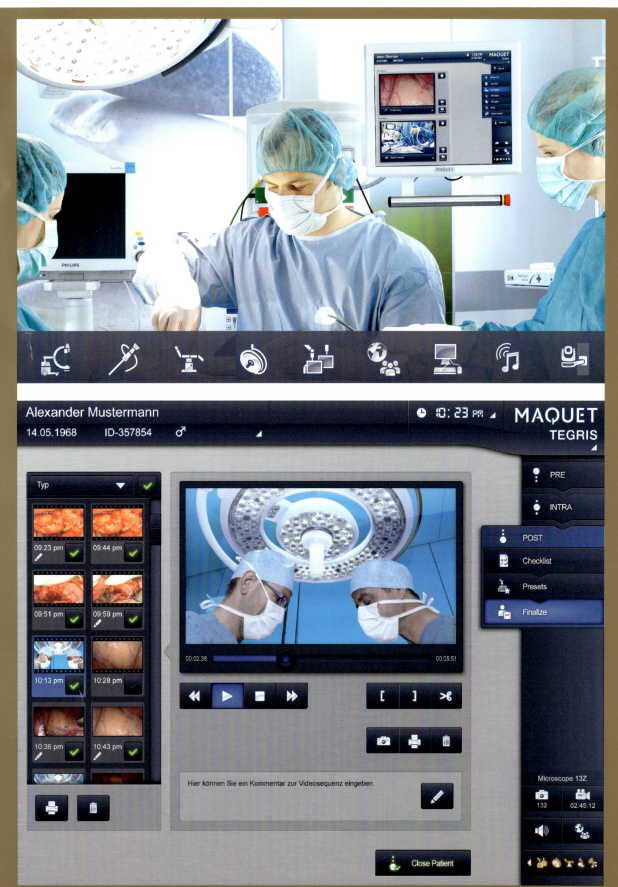

client
Maquet GmbH OR Integration, Rastatt

design
CaderaDesign, Würzburg

→ clip on DVD
→ designer portrait: p. 398

Red Dot: Best of the Best

Bedside Station

[Interface Design for Inpatient Medical Services]

Bedside Station is a personalised medical service platform installed at the bedside for hospital inpatients. Its streamlined timeline interface provides access from a single platform to each patient's personal schedule as well as timely and relevant information on the various hospital services and treatments. Thereby, patient wait and travel times can be reduced and, at the same time, their hospital experience can be improved. The simple and intuitive interface makes it user-friendly for all ages, from children to the elderly, and the cheerful, relaxing design adds a level of warmth and comfort to the otherwise clinical hospital environment. The icons for TV, Internet or new linen, for example, are self-explanatory and immediately understandable. Thus, the Bedside Station application aims to enhance the experience and satisfaction of inpatients and their caregivers, improving the overall quality of medical treatment and services.

Statement by the jury

»Alongside offering comprehensive information, this patient information system for hospitals also facilitates an easy way of mutual communication between patients and care staff at all times. The design of the device is intuitive in use, marked by plain clear user guidance, and imparts an overall highly friendly and appealing look.«

Interface Design | Mobile & Apps | Game Design | Sound Design | Red Dot: Junior Award | Designer Portraits

client
Center for Medical Informatics,
Seoul National University
Bundang Hospital

design
pxd, Inc.,
Seoul

concept
Park Kihyuck,
Hawer Euree,
Hwang Hyunho,
Jin Hyunjung

graphic design
Noh Gyeongwan,
Kang Boa,
Lee Seungwoo,
Lee Bom,
Kim Youri

project management
Jeongwan Seo,
Health Connect

programming
PLNC

product design
Martha Doh,
MOD

→ designer portrait: p. 429

Event Design | Information Design & Public Space | Corporate Films | TV, Film, Cinema & Animation | Online World

RaySafe S1
[Cloud-Based Radiation Management Solution]

client
Unfors RaySafe,
Billdal

design
Lots,
Göteborg

design team
Hanna Ljungström,
Jesper Jonsson

→ designer portrait: p. 419

Interface Design   Mobile & Apps   Game Design   Sound Design   Red Dot: Junior Award   Designer Portraits

RaySafe S1 is a cloud-based radiation management solution for hospitals, supporting procedures like CT scans or other X-ray methods. It collects patient's radiation dose data over time and guides each user (e.g. referring doctor, radiologist, nurse) in giving the most suitable examination and the lowest possible dose to the patient. Used successfully to justify, optimise and control patient doses, RaySafe S1 leads to greater patient safety, supports the hospital staff in stressful situations with difficult decisions and secures efficiency in day-to-day hospital operation. All relevant data is displayed in an intuitive graphical user interface, where the design is adapted to the radiation environment, featuring clear guiding elements. Thanks to its responsive design, this web client is prepared for a variety of screen resolutions, including tablets.

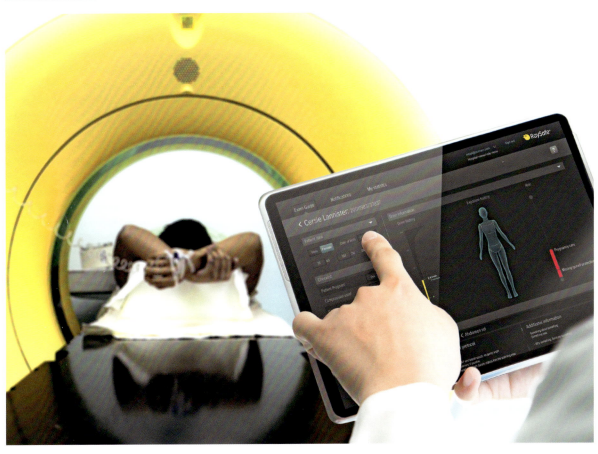

Volvo Sensus Connected Touch

[Car Infotainment System]

client
Volvo Car Corporation, Göteborg

design
Interaktionsbyrån, Göteborg

creative direction
Joel Rozada

design director
Emma Rozada

lead designer
Hanne Marte Holmøy

→ clip on DVD
→ designer portrait: p. 411

| Interface Design | Mobile & Apps | Game Design | Sound Design | Red Dot: Junior Award | Designer Portraits |

This application platform integrates seamlessly into Volvo's cars. It enables users to utilise the benefits of smartphone apps, such as digital music services, without compromising on safety. The integration of Spotify is just one of the many smart features. The touch-based interface is laid out horizontally with a focus on the circle in the middle. Apps are accessed by swiping left or right and tapping on large, distinctive icons. It is designed with a less-is-more approach, so that attention is directed to important information, enabling the driver to keep their attention on the road. This is further enhanced by the implementation of an intelligent voice-activation feature.

MyLook Magic Mirror
[Consumer Kiosk]

This consumer kiosk makes shopping for a new pair of glasses easier. The custom-built digital mirror captures photos of customers in new store frames, which they may then view while wearing their prescription glasses. Multiple frames can be compared from various angles, and the customer can even share different looks with friends on Facebook or via e-mail for added validation. The kiosk's interface is big and bold, relying on simple language, animation and colour cues, which makes it easy for anyone to use.

client
Luxottica Retail,
Mason, Ohio

design
SapientNitro,
Boston, Massachusetts

creative direction
Pete Tschudy

art direction
Josh Bean

text
Lynn Bossange

project management
Peter Cundall

account management
Scott Cleversey

technical direction
Vivek Agrawal

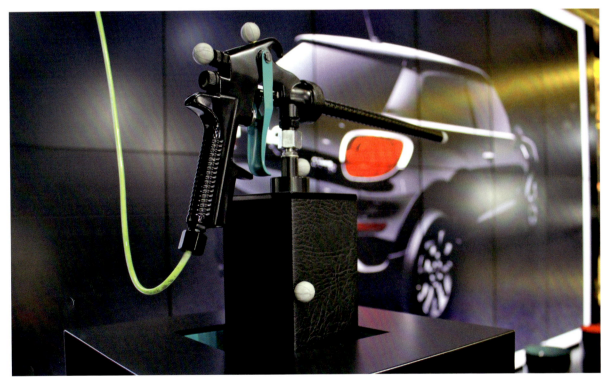

MINI Bodypaint
[Interactive Exhibit]

This interactive exhibit enables visitors to engage with the MINI in a way that reflects the car's typical "twinkle in the eye". As the vehicle moves and bounces on screen, visitors can paint it using digital aerosol devices. By pointing the spray can at paint buckets, different colours may be selected. Tilting the can activates tricks similar to graffiti spraying in street culture, such as blowing wind. Once the paint job is done, visitors can share pictures of themselves in action, as well as of the body-painted MINI, at a touchscreen terminal.

client
BMW Group, Munich

design
MESO Digital Interiors GmbH, Frankfurt/Main
Meiré und Meiré, Cologne

creative direction
Carsten Goertz,
Sebastian Oschatz

realtime 3d design
Thomas Eichhorn,
Johannes Lemke

product design
Xiaojia Yao

architecture
Simon Schmolling,
Aksinja Kutschera

social media
Claudius Coenen,
Benjamin Baum

project management
Klaus-Peter Texter,
Sarah Bamberg

→ clip on DVD

| Event Design | Information Design & Public Space | Corporate Films | TV, Film, Cinema & Animation | Online World |

Melitta bar-cube touch Fully Automatic Coffee Machine

[Graphical User Interface]

client
Melitta SystemService
GmbH & Co. KG,
Minden-Dützen

design/programming
macio GmbH, Kiel

creative direction
Stefanie C. Zürn

Interface Design   Mobile & Apps   Game Design   Sound Design   Red Dot: Junior Award   Designer Portraits

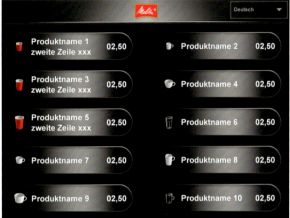
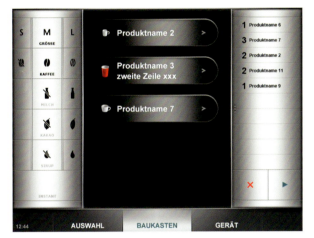

The Melitta bar-cube touch is a fully automatic coffee machine for professionals in the catering industry. It features a graphical user interface operated via a touchscreen. The interface is highly customisable and can be changed to fit the mood of the café where it is used. This easy-to-operate coffee machine is divided into two operating modes: a public one, for quick and easy selection of coffee specialties, and a sub-level for caterers and personnel, for individual recipe selection, maintenance and statistical evaluation. Thanks to well-structured navigation, users do not get lost, despite the machine's functional density. All relevant states, parameters and operating steps are displayed on the 8.4-inch touchscreen display.

Gaggenau Product Family Series 200/400

[Holistic User Interface Design]

client
Gaggenau Hausgeräte GmbH, Munich

design
HID Human Interface Design, Hamburg

creative direction
Claudia S. Friedrich,
Prof. Frank Jacob,
HID
Sören Strayle,
Markendesign Gaggenau

art direction
Kristina Wisch,
HID

concept
Simone Schramm,
Mette Mark Larsen,
HID

graphic design
Andi Kern,
Simone Schramm,
HID

music/sound design
Nils Kacirek

interactive prototyping
Carsten Ziegenbein,
HID

→ clip on DVD
→ designer portrait: p. 408

In creating the user interface design of the Gaggenau Product Family Series 200/400, strong emphasis was placed on striking a harmonious balance between physical haptics and concise graphics. The main functions are controlled through two rotary knobs, with a TFT touch display conveying the information. Secondary functions are only shown when needed and can be easily accessed via the touchscreen. Information is either magnified to draw the user's attention or reduced in size in the background, thus graphically reflecting the rotary motion of the knobs. Individual operating steps are furthermore highlighted through the discreet use of colour.

Nikon D5200 Camera
[Graphic Info Display]

The info display of the Nikon D5200 DSLR camera shows the three most important elements in determining exposure at a quick glance. Shutter speed, aperture value and ISO sensitivity are represented through animated, camera-like graphic representations, while other settings are displayed at the bottom. As settings are adjusted, the respective dials rotate, thus graphically indicating the user's actions in a natural and intuitive way. The option of changing the info display to Nikon's classic layout caters to experienced photographers.

client
Nikon Corporation, Tokyo

design
Nikon Corporation, Tokyo

design team
Chihiro Tsukamoto, Misao Miura

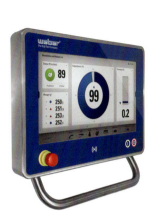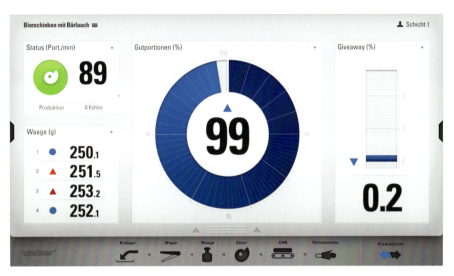

Weber Power Control

[Touch-Optimised
User Interface Design
for High-End Slicing Machines]

This modular touch-based user interface for high-end slicing machines can be adapted to various machine types. At its heart is a dynamic layout that enables the user to monitor the most important key figures at a glance. Frequently used values can be accessed quickly through swipe gestures, while production parameters are grouped according to product-processing steps or machine components in a workflow-oriented menu. Thanks to the Weber Power Control's ergonomic and coherent interface design, handling a machine is quick and easy to learn.

client
Weber Maschinenbau GmbH,
Breidenbach

design
HMI Project,
Karlstadt

creative direction
Markus Buberl

concept
Markus Buberl,
Christian Rudolph

graphic design
Werner Goldbach,
Christian Nath

project management
Christian Rudolph

programming
Philipp Kruse

| Event Design | Information Design & Public Space | Corporate Films | TV, Film, Cinema & Animation | Online World |

Smart Washing Machine Interface Design

The Smart Washing Machine interface design reflects the cleanliness and freshness of laundry through its graphical user interface. Animations and images reminiscent of clothes washing illustrate the different steps, for example rinsing water or washing machine drums that are spinning. The various cycles are selected via a touchscreen display, with the icons showing images taken from the laundry context, thus easing recognition and navigation. Additional cycles can be downloaded and edited – even on the go – thanks to a mobile companion app.

client
LG Electronics Inc.,
Seoul

design
LG Electronics Inc.,
Seoul

user interface design
Jeong-Hwa Yang,
Jin-A Lee,
You-Jin Lee,
Jung-In Park,
Eun-Gyeong Gwon

Emotional Unlock GUI
[Smartphone Graphical User Interface]

The lock screen is what smartphone users see first when they activate their device. Instead of the standardised swipe-to-unlock feature with specific unlock spots, LG utilises a peephole method that engages the entire screen. When the screen is touched, a small circle appears, allowing the user to view the home-screen layer beneath. The circle enlarges with the swiping motion, as if a door were being opened. Various design patterns, such as a white hole or a dewdrop, provide a new and engaging way to interact with one's smartphone.

client
LG Electronics Inc.,
Seoul

design
LG Electronics Inc.,
Seoul

user interface design
Kwon-Han Bae,
Kun-Ho Lee,
Yong-Deok Lee,
Insu Hwang,
Kwanju Jung

| Event Design | Information Design & Public Space | Corporate Films | TV, Film, Cinema & Animation | Online World |

Intel,
My Media Library

[Mobile Interface Design]

My Media Library (MML) is an entertainment media access, discovery and commerce service. The service was created to help users catalogue, manage, purchase, and enjoy media of all types – music, movies, TV shows and photos – and to access them on all their devices regardless of location or operating system. MML takes the point of view that people treat their media as cherished, social objects – and that each piece of media can be the start of an immersive experience (in-depth information), social connection (community) and exploration (serendipitous discovery of new media).

client
Intel,
Santa Clara

design
Ammunition LLC,
San Francisco

**user experience/
user interface design**
Brett Wickens,
Michael McQueen,
Monica Gautier,
Alex Carter,
Darcy DiNucci,
Anne Kitzmiller

CalendarWatch
[App]

This app is a unique combination of diary and clock, which synchronises with all standard smartphone calendars. An outer circle displays the time in a 24-hour format, while small triangles inside the circle visualise appointments. By swiping left and right, users can browse through the days of the week, whereas swiping up and down brings up the calendar weeks. The app's flat design, with full colour backgrounds and clean typography, highlights what is important in a highly aesthetic way.

client
denkwerk GmbH,
Cologne

design
denkwerk GmbH,
Cologne

**creative direction/
art direction**
Alina Schlaier

programming
Christian Neuls,
Mohammad Irani

Aura
Horizon Table PC
[Interface Design]

Aura is a graphical user interface for Lenovo's Horizon Table PC. Designed as a multi-user, multi-touch device, it can be operated by several family members at the same time. Its 360-degree dial navigation enables users to easily access content from every corner of the device. Pictures, videos and music files unfold in a ring around the dial and can be interacted with through touch gestures, such as swiping, pinch-to-zooming, and more. This unique and intuitive control concept is launched when the PC is laid flat on a surface.

client
Lenovo (Beijing) Ltd.,
Beijing

design
Lenovo (Beijing) Ltd.,
Innovation Design Centre,
Beijing

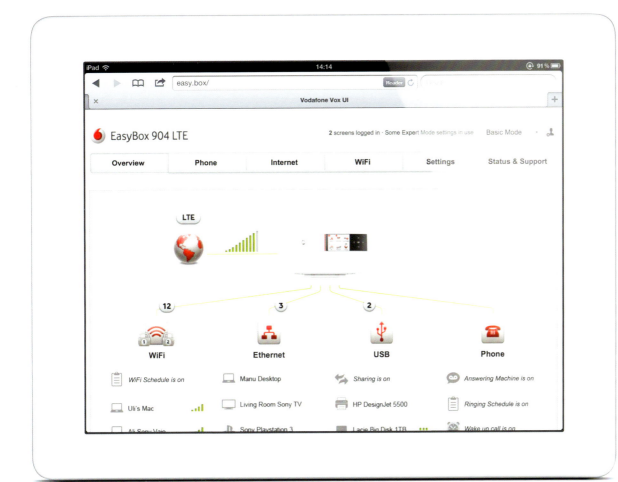

Vodafone EasyBox Router

[Graphical User Interface]

This graphical user interface for Vodafone's EasyBox router suits not only experts but also those averse to technology. The tablet-optimised web interface offers simple, step-by-step setup and features an uncluttered layout. Large icons and graphic elements, as well as its clean look, further contribute to the EasyBox interface being approachable for just about anyone. The complexities of network administration take a back seat to simplicity and ease of use, yet without losing any functionality.

client
Vodafone Group Services
Deutschland, Düsseldorf

design
Ziba Munich

project management
Oliver Lang

user interface design
Oliver Lang,
Manuel Perez Prada,
Eunggyu Lee,
Michael Friebe

programming
Andreas Daoutis,
Hozefa Indorewala

IWC Watch International 01/2013

[iPad App]

client
IWC Schaffhausen

brand publisher
Marion Willam

editor-in-chief
Medard Meier

design
ringzwei,
Hamburg

creative direction
Dirk Linke

art direction
Stefan Kaetz

art buying
Trine Skraastad

programming
Swipe GmbH,
Hamburg

| Interface Design | Mobile & Apps | Game Design | Sound Design | Red Dot: Junior Award | Designer Portraits |

Watch International is the magazine of the Swiss watch manufacturer IWC Schaffhausen. Revolving around timepieces, watchmakers and renowned personalities, the iPad version of the magazine goes beyond the paper edition. Interactive features, as well as additional material, bring Watch International to life. Different layouts and content in both portrait and landscape modes lend the magazine a certain playfulness, as does the use of parallax scrolling. The interface invites users to explore the content, without them ever feeling lost.

ChineseCUBES AR

[Language-Learning Software/ Game]

ChineseCUBES AR is a language-learning utility that uses augmented reality technology to provide an interactive environment in which to study Chinese. Students place physical cubes on a felt mat, which are captured by a webcam and automatically augmented through software, offering audio and video feedback on the characters. By combining various cubes, new and meaningful phrases can be created, which are represented on screen in colourful pop-ups. The software's vivid look adds a level of playfulness to the otherwise dry subject of language learning.

client
ChineseCUBES,
Taipei

design
ChineseCUBES,
Taipei

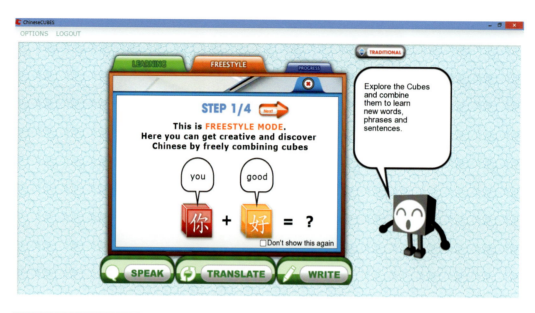

SAP HANA
Data Visualisations
[Realtime Multimedia Visualisations]

SAP HANA is an in-memory appliance for realtime data generation. Instead of showing this data in slide shows with bullet points, lists and tables, the information can now be shown via interactive 3D objects, self-explanatory graphics and other appealing visual media. These realtime visualisations of SAP HANA data can be custom-built to suit every customer's needs. The understanding of the displayed data is improved thanks to the combination of optical, auditive and haptic impulses.

client
stereolize. GmbH,
Munich

design
stereolize. GmbH,
Munich

→ designer portrait: p. 432

Event Design | Information Design & Public Space | Corporate Films | TV, Film, Cinema & Animation | Online World

fiat500.de
[Website]

The Fiat Cinquecento is a compact car that is best described as vibrant and full of life. And so is its website fiat500.de. In lieu of traditional click-through navigation, users simply swipe through the website. Features are presented in a playful way, with interactive elements scattered around. Thanks to HTML5 technology and state-of-the-art parallax scrolling, the stop-motion animation also runs on mobile devices, so that users can configure their individual Fiat 500 anytime, anywhere.

client
Fiat Group Automobiles Germany AG, Frankfurt/Main

design
Leo Burnett, Frankfurt/Main

creative direction
Andreas Pauli

art direction
Ronald Kraft, Marcel Günthel

text
Axel Tischer, Christian Vonscheidt

strategic planning
Björn Brockmann

project management
Axel Käser, Christiane Fritsch

programming
Marco Randi, Sergio Georgalli, Oliver Goertz

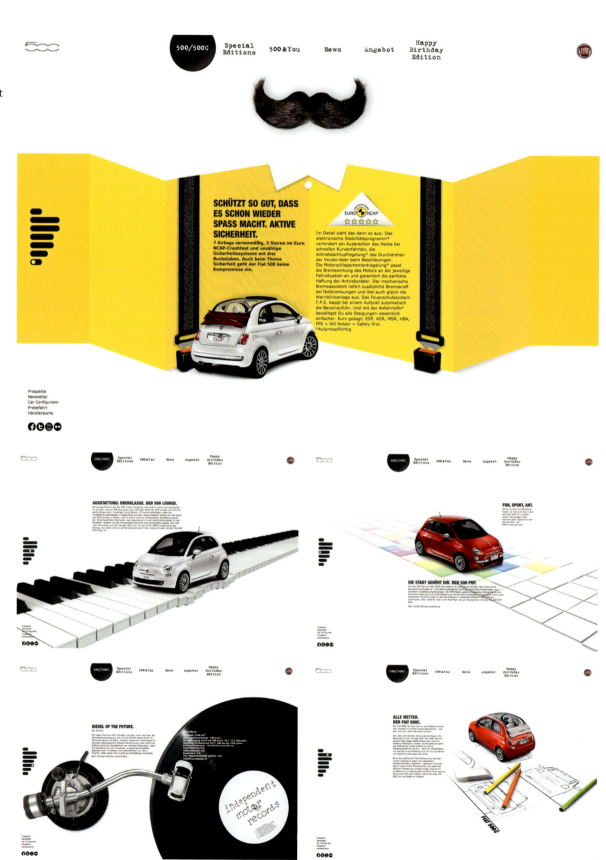

Visualisation of the German Federal Budget

[Website]

The German federal budget involves an enormous amount of money – over 300 billion euros. The budget plan covers more than 2,700 pages. In collaboration with the Bundesministerium der Finanzen (German Federal Ministry of Finance), Pixelpark has succeeded in making this data volume accessible to everyone. All revenue and expenditure can now be found in an easily accessible data visualisation that can also be viewed on smartphones and tablets. This makes the budget understandable – even for non-specialists.

client
Bundesministerium der Finanzen, Berlin
Dominik Grobien, Udo Fenchel
(Referat Öffentlichkeitsarbeit)

design
Pixelpark/Elephant Seven, Berlin

concept
Christoph Krebs

graphic design
Michael Ledwig

account management
Stefan Schopp

project management
Nikola Kinsler

programming
Heiko Hardt

→ designer portrait: p. 428

| Event Design | Information Design & Public Space | Corporate Films | TV, Film, Cinema & Animation | Online World |

Nevaris

[Software Solution for Construction (TAI - Tender, Assignment and Invoicing)]

client
AUER – Die Bausoftware GmbH
(Part of the NEMETSCHEK GROUP), Wals-Siezenheim/
Salzburg

project management
Helmut Houdek

programming
Roland Dorfer

design
CUP GmbH,
Stuttgart

concept
Markus Weidemann,
Hanspeter Hüttisch

graphic design
Katrin Schmuck

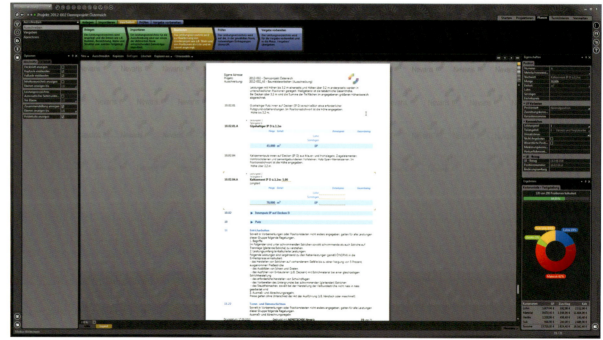

| Interface Design | Mobile & Apps | Game Design | Sound Design | Red Dot: Junior Award | Designer Portraits |

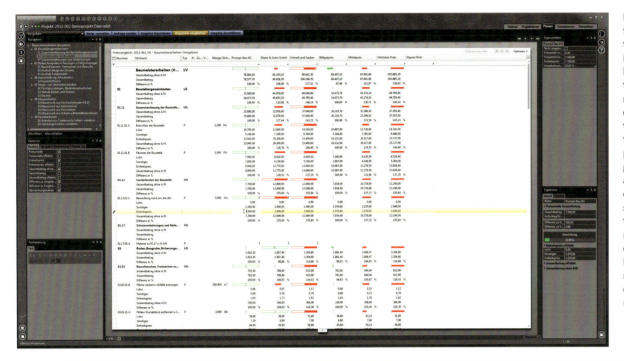

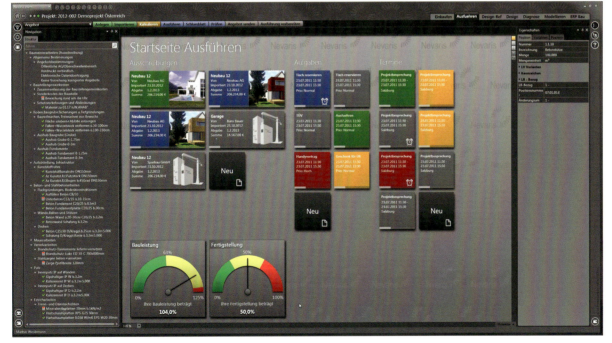

Nevaris is a software solution for architecture and construction. As a replacement for three individual products, it combines cost planning, calculation, tenders, contract awards, settlement and controlling in one solution. Broken down into task-related workflows in order to ensure effective and efficient processing for different user groups, the interface provides an intuitive and uniform user experience. The software is scalable without loss of quality, thus ensuring optimum usability, regardless of screen size. The colour-coded navigation and a high degree of data visualisation serve to facilitate orientation, despite the high density of information and functions.

INTERNATIONAL YEARBOOK COMMUNICATION DESIGN 2013/2014

VOL. 2

MOBILE & APPS

Red Dot: Best of the Best

Leeum Interactive Project
[Interactive Installation for Exhibitions]

The Leeum Interactive Project was conceived to enhance exhibitions through digital media installations that allow visitors an in-depth exploration of elaborate traditional artworks on display. High-resolution photographs of the works are transferred into digital images and shown on a large screen. The visitors are invited to freely reduce, enlarge or move the images with the help of a tablet device. In addition, 360-degree spin photographs are taken to create quasi-sculptural objects that can be rotated, enlarged and adjusted freely to the desired viewing angle. Consisting of a simple navigator and a wheel button, the intuitive-to-use touch interface not only enables easy control of the images, but also helps visitors gain a fascinating, virtual hands-on experience of the artwork. Vibrantly standing out against a black background, the items are complemented by additional information explaining the characteristics of each object to foster a deeper understanding of them. The display monitor and the tablet are connected via Wi-Fi and are easily adaptable to different exhibition environments.

Statement by the jury

»In an impressively staged setting, the interactive installation for the Leeum museum presents exhibits with which users can directly interact. What is outstanding about this is the technical implementation on the one hand, and the high aesthetic and creative quality on the other, a quality that helps focus on and illuminate historical works in particular in a way that is hardly possible by other means.«

| Interface Design | **Mobile & Apps** | Game Design | Sound Design | Red Dot: Junior Award | Designer Portraits |

client
Leeum, Samsung Museum of Art

project management
Seong-Tae Kim,
Doonam Lee

exhibition design
Leeum, Samsung Museum of Art

interface design
Tangomike

**creative direction/
graphic design**
Kyungseok Hahm

programming
Kwanseok Hahm,
Kyungseok Hahm

image editing
Hyojin Park,
Sangwon Lee

→ clip on DVD
→ designer portrait: p. 435

| Event Design | Information Design & Public Space | Corporate Films | TV, Film, Cinema & Animation | Online World |

Red Dot: Best of the Best

Das Auto. Magazine
[iPad App]

The development of the brand car magazine "Das Auto. Magazine" by Volkswagen started with the goals of being approved by different markets in the world, contributing to the enhancement of the global recognition of the brand and improving customer communication. In accordance with its cross media concept, the editorial content management utilises the specific strengths of the channels and complements the print edition, and in particular the content-related features programmed for the iPad app, with a responsive web design. Facilitated by a versatile layout that is marked by vibrant photo spreads, each brand area thus has the possibility of placing individual content and compiling the magazine into a clearly outlined form that is specifically targeted to reflect regional differences. The area editors thus can choose not only the channels but also the extent to which they want to adapt this magazine with its clear typography and variable design to their needs.

Statement by the jury

»This brand magazine is convincing because it not only allows for simple, intuitive navigation and orientation, but also offers an entertaining novel approach for staging the content. The multitude of interaction possibilities and animations, as well as the specific content modules that keep appearing and disappearing, lend it an overall lively and inspiring appearance.«

| Interface Design | **Mobile & Apps** | Game Design | Sound Design | Red Dot: Junior Award | Designer Portraits |

client
Volkswagen AG,
Wolfsburg

design
KircherBurkhardt GmbH,
Berlin

→ designer portrait: p. 415

Red Dot: Best of the Best

Time Travel
[iPad In-App Ad]

For the Mercedes-Benz SL's new edition, an iPad ad for large daily newspapers was developed as a special means to promote the legendary luxury roadster on mobile devices. Together with the latest models, it celebrates the sixty-year-old SL history by inviting users on a fascinating trip into the past. With the help of an intuitive-to-handle "time machine", the users can discover milestones in the contemporary history of car design through text and images. Complemented by important headlines from past decades, all former SL models are gathered on one dedicated newspaper page of authentic historic look which takes the users on a journey backward in time through various decades – all the way back to 1952 when the first SL was born. Echoing the styles of past decades, the design piques curiosity and lets users explore the full details of all former SL models – from the 300 SL sports car to the legendary "Pagoda".

Statement by the jury

»Generated on the basis of the past Mercedes-Benz SL models, the iPad ad has the particular effect of virtually taking users back to past decades, which come to life through real information and an aesthetic look inspired by those times. The solution is outstanding in technique and design and thus instantly stimulates interest in the new SL.«

Interface Design Mobile & Apps Game Design Sound Design Red Dot: Junior Award Designer Portraits

client
Mercedes-Benz Vertrieb
Deutschland, Berlin

design
Pixelpark/Elephant Seven,
Berlin

creative direction
Oliver Baus

art direction
Katja Borsdorf

text
Julia Molina,
Nils Liedmann

programming
Christian Beyer,
Christian Häringer

→ designer portrait: p. 428

Event Design | Information Design & Public Space | Corporate Films | TV, Film, Cinema & Animation | Online World

Red Dot: Best of the Best

The Opel ADAM App

The iPad app ADAM&YOU enables virtual test drives, supporting the configuration and decision-making process. As high-end 3D visualisation solution, this configurator app was created in the style of a computer game for the launch of the new Opel ADAM in Europe. In doing so, it combines technologies such as the Unity 3D game engine with high-end 2D visualisations of the model and its surroundings. By including a virtual test drive function, ADAM&YOU provides a wholly new, dynamic experience of the automobile during the configuration process. The result can be shared and discussed with friends via various social media channels. Available in seven languages, the app's successful launch and the extremely positive user response have now led to develop other app versions for Android-based mobile end devices and the iPhone.

Statement by the jury

»The Opel ADAM configuration app is fascinating because it pushes the boundaries of what comparable configurators have to offer. The playful aspect of allowing users to virtually customise and then test-drive their personal car model, by turning the iPad into a steering wheel, is highly original. The design convinces with its clear layout and appealing appearance.«

client
Adam Opel AG

project management
Thomas Bernd
(Project Manager
Digital Marketing)

game integration/visualisation/
model preparation
RTT AG

design/creative direction/
concept
Gunnar Menzel,
g-p-u-n-k

sound design/production
Bram van der Poel

2d programming
Sevenval

→ clip on DVD

Event Design | Information Design & Public Space | Corporate Films | TV, Film, Cinema & Animation | Online World

Red Dot: Best of the Best

STILL EASY
[iPad App]

This iPad app was developed to support the field organisation of the intralogistics provider STILL in sales and consulting. It comprises four major content areas – PartnerPlan (the service portfolio at a glance), ProductSelector, This is STILL (the company history) and News – and offers eye-catching, interactive 360-degree views and gyro sensor controlled interior views of the forklift trucks. All 46 product families are covered by high-quality images and videos with a total of over 1,400 individual views, implemented in a gamification approach. The ProductSelector thus allows to select and filter the forklift trucks quickly and easily, view them from all sides and test-drive them in a virtual environment. The innovative tool offers intuitive operations guiding the user through the application. Marked by a simple and sophisticated design in premium anthracite colours, the app also provides users with in-depth information on the history and the self-image of the brand.

Statement by the jury

»The STILL EASY iPad app impresses both with its reduced yet elegant design and by implementing a refreshingly novel concept using 360-degree images for the virtual presentations. At the same time, it allows various mobile devices with gyro and tilt sensors to view the products in a playful way.«

Interface Design   Mobile & Apps   Game Design   Sound Design   Red Dot: Junior Award   Designer Portraits

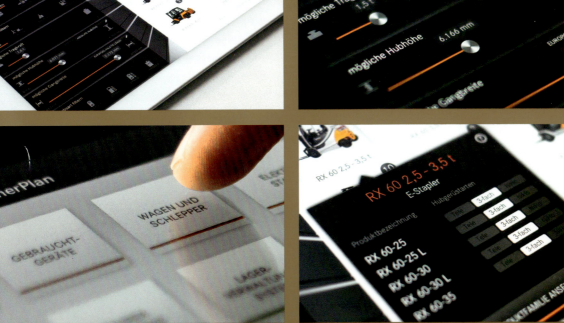

client
STILL GmbH,
Hamburg

design
melting elements gmbh,
Hamburg

→ designer portrait: p. 421

| Event Design | Information Design & Public Space | Corporate Films | TV, Film, Cinema & Animation | Online World |

Volkswagen AG Annual Report 2012 – Experience D(r)iversity

[iPad App]

The iPad version of the Volkswagen AG Annual Report 2012 Experience D(r)iversity is the digital extension of the printed annual report. Layout and navigation mechanisms have been conceptualised to take advantage of the iPad. The eighteen stories are accessed through a horizontal navigation menu, while the editorial content is laid out vertically. Users can interactively discover the twelve brands of the VW Group thanks to clips, sounds and animations. From the new Golf touring through Berlin to the virtual showroom at London's Piccadilly Circus, this annual report takes the user through the varied facets of the group.

client
Volkswagen AG, Wolfsburg

design
3st kommunikation GmbH, Mainz

creative direction
Marcel Teine

art direction
Sebastian Eberstaller, Maximilian Kostopoulos

concept
Thilo Breider

programming
Alex Knaub, Tobias Rehn, Stanislav Müller, Florian Kosiol, 3st digital GmbH, Mainz

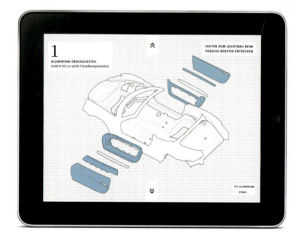

Interface Design | **Mobile & Apps** | Game Design | Sound Design | Red Dot: Junior Award | Designer Portraits

Kia Sportage
[iPad App]

This iPad application invokes digitised descriptions and 3D video clips to present the Kia Sportage with its many features. The showroom portion of the app displays descriptions of specific car features, such as the stop and go system or the electrochromic mirror. Both the exterior and the interior of the car are presented in a detailed 360-degree view. The car's features can be experienced through photo and video galleries, as well as interactive elements. Furthermore, a customisation tool allows users to browse all available colour and wheel options.

client
Kia Motors Corporation, Seoul

design
Design and Communication, Seoul

head of marketing
Sang-Kyoon Woo

**creative direction/
strategic planning**
Seokhoon Jeong

art direction
Yongho Jeong

graphic design
Sunghoon Hong

project management
Youngsuk Jeong, Deokgeun Yoon

film direction
Sangyeul Lee

| Event Design | Information Design & Public Space | Corporate Films | TV, Film, Cinema & Animation | Online World |

myAudi Mobile Assistant
[App]

This app gives Audi drivers access to the content of their myAudi online account and connects them to the car's multimedia interface. For instance, users can take a picture of a point of interest with their smartphone and submit it to the car's navigation system, allowing drivers to select destinations visually and intuitively. Other features include routing and scheduling, as well as the analysis of car information. The app's design is clean, using knocked-greys and the reduced but characteristic Audi aesthetics, which perfectly addresses the target group.

client
AUDI AG,
Ingolstadt

design
Razorfish GmbH

creative direction
Carsten Lindstedt,
Razorfish GmbH

art direction
Frank Lazik,
Razorfish GmbH
Marc Benz,
SapientNitro

concept
Felix Oberhage,
Razorfish GmbH
Stefan Schröder,
SapientNitro

implementation
SapientNitro

Meine Fahrzeuge **Tankbuch** **Verkehrsinfo**

Mein Händler **Mein Abholtag**

Interface Design Mobile & Apps Game Design Sound Design Red Dot: Junior Award Designer Portraits

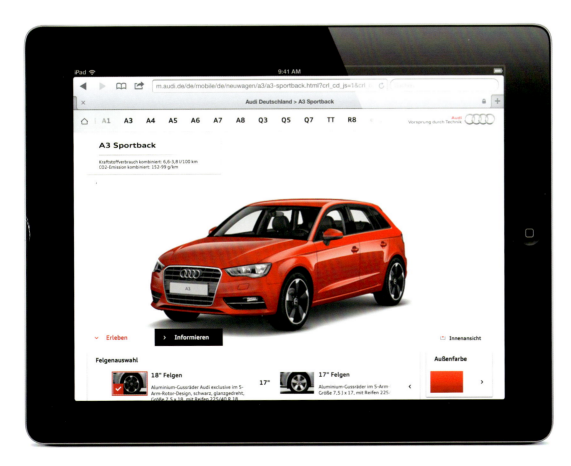

Audi Website
[Tablet App]

Bearing in mind the needs of tablet users, the Audi tablet-optimised website offers a truly responsive design. Every element of the site has been optimised for touchscreen use, accommodating different views: landscape, portrait and a car's 360-degree view. Users can configure car models, locate dealers, search for used models and add vehicles to their wish list. Using light elements, knocked-back greys and smart sliders, a high-quality brand experience is achieved, which follows Audi's "pure and clean" visual approach.

client
AUDI AG,
Ingolstadt

mobile marketing
Bettina Rühle

design
SapientNitro,
Cologne

creative direction
Carlo Wirth

art direction
Marc Benz

information architect
Stefan Schröder

mobile developer
Rainer Friesen

account management
Bahar Eris

Event Design | Information Design & Public Space | Corporate Films | TV, Film, Cinema & Animation | Online World

Kia Carens
[iPad App]

client
Kia Motors Corporation,
Seoul

design
JNS communications,
Seoul

head of marketing
Sang-Kyoon Woo,
Yong-Tae Shin

creative direction
Seung-Ho Cho,
Seokhoon Jeong

art direction
Jun-Young Choi

graphic design
Ji-Hey Choi,
Su-Ji Lim

film direction
Do-Gyun Kim,
GRAPHITE,
Seoul

programming
Kyoung-Kook Kim

→ clip on DVD
→ designer portrait: p. 413

Interface Design　　　Mobile & Apps　　　Game Design　　　Sound Design　　　Red Dot: Junior Award　　　Designer Portraits

This app allows users to experience the MPV car, Kia Carens. The car is presented in four interactive videos, which focus on the aspects of design, performance, space and safety. Through a clear and intuitive user interface with central dial, these clips highlight the main features of the car. Furthermore, users can experience not only exterior and interior of the car in interactive 720-degree view, but also various customisation options.

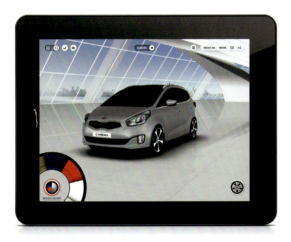

Event Design   Information Design & Public Space   Corporate Films   TV, Film, Cinema & Animation   Online World

Dell Quick Resource Locator (QRL)

[System Information Solution]

The Dell Quick Resource Locator is a powerful utility for IT professionals. Utilising a QR code on twelfth-generation Dell PowerEdge servers and a smartphone app (iPhone and Android), a scan of the QR code directly links to critical service information. IT professionals thus gain immediate access to concise how-to videos, reference materials, configuration information and mobile-optimised user's manuals. Thanks to the app's clean interface, the many different options are easily accessible.

client
Dell Inc.,
Round Rock, Texas

design
Dell Inc.,
Experience Design Group

photography
Dell Photo Studio

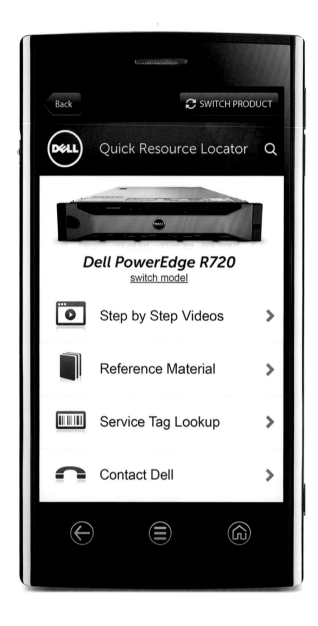

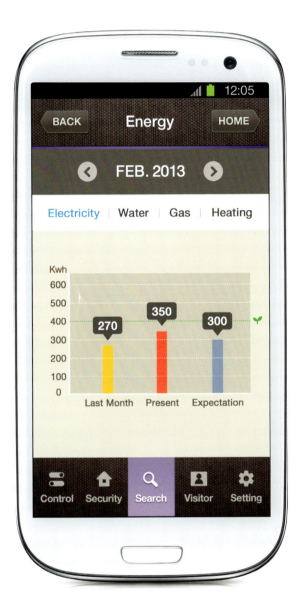

Smart Home
[Smartphone App]

"Smart Home" is an application which provides in-house care and control services that are accessible via smartphone or tablet anytime, anywhere. With the network system installed at home, gas valves, heating systems and lights can be controlled via any personal mobile device. In addition, if you were to leave, you would receive alerts about intrusions, gas leaks, and any other situation that may arise via SMS or mobile notification.

client
Samsung SNS Co., Ltd., Seoul

design
Samsung SNS Co., Ltd., Seoul

art direction
Jeong-Hoon Ha

graphic design
Go-Eun Han,
Hye-Won Suh

project management
Soo-Yeon Chung

| Event Design | Information Design & Public Space | Corporate Films | TV, Film, Cinema & Animation | Online World |

Laplication
[App]

The Northern Lights are visible for up to 200 nights per year in Finnish Lapland. With the Laplication app for iPhone, iPad and iPod touch, users do not have to travel to the northern edge of Finland in order to experience it for themselves. Utilising augmented reality technology, users simply point their smartphone camera at the sky, while GPS data and the phone's compass provide the distance and directions to Lapland. Furthermore, the application includes travel information and pictures from the region.

client
Regional Council of Lapland

marketing director
Hanna-Mari Talvensaari

marketing coordinator
Pauliina Silven-Alamartimo

design
SEK & GREY Finland
(Lead Creative Agency)
Great Apes Ltd
(Digital Design & Development)

art direction
Sami Kelahaara, SEK & GREY
Niko Sipilä, Mika Mäkinen,
Great Apes

copywriting
Suvi Lähde, SEK & GREY

account director
Laura Mertano, SEK & GREY

strategic planning
Sami Lanu, SEK & GREY

project coordination
Mikko Sairio,
Great Apes

development
Mikko Saario, Antti Kaukinen,
Great Apes

3d production
Fake Graphics (winter animation),
Pinata (summer animation)

| Interface Design | **Mobile & Apps** | Game Design | Sound Design | Red Dot: Junior Award | Designer Portraits |

9292 – Your personal public transport planner

[Mobile App]

The 9292 app is a personal travel planner for public transportation in the Netherlands that is designed to work on various smartphone systems, including iPhone, Android, BlackBerry 10 and Windows Phone. Users can enter their departure location by using GPS, points of interest, a bus stop or an address. Frequently searched locations are stored for quicker access. Travel routes can even be synchronised between a PC and the mobile device. Implementing a flat design and a colour palette of grey, white and light blue, the app puts travel data front and centre.

client
9292,
Utrecht

design
Fabrique
[brands, design & interaction],
Delft

Event Design | Information Design & Public Space | Corporate Films | TV, Film, Cinema & Animation | Online World

sportcast APP

client
SportCast,
Taipei

design
JamZoo Inc.,
Taipei

director
Chuang Scott

creative direction/art direction
Chiu Sheng-Yu

concept/film direction
Chang Chu Ting

animation/motion design
Lin Hsuan Yi

final artwork
Chang Chu Ting

production
Jay Chang

→ clip on DVD

The sportcast app combines the convenience of watching sports on the go via a smartphone with the joy and excitement of a public sports bar. Users can share their feelings while watching a game, using standardised symbols like smiley faces or the thumbs down icon. Once the click count exceeds a certain threshold, an animation will be displayed on the user's device, spreading the emotion of other fans. In addition, users can combine their smartphones to create a bigger screen. With its clear blue-and-grey design and its cut-and-dried navigation, this feature-laden app is easy to use.

| Event Design | Information Design & Public Space | Corporate Films | TV, Film, Cinema & Animation | Online World |

AppsPlay
[Smart TV App]

AppsPlay Smart TV is the television extension of Pantech's mobile and web app store. As is evident here, South Korea's second largest mobile handset maker has put heavy emphasis on the user experience. Since navigation generally takes place via the remote control, the routes for the cursor have to be short in order to ensure quick and easy access to the key functions of the TV. The guided user interface, with its modern look, uses colour-coded navigation elements for further ease of use.

client
Pantech,
Seoul

design
NINEFIVE,
Seoul

creative direction
Younghee Jo

graphic design
Suwoong Byun,
Kihan Kim,
Yujin Kwon

account management
Yujin Won

→ designer portrait: p. 425

2013 Samsung Smart TV AR

[Mobile App]

Finding the television that fits best in one's own home is not an easy task. Samsung's augmented reality application for Android enables users to preview their desired TV where it is supposed to be placed without it physically being there. Using everyday objects as a marker, such as credit cards or playing cards, the app digitally creates a simulation of the TV that is close to life size. By tilting the smartphone in various directions, users can examine the television from different angles. In addition, they can capture images and share them via social media and e-mail.

client
Samsung Electronics Co., Ltd., Suwon

head of advertising
Yongku Kim

design
designfever, Seoul

creative direction
Juhwan Lee

graphic design
Sanghun Lee

project management
Heehyun Kim

programming
Hyungju Shin

animation
Hyunggon Kim

Acousticons

[Mobile App]

This app is a messenger for the iPhone with a twist: instead of emoticon smiley faces, it uses so-called "Acousticons". Created for and played by the Hamburg Philharmonic Orchestra, these little icons give musical expression to a wide range of emotions. Acousticons such as "Amabile" (lovely), "Giocoso" (funny) and "Furioso" (angry) illustrate the respective emotion not only through distinct icons in the shape of notes, but also through full orchestral accompaniment.

client
Philharmoniker Hamburg

design
Draftfcb Deutschland GmbH, Hamburg

creative direction
Dirk Haeusermann,
Patrik Hartmann,
Michael Okun

art direction
Vitali Nazarenus,
Markus Schmidt,
Semjon Janzen,
Elena Balzer

text
Saemi Sebastian Bouchareb,
Verena Kessler,
Elena Praetze

film production
Estelle Bolin,
Holger Siegle,
onehousemedia,
Optix Digital Pictures

music/sound design
Loft Tonstudios Hamburg

programming
Akryl Digital Agency

→ designer portrait: p. 403

Interface Design | **Mobile & Apps** | Game Design | Sound Design | Red Dot: Junior Award | Designer Portraits

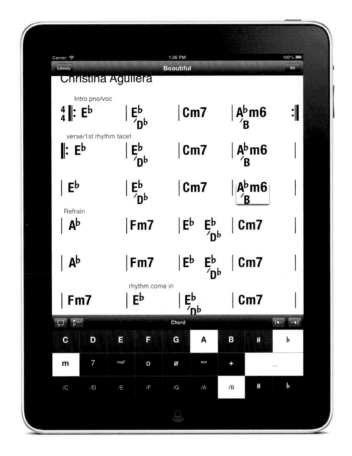
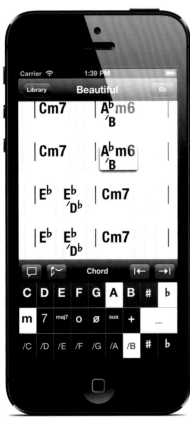
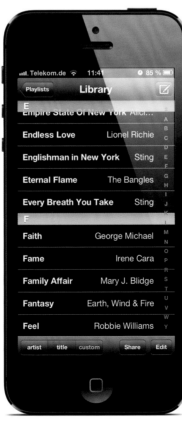

Chord Sheets
[App for Pop Sheets]

This iPhone and iPad app offers two things at the same time. On the one hand, it compiles a comprehensive collection of chord sheets, with the most important pop songs starting from the 1970s and ranging to the current charts. Songs can be played back and transposed into the key of the singer. On the other hand, the app Chord Sheets features an editor, which enables users to edit the existing sheets and create new compositions from scratch. In order to make the app simple and easy to use, only the elements and buttons applicable to the current context are shown.

client
wysiwyg* software design gmbh, Düsseldorf

design
wysiwyg* software design gmbh, Düsseldorf

art direction
Alex Koch

concept
Marcus Schinkel,
Pattrick Kreutzer,
Alex Koch

programming
Moritz Pipahl,
Pattrick Kreutzer

account management
Florian Breiter

| Event Design | Information Design & Public Space | Corporate Films | TV, Film, Cinema & Animation | Online World |

City Shopper
[iOS App]

With this app, a personal shopper is always available. Utilising tags and sophisticated filters, City Shopper enables users to filter shops according to their individual needs and to compile their own shopping tours. The app features an elegant, feminine design and a simple, straightforward user interface, thus perfectly addressing the target group. Detailed information on individual shops is provided and includes pictures, while sightseeing tips and recommendations for cafés and restaurants round off the app.

client
Raukamp & Raukamp GbR, Berlin

concept
Johara Raukamp,
Smart Mobile Factory GmbH, Berlin

design/programming
Smart Mobile Factory GmbH, Berlin

head of marketing
Jana Wittkowski

graphic design
Sabine Brambach

project management
Tobias Fuchs

→ designer portrait: p. 431

| Interface Design | Mobile & Apps | Game Design | Sound Design | Red Dot: Junior Award | Designer Portraits |

Evernote 5 for iPhone, iPad and iPod touch

[Mobile App]

Evernote 5 is a fully fledged notebook app for the iPhone, iPad, and iPod touch. The app lets users take notes, capture photos, create to-do lists, record voice reminders and make these notes available across all of the user's devices. The completely redesigned application makes all major functions accessible within two taps. Along the top of the app are the quick note buttons for creating new notes, starting a snapshot and digitising physical documents. Below the buttons are hanging file folders sorted by notes, notebooks, tags and places to make it easy for users to find the content they are looking for.

client
Evernote,
Redwood City, California

design
Evernote,
Redwood City, California

255

GameMate

[Game Capture App]

client
AVerMedia Technologies, Inc.,
New Taipei City

design
AVerMedia Technologies, Inc.,
New Taipei City

concept
Johnson Chao,
Daniel Dai

graphic design
Dona Yen,
Aline Hsu

text
Charity Liu

project management
Daniel Dai

animation
Peter Chang

motion design
Neo Hsu,
Eling Hsu

The GameMate app for iOS devices is designed to remotely control AVerMedia's Game Capture HD video capture box. It enables users to record their gaming triumphs on video game consoles with the tap of a button. The interface aims to transcend its peers with its futuristic look, resembling a modern video game. Fluid animations and transitions highlight the app's high-tech appeal. It uses distinct neon colours as a visual cue for the four main modes – record, playback, snapshot and stream – with text overlays and gradients in the respective colour highlighting the mode selected. Arranged around the central control button, the app's features can be accessed intuitively with a tapping or swiping motion.

| Event Design | Information Design & Public Space | Corporate Films | TV, Film, Cinema & Animation | Online World |

Teemo
[App]

Teemo is a fitness adventure game that combines proven training techniques, social connection, and entertaining adventures to help small groups of friends get and stay moving. From an interaction design perspective, Teemo is above all an experiment in moving beyond conventional approaches to gamification and social computing. From the start, the project team set its sights on providing something less stressful than points schemes, leaderboards, peer pressure, lifelogging, and self-quantification, instead encouraging people to get together with friends to have fun in ways that also happen to increase overall fitness.

client
Bonnier R&D,
San Francisco

design
Ammunition LLC,
San Francisco

**user experience/
user interface design**
Matt Rolandson,
Brett Wickens,
Aaron Poe,
Michael McQueen,
Darcy DiNucci,
Anne Kitzmiller,
Ryan Lauer,
Jenny Shears,
Chona Reyes,
Vivian Wu

Interface Design Mobile & Apps Game Design Sound Design Red Dot: Junior Award Designer Portraits

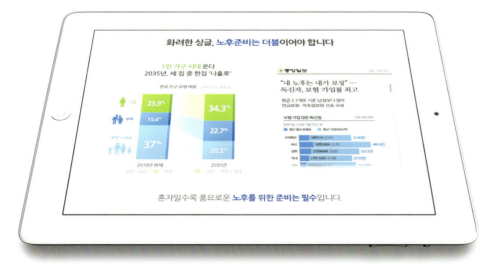

Kyobo Life Insurance's Dream Planner – the ESS (EDA Sales Suite)
[App]

Forms, brochures and lots of paper in general play a huge role in the lives of life insurance salespeople. This iPad app renders most of it obsolete. By giving salespeople the tools to create their own presentations and bundling them with digital forms, they can provide their customers with effective and creative advice. Swiping through and interacting with the sales material helps customers understand complicated insurance planning forms more easily. Necessary papers and informational materials can then be sent by e-mail.

client
Kyobo Life Insurance Co., Ltd., Seoul

design
EDA Communications, Inc., Seoul

art direction
Kang Myung-Soo

graphic design
Lee Seung-Hyun,
Chae Song-Hwa

artwork
Jeon Kang-Hwan

editor
Kang Ji-Hye,
Moon Hye-Won,
Han Dong-Wook

project management
Kim Sung-Yong

programming
Han Yo-Han,
Park Sung-Won,
Park Sang-Hyun

→ clip on DVD

Event Design | Information Design & Public Space | Corporate Films | TV, Film, Cinema & Animation | Online World

E.ON
Key Account App

client
E.ON Vertrieb Deutschland GmbH

brand communication
Annette Dudenhausen

design
zeros+ones GmbH,
Munich

creative direction
Michael Teltscher,
Luca Capelletti

art direction
Luca Capelletti

graphic design
Thomas Uebe

project management
Tobias Bauer

programming
Henrik Lang,
Nils Distler
(native iOS programming)
Alexander Schenker,
Kristof Dreier

motion design
Martin Mühle

→ clip on DVD
→ designer portrait: p. 437

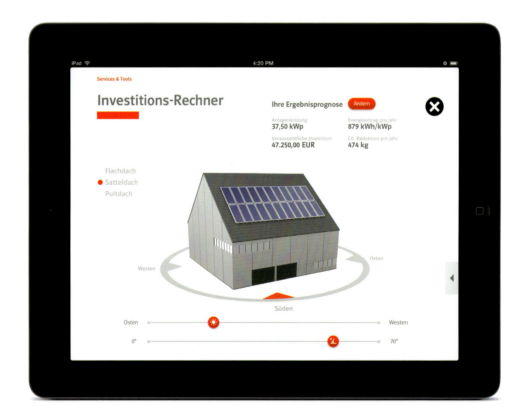

Interface Design   **Mobile & Apps**   Game Design   Sound Design   Red Dot: Junior Award   Designer Portraits

The E.ON Key Account App is a professional tool for key account managers, enabling them to easily create custom-made presentations for customer pitches. The app acts as a visual conversation guide, highlighting selected client data in diagrams, such as clients' past electricity or natural gas consumption. Instead of encountering sheets and tables, the users are greeted with interactive elements, animations and digital tools. By doing away with piles of paperwork, a relaxed dialogue between the key account manager and the customer may be established. Thanks to various theme packages, each presentation can be matched to the respective small or medium enterprise.

| Event Design | Information Design & Public Space | Corporate Films | TV, Film, Cinema & Animation | Online World |

CREON MTS
[Mobile Trading App]

client
Daishin Securities,
Seoul

design
NINEFIVE,
Seoul

creative direction
Younghee Jo

graphic design
Suwoong Byun,
Kihan Kim,
Yujin Kwon

project management
Moonsoo Kim

account management
Yujin Won

→ designer portrait: p. 425

| Interface Design | **Mobile & Apps** | Game Design | Sound Design | Red Dot: Junior Award | Designer Portraits |

This trading app for the Korean company Daishin Securities was designed to simplify mobile trading. With a heavy focus on usability and user experience, the Creon MTS app accomplishes the feat of offering a multitude of features in a neat package, while maintaining the brand identity. The distinct brand colour Creon Magenta is used throughout the app, with even the glossiness of the company logo being reflected through gradients on basic menu and action buttons. By using intuitively recognisable icons, the complexity of trading is further reduced. The guided user interface – with its quick menu, history buttons and user-enabled filters – minimises the number of actions a user must perform in order to obtain the desired information.

Event Design | Information Design & Public Space | Corporate Films | TV, Film, Cinema & Animation | Online World

Star Alliance Navigator

[iPad App]

This iPad app is an interactive portal for customers of airlines that are part of the Star Alliance network. Its distinguishing feature is a 3D globe, which visualises the route network of Star Alliance's 27 airlines, enabling voyagers to keep track of their travels. Depending on the traveller's time and place, additional information is displayed, including weather data, details on the destination airport and up-to-date information about flights.

client
Star Alliance Services GmbH, Frankfurt/Main

design
SapientNitro, Cologne

art direction
David Stoll

project management
Marie-Christin Anthony

information architect
Sonja Geissler

app development
Nils Martens

account management
Wolfgang Katsch

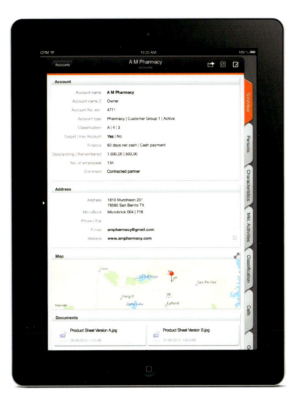

update CRM.pad
[B2B App for Sales Representatives]

The CRM.pad app allows sales representatives to access their customer data anytime, anywhere. The mobile version of update's customer relationship management solution provides the functional essentials, while taking advantage of the benefits of the iPad. The dashboard displays CRM data and an overview of current tasks, visits and locations. With customer master data and contact histories at their fingertips, sales representatives can focus on what they do best: engaging with customers.

client
update software AG,
Vienna

design
Martin Zopf,
update software AG,
Vienna

project management
Christian Puhr,
update software AG,
Vienna

→ clip on DVD

Event Design | Information Design & Public Space | Corporate Films | TV, Film, Cinema & Animation | Online World

hochfünf Magazine
[App]

client
hoch5 next GmbH & Co. KG, Bünde

design
hoch5 next GmbH & Co. KG, Bünde

creative direction
Tobias Heyer

art direction
Michael Stüker,
Miriam Weck

project management
Anne Lüneburg

As a magazine app that tells stories about people – what affects them and how they affect others – the hochfünf Magazin app for iOS and Android devices builds on the print version. With rich media enhancements, such as additional images, sounds and videos and a wild layout, the app conveys its content in a unique and fitting way. Typography, photography and graphic design are implemented without following any specific pattern or category. Dynamic and interactive elements make the stories even livelier.

Event Design | Information Design & Public Space | Corporate Films | TV, Film, Cinema & Animation | Online World

Evonik Magazine
[iPad App]

Evonik Magazine's app for the iPad opens up the possibilities of multimedia storytelling. Reporting on topics such as resource efficiency, health and nutrition, as well as globalisation, the interactive iPad version enhances the print magazine. Interactive infographics, videos, picture galleries and audio elements can be tapped and swiped to reveal content. The app's intuitive mechanics make it easy for users to navigate through the magazine. The kiosk app is constantly updated and also offers PDF versions of previous issues, thus giving users access to a digital archive of the publication.

client
Evonik Industries AG,
Essen

publisher
HOFFMANN UND CAMPE
Corporate Publishing,
Hamburg

project management
Kim Krawehl

design/programming
Redaktion 4,
Hamburg

1890
[Customer Magazine, App]

Named after the year the Allianz insurance group was founded, 1890, this iPad knowledge magazine offers anything but dry insurance data. Revolving around culture and science, the app utilises many of the iPad's unique features to deliver the magazine's content. Videos and picture galleries enhance the articles, while special features such as interactive personality tests add a certain degree of playfulness. Both the imaginative layout and the multi-dimensional navigation, which enables users to swipe through the content, do away with the conventions of print magazines.

client
Allianz Deutschland AG, Munich

design
KircherBurkhardt GmbH, Berlin

| Event Design | Information Design & Public Space | Corporate Films | TV, Film, Cinema & Animation | Online World |

Das ist mein Körper – Anatomie für Kinder
This is my body – Anatomy for kids
[iPad App]

This educational app gives children an understanding of the principles of human anatomy. By playfully tapping and swiping colourful illustrations, children discover and learn about the nervous system, the senses, the skeleton and much more. To ensure that even younger kids can enjoy the app, its elements are represented visually using colour and shapes, while text is read out loud. Older children, who can already read, have the option of digging deeper into the content with extensive textual information.

client
urbn; interaction, Berlin

design
urbn; interaction, Berlin

creative direction/ project management
Franka Futterlieb

art direction
Anna Mentzel

illustration
Anna Mentzel, Franka Futterlieb

programming
Benjamin Müller

animation
Jörn Alraun

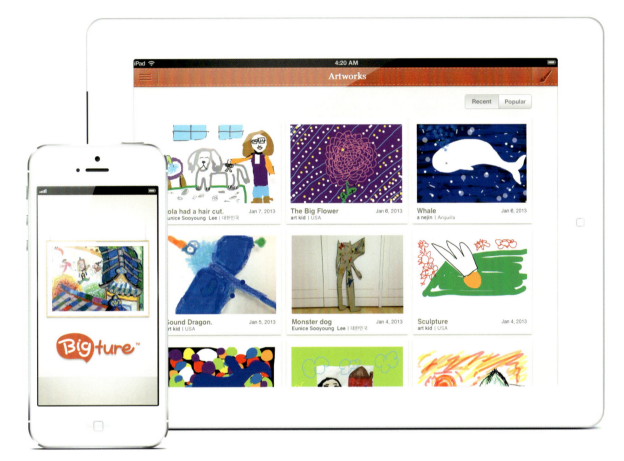

Bigture
[Art SNS App for Kids]

Bigture is an art-centric social network app that enables children to express their creativity without limitation. Consisting of a sketchbook and special kits for obtaining additional materials, they can draw on the iPad using merely their fingers. Once done, children can share their creations with the Bigture social network. Professional designers, artists, curators and teachers will leave critiques and give feedback on the submitted pictures. Other users can then rate the creations using stickers and words.

client
The Clockworks Innovate, Seoul

design
The Clockworks Innovate, Seoul

art direction
Cheong Hyun Lee,
Hyejin Ahn,
Hoonsil Jeong

film direction
Taeyeon Kim

artwork
Misun Jin,
Miyeon Ahn,
Mijin Kim,
Kayoung Seo,
Hyunyoung Ki

→ clip on DVD

SMART Project – Pediatric Growth Chart App

client
Harvard Medical School, Boston

development
MedAppTech, Boston

design
Fjord, New York

Interface Design   Mobile & Apps   Game Design   Sound Design   Red Dot: Junior Award   Designer Portraits

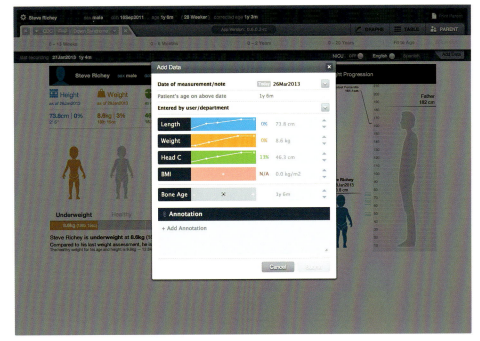

Developed for the SMART Project, this pediatric growth chart app helps clinicians get an accurate overview of a child's growth patterns, yet it is simple enough to communicate data meaningfully to parents. The app combines the best parts of the old analogue tool with all the benefits of modern information technology. Personal growth charts can be overlapped with several different growth chart standards, including those from the World Health Organization, the Centers for Disease Control and Prevention, and for children with Down's syndrome. A clear view of the data is offered, making vital information available in an intelligible way, without neglecting the complexities of pediatrics. A "parental view" further breaks down the charts and presents data with simple visuals in an engaging way.

INTERNATIONAL YEARBOOK COMMUNICATION DESIGN 2013/2014

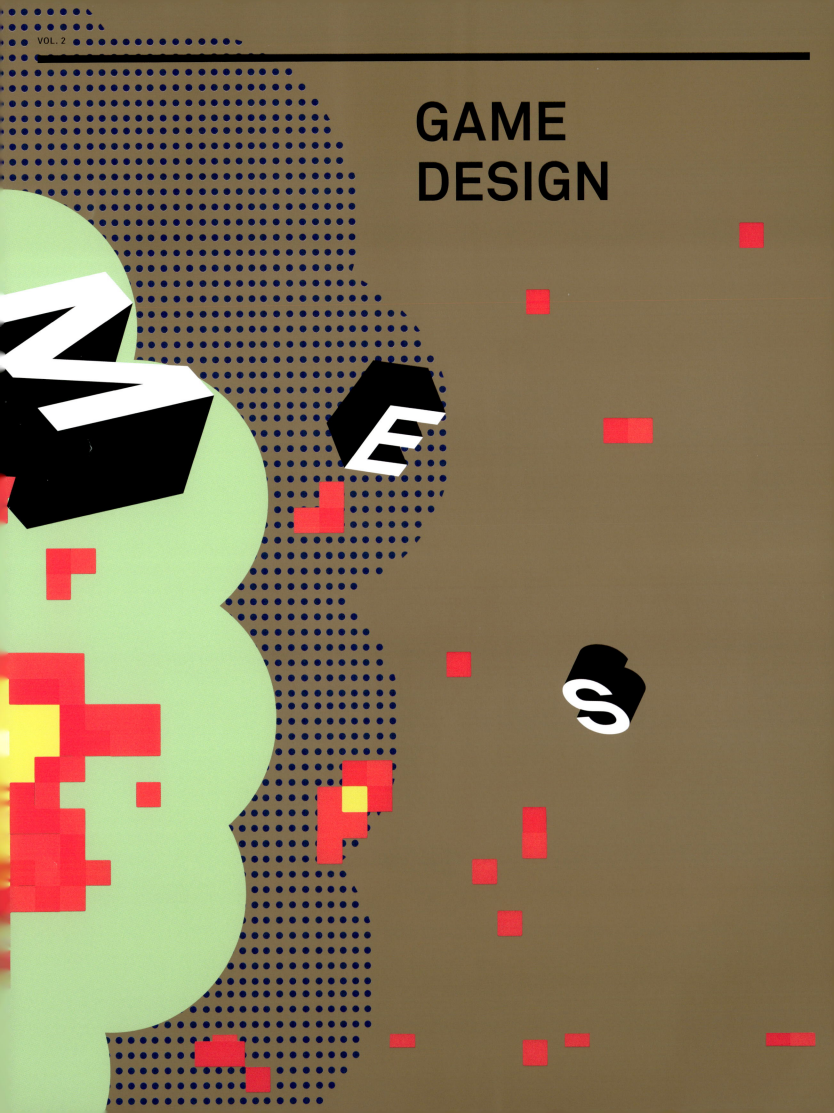

Red Dot: Grand Prix

Crysis 3
[Video Game]

The multi-platform video game Crysis 3 envisions a spectacular future for New York City, a future in which the armed henchmen of the corrupt Cell Corporation have seized power. Envisioned in elaborately crafted animations full of rich details, the metropolis is dominated by seven natural wonders including turbulent rivers, deep canyons and lush jungles that all offer distinctive visual impressions and hold different challenges. Players have the freedom to pick their own path and play-style, check out versatile weapons such as the Predator Bow with the powers of the famous Nanosuit, and thus experience fascinating adventures in this immersive first-person shooter game. The Nanosuit acts as the player's high-tech window on the world in this video game, affording them the opportunity to become invisible or ultra powerful as they explore the futuristic interpretation of New York City, and later in the game the sunlight-flooded grasslands and the impressively visualised water dam.

Statement by the jury

»Particularly impressive in the third part of Crysis are the distinctively lush graphics that characterise the fascinating scenarios, as well as the cinema-like sound and the multiplayer mode. The plot becomes ever more enthralling in the course of the game and, alongside manifold opportunities for exploring and acting in this world, it offers outstandingly staged settings in terms of game graphics design.«

Interface Design | Mobile & Apps | **Game Design** | Sound Design | Red Dot: Junior Award | Designer Portraits

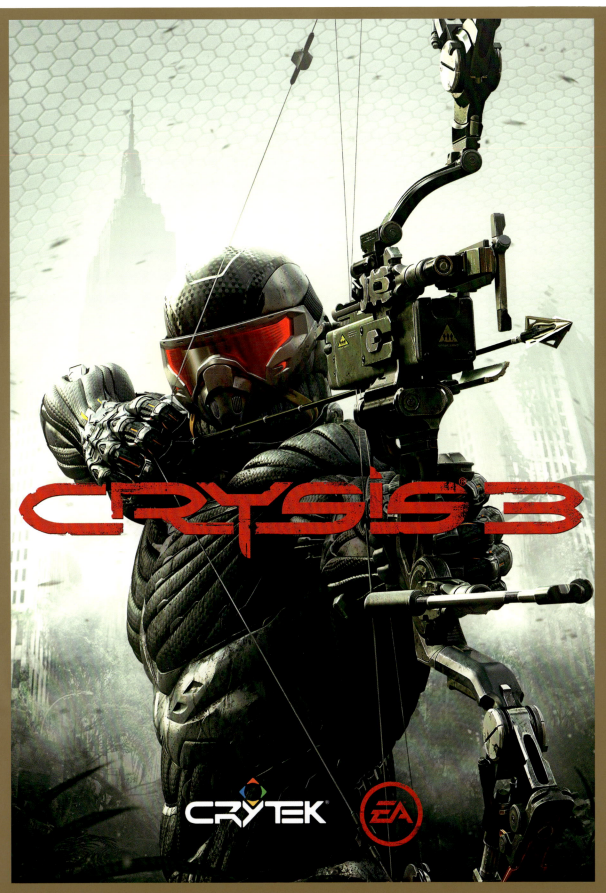

client
Crytek,
Frankfurt/Main

design
Crytek,
Frankfurt/Main

creative direction
Cevat Yerli

art direction
Magnus Larbrant

project management
Jan Lechner

music/sound design
Borislav Slavov

animation
Steven Bender

level design director
Chris Auty

→ clip on DVD
→ designer portrait: p. 399

reddot design award
grand prix 2013

Red Dot: Best of the Best

Chaos on Deponia
[PC Game]

"Chaos on Deponia" follows the path of a classic point-and-click adventure while exploring the possibilities of interactive narrative. The second instalment of the trilogy leads back to the planet Deponia on an epic storyline, in which the player in the role of the antihero Rufus fights to rescue this junk planet and improve his living conditions. Filled with engaging peculiar characters, bizarre locations and strange creatures, all staged in a congenial cartoon style, the complex setting not only provides manifold themes with a lot of references to real life but also off-beat humour and great depth. Characterised by a unique visual design with affectionately hand-drawn scenes, the Deponia Series is a parody and reflection of social conventions and grievances. The whole planet is a single junkyard, and therefore a huge playground for adventure gamers as well as a childhood dream that has come true.

Statement by the jury

»"Chaos on Deponia" offers a complex storyline in which the tragic hero Rufus on his mission to save the junk planet experiences many adventures and faces difficulties. The game surprises with imaginative settings and twists in plot, spirited wordplay and witty dialogues, as well as a highly appealing graphic style. Informed by the narrative talent of the developers, the many strange and peculiar characters in the game are outstanding.«

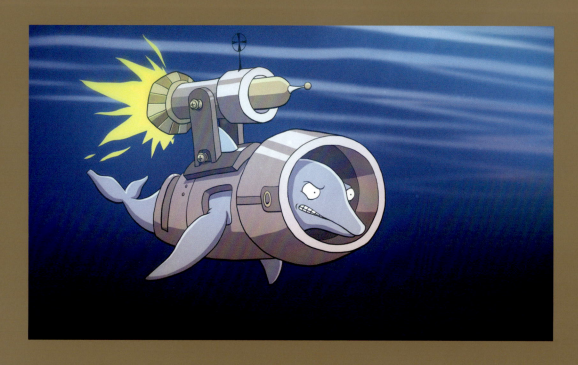

client
Daedalic Entertainment,
Hamburg

design
Daedalic Entertainment,
Hamburg

creative direction
Jan Müller-Michaelis

art direction
Simone Kesterton

programming
Eduard Wolf

animation
Gunnar Bergmann

executive producer
Carsten Fichtelmann

→ clip on DVD
→ designer portrait: p. 400

Event Design · Information Design & Public Space · Corporate Films · TV, Film, Cinema & Animation · Online World

Magic Seeds
[iPad App]

design
BiBoBox Studio,
Dalian Nationalities University,
Dalian

creative direction
Bo Liu

art direction
Xiaofang Li

music/sound design
Yilin You

artwork
Songling Zhang,
Xiaoshuang Guo,
Yajuan Mao,
Yichao Wu,
Na Zuo,
Mengtan Liu,
Bowen Li

programming
Jiansheng Jiang,
Tao Fang

→ clip on DVD
→ designer portrait: p. 397

280

Interface Design Mobile & Apps **Game Design** Sound Design Red Dot: Junior Award Designer Portraits

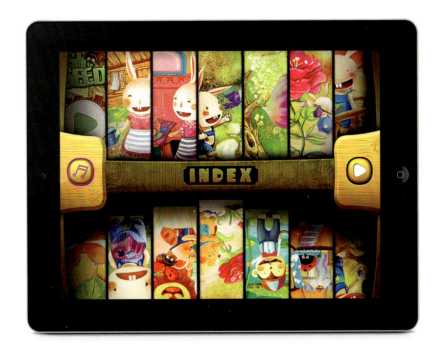

Magic Seeds is a fully interactive iPad app for children. Its colourful illustrations and non-verbal aspect of storytelling make it accessible to a broad audience. The game aims to encourage children's imagination and creativity through puzzle solving and engaging with more than 100 interactive elements and sounds. By touching, dragging and rotating the illustrations, hidden collectibles are discovered, which can then be used to create unique flowers and plants. These creations can be edited, saved and shared through social networks.

Event Design | Information Design & Public Space | Corporate Films | TV, Film, Cinema & Animation | Online World

Meltdown
[Board Game]

client
Gruner + Jahr AG & Co. KG,
Hamburg

design
Kolle Rebbe GmbH,
Hamburg

executive creative director
Sascha Hanke

creative direction
Rolf Leger,
Thomas Knüwer

text
Oliver Ramm

game development
Thomas Knüwer

consulting game development
Tom Schoeps

production
Martin Lühe

→ clip on DVD

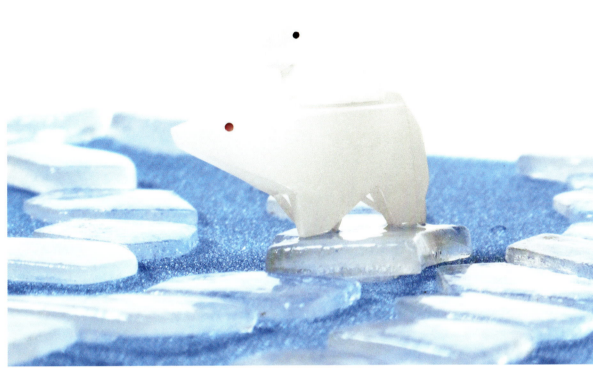

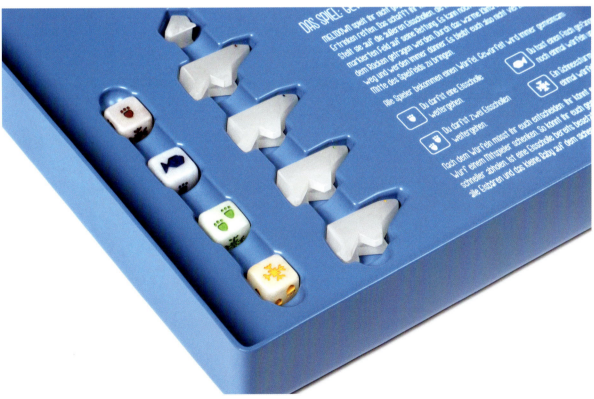

Global warming is a complex issue that is difficult to convey to primary school children. GEOlino, the children's science magazine from one of the largest publishing houses in Europe, Gruner + Jahr, set out to change this and introduced the first-ever melting board game. Children create ice floes by filling a moulded tray with water and freezing it. The floes are then placed on a spongy game board, where players have to rescue polar bears while the ice floes are melting away. By positioning the imminent danger of real-world polar bears as the key game element, Meltdown makes global warming palpable.

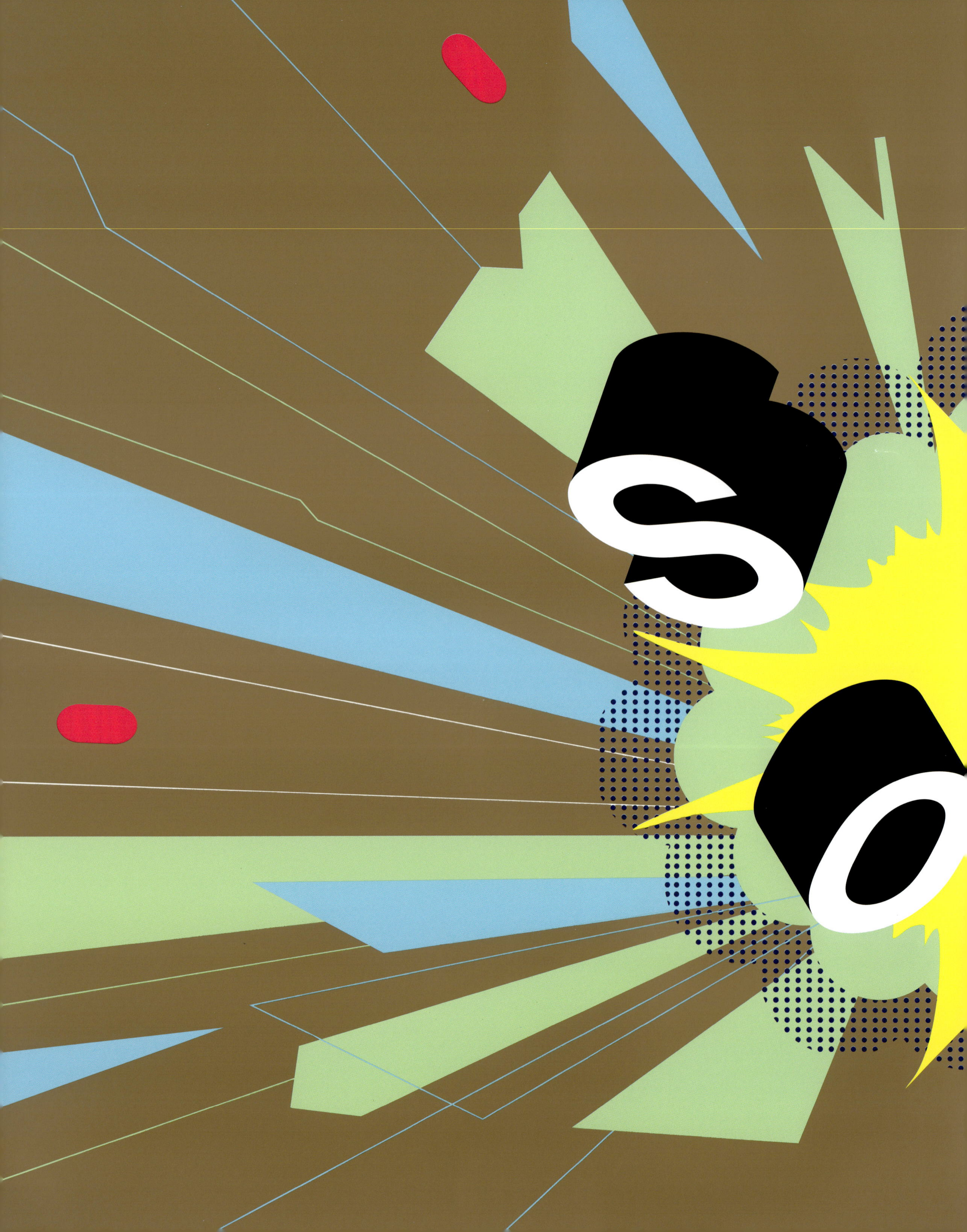

INTERNATIONAL YEARBOOK COMMUNICATION DESIGN 2013/2014

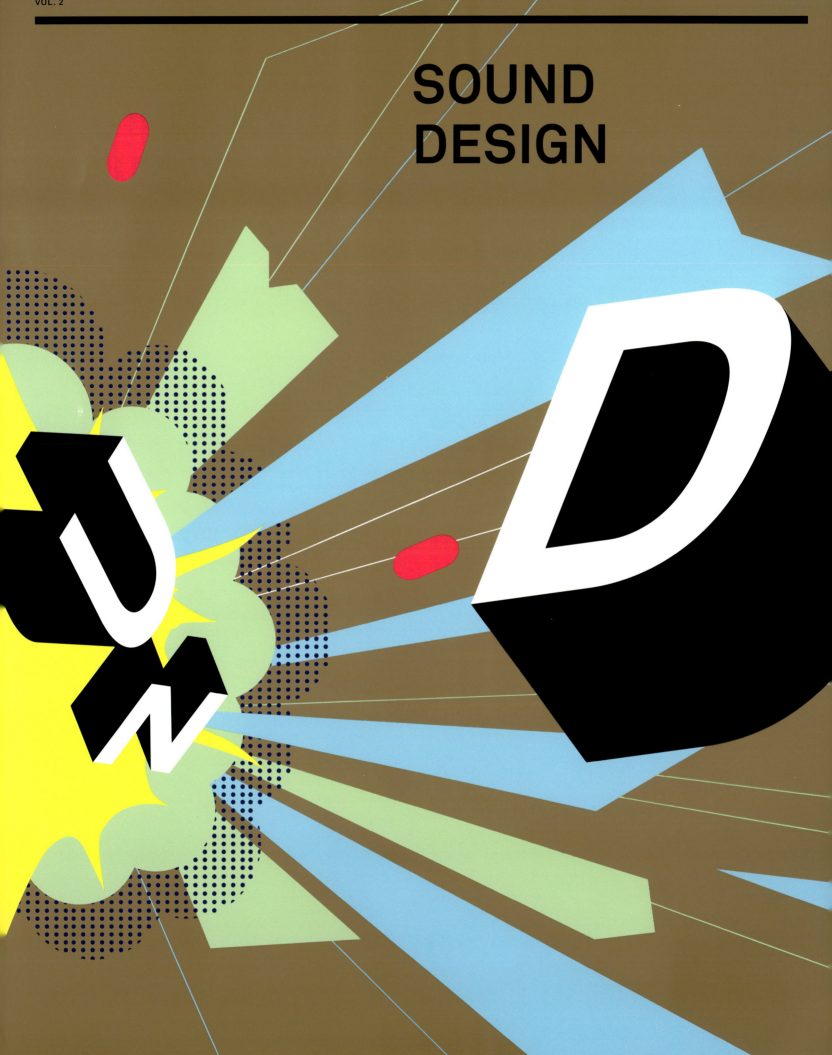

Red Dot: Best of the Best

Tree Concert
[Interactive Installation]

Berlin loses thousands of city trees every year. In order to stop this trend and raise public awareness of the need to protect trees, the Friends of the Earth Germany (BUND) organisation put on an unusual charity concert. The idea was to stage a "Tree Concert" and have a chestnut tree perform as a musician in order to collect donations. A unique instrument was built that made each falling chestnut become part of an artistic composition created by the impact of the chestnut as it triggered a combination of sound and light effects. The instrument consisted of cloth membranes stretched over a steel frame. Attached sensors responded to any vibration on the membrane caused by the falling chestnuts and translated them into harmonic sounds. In addition, the sounds made by the tree itself, such as branches creaking and leaves rustling in the wind, also became part of the composition. The tree could thus "play" for its companions and attracted a large audience with the aim of collecting donations for the cause.

Statement by the jury

»The idea of promoting and staging the issue in the form of a musical performance, and thus conceive of it as sound, is outstanding. As a means of raising awareness about the problems concerning trees, this installation was not only implemented to be visually attractive, but also to create an experience that leaves a lasting impression on the audience.«

Interface Design · Mobile & Apps · Game Design · **Sound Design** · Red Dot: Junior Award · Designer Portraits

client
BUND Bund für Umwelt und Naturschutz Deutschland, Landesverband Berlin e.V., Berlin

design
BBDO Proximity Berlin GmbH
Gang of Berlin

creative managing director
Jan Harbeck, David Mously

creative direction
Jan Harbeck

art direction
Daniel Schweinzer

text
Lukas Liske

account management
Dirk Spakowski, Sebastian Schlosser, Joris Jonker, Mia Lücker, Frank Hägele, Emily Dietzsch, Christof Biggeleben, Monika Groewe

production
Mat Neidhardt, Friederike Seifert, Gang of Berlin

production assistance
Kirsten Schulz

design/architecture
Steve Bergmann, Alexej Alschiz, Gang of Berlin

digital design
Kamil Garbacz

music/sound design
Philipp Tögel

lighting design
Sandra Glaser

illustration
Robert Bilz

concept online
Yassin Taibi, René Bieder

→ clip on DVD
→ designer portrait: p. 396

Offroad

[TV Spot]

Visualising weakness in a humorous way, this TV spot emphasises the advantages of the smart fortwo as a car that was made for the city. First, the smart fortwo is challenged by desert-like terrain and fails miserably. But the next scene shows it in a city, where it effortlessly drives into a tiny parking space. The sound design underscores the bold manoeuvres through the dramatic rise and fall of powerful music. This tension-building acoustic atmosphere is intensified by individual sounds, such as the rippling of water.

client
Daimler AG,
Böblingen

design
BBDO Proximity Berlin GmbH

creative managing director
Jan Harbeck,
David Mously

creative direction
David Mously,
Ton Hollander,
Jens Ringena

art direction
Daniel Schweinzer

text
Lukas Liske,
Momme Clausen

account management
Dirk Spakowski,
Sebastian Schlosser,
Jan Hendrik Oelckers,
Joris Jonker,
Mia Lücker

film production
Bigfish Filmproduktion GmbH

film direction
Daniel Warwick

music/sound design
Eardrum Music & Sound Design

→ clip on DVD
→ designer portrait: p. 395

>> So gut im Gelände wie ein Geländewagen in der Stadt.

Interface Design   Mobile & Apps   Game Design   **Sound Design**   Red Dot: Junior Award   Designer Portraits

THE
REVOLUTION
OF
CINEMA
DER BESTE SOUND IM CINEPLEX

The Evolution of Sound – The Revolution of Cinema
[Cinema Spot]

In the course of converting the sound system of a major cinema chain from 5.1 to 7.1 surround sound in all its German branches, this cinema spot campaign opens up new vistas of sound and imagery to viewers. Seemingly unremarkable, almost invisible things and events are turned into exciting audible experiences. The aim of this acoustic realisation was to use the new sound system to the fullest, giving the Dolby 7.1 sound a new dimension of brilliance and spatiality.

client
Cineplex Deutschland
GmbH & Co. KG,
Wuppertal

design
GUCC GmbH,
Münster

art direction
Carsten Christochowitz,
Christian Hund

graphic design
Jessica Comes

music/sound design
Thomas Bücker

camera
Karsten Jäger

editor
Christian Hund

→ clip on DVD

| Event Design | Information Design & Public Space | Corporate Films | TV, Film, Cinema & Animation | Online World |

LZF
High Fidelity
[Sound Design]

The compact disc "High Fidelity – Rithma Sounds" was produced as part of a promotional campaign for LZF Lighting that pays tribute to the aesthetics of old jazz cover art. 12 new lamp designs are each graphically represented by a different record cover. Each graphic was then used by The Own, Barcelona, to create a retro motion graphics masterpiece for the presentation of the lighting collection. LA-based musician and producer Rithma was then fused into the project, composing a jazz-inspired soundtrack for the film. The result was so successful that it turned into a 12-song CD, which was constantly used as the soundtrack accompanying the whole campaign, as well as being a key component to the campaign merchandising.

client
LZF LAMPS,
Valencia

music/sound design
Rithma Music
(Etienne Stehelin),
Los Angeles

**creative direction/
project management**
Marivi Calvo,
Sandro Tothill,
LZF LAMPS

**cover art/
motion graphics animation**
LekuonaStudio,
The Own,
Barcelona

→ clip on DVD
→ designer portrait: p. 420

BMW Sound Logo

The BMW sound logo was developed with the aim of creating an acoustic business card for the brand. It is characterised by a catchy melody, which has strong recognition value thanks to an innovative mix of sounds. Acoustic elements are played forwards and backwards in a way that symbolises flexible mobility. The melody is introduced by rising, resonant sound and underscored by two distinctive bass tones that form the logo's melodic and rhythmic basis.

client
BMW Group,
Munich

design/production
Hastings media music,
Hamburg

creative direction
Olaf Weitzl,
Thomas Burhorn

strategic planning
Joachim H. Blickhäuser,
Konstantin Lauber,
Paul Steiner

project management
Paul Steiner,
Thomas Burhorn

music/sound design
Thomas Kisser

post-production
Jan Finck,
Oscar Meixner

→ clip on DVD

INTERNATIONAL YEARBOOK COMMUNICATION DESIGN 2013/2014

Event Design | Information Design & Public Space | Corporate Films | TV, Film, Cinema & Animation | Online World

Red Dot: Junior Prize

Women's Rights
[Poster Campaign]

This poster campaign deals with the topic of women's rights in today's society and in different cultures. Created in the spirit of social graphic design, it focuses on the massive oppression of women in different culture groups and countries around the world with the aim of raising awareness of the serious issue of the ongoing violence and assaults committed against women. The individual posters symbolically represent the suffering inflicted on women through the motif of a flower, the calla lily, shown in various renditions. Serving as a symbol of innocence and love, the flower is manipulated artistically on each poster and shows foreign interference that hurts and even destroys them, such as a rope used to tie down and thus oppress women or acid used for mutilation. Each modification on the flower points to a form of violence that still continues to be committed against women on a daily basis without being avenged.

Interface Design   Mobile & Apps   Game Design   Sound Design   **Red Dot: Junior Award**
Posters   Designer Portraits

university
University of Applied Sciences and Arts Dortmund

supervising professor
Prof. Dieter Ziegenfeuter

design
Mustafa Karakaş, Dinslaken

→ designer portrait: p. 449

reddot design award
junior prize 2013

| Event Design | Information Design & Public Space | Corporate Films | TV, Film, Cinema & Animation | Online World |

Red Dot: Junior Prize

The poster series "Women's Rights"

[Statement by the jury]

In view of the dominance and influence of moving and digital media, the spectre of the end of the classical poster has, in the last few years, repeatedly been painted on the wall. However, the eight-part poster campaign "Women's Rights" proves that the expressiveness of this traditional medium continues to be utterly alive and contemporary. Just like all the other forms of communication, whether they be digital or analogue, it by no means leads an existence in the shadows.

There are reasons for the uninterrupted relevance and topicality of posters: they offer a unique way to condense information. Image and text statements have to get straight to the point so that viewers can absorb and understand them the moment they see them. The great challenge for the designer is the limited options the poster offers. They make reduction and concentration unavoidable – and bring real talent for innovative, creative image ideas to the fore, as is apparent in an exemplary fashion in the "Women's Rights" poster series. As social graphic design campaign, this series tackles the controversial topic of women's rights in different cultures of the world. In doing so, it uses imagery with exceptional symbolic power that is also captivatingly simple. It is so striking and disturbing that it immediately won us over. We were almost unanimously convinced that it deserved this year's Red Dot: Junior Prize.

In a way that leaves viewers reeling, the eight designs successfully portray the cruel, inhuman violence experienced by women in certain cultures on a daily basis without the perpetrators being sanctioned. The focal point – the oppression and abuse – is symbolically depicted by the calla lily, a flower that stands for beauty and innocence. The designs show how different "external influences" damage or disfigure the flower. Designer Mustafa Karakaş has illustrated abuse such as stonings, isolation, torture, mutilation and forced marriages so incisively that the subject is clear without needing any words. The message is unambiguous and gets right under the viewer's skin. The simplicity of the flower, formally without any frills, on a plain white background and the expressiveness with which violent attacks are depicted using simple means such as cuts to the flower or a cord used to constrict it, are moving. It is precisely the subtlety behind the disturbing combination of violence and beauty that creates a deeply emotional and lasting impression. We particularly value this subtlety in a time when it is usually only the loud and the shrill that are well received.

Both the concept and the implementation of this socially sensitive topic have been solved magnificently. We were just amazed that a student, who had none of the experience of a professional designer to fall back on, was already able to develop and design an equally thought-out, emotional and aesthetic piece of work. Mustafa Karakaş' aim: to draw attention to the continuing cruelties still meted out to women and to call for the outlawing of such practices and for help, has been achieved with brilliance. Our heartfelt congratulations on this distinctive, as well as memorable achievement.

Red Dot: Best of the Best

Morphogen – The Crystallisation of Acoustics

[Conceptual Design]

"Morphogen" deals with the idea of translating musical content into visual representations and thus explores how morphing can help develop new formal approaches. Derived from the 18 parts of the musical piece "Music for 18 Musicians" by Steve Reich, different approaches were developed and visualised as a series of sketches that document the complex interrelations in abstract geometric drawings, patterns and graphics, all compiled into a specifically designed book and website. The experiment of analysing the fractal character of the musical piece by correlating it to the structure of a crystal led to the development of a system for displaying individual bars of the notation in space and object, as well as to a two-dimensional grid for designing new applications. The sophisticatedly visualised details of this work thus translate the acoustic dimension of the composition and extend it with visual coding, an approach that ultimately blurs the boundaries between science and design.

Statement by the jury

»"Morphogen" incorporates a highly interesting approach of translating music into a graphical system that thus allows the composition by Steve Reich to be experienced as a visual representation. The complex solutions projected by the work manifest themselves in systems and formations that possess outstanding expressivity with regard to the various design possibilities of the respective media used.«

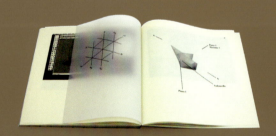 

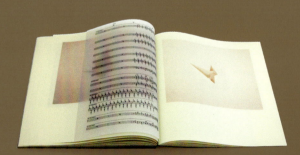 

university
FHNW, Academy of Art and Design Basel

design
Susanne Hartmann, Basel

programming
Philipp C. Adrian, Wanja Chresta

technical support
Roland Pavloski

→ designer portrait: p. 447

Red Dot: Best of the Best

Endless
[Packaging]

"Endless" is the packaging design of a case for an HTC mobile phone, including an urBeats headset, a battery charging set and a product description. Pushing the packaging case out of its cardboard sleeve reveals a series of sketched comic faces which appear in the round hole on the top and, once fully taken out, the spring fold design structure makes it unfold into a long cardboard band. Individual "pockets" in the case band present the mobile phone and accessories in respectively sized punch-outs that snugly hold them in place without fasteners and allow them to be taken out by simply pushing with a finger. Following the concept of "small phone, big world", on the one hand, the environmentally friendly cardboard itself serves to tell the story through comic illustration of the endless possibilities using a mobile phone and it reduces waste paper. On the other hand, the surface on the spring fold paper also features product descriptions printed in environmentally friendly soy ink, which consumers may read while turning the folding paper to take out the product and accessories. This saved having to print and include a separate product instruction manual.

Statement by the jury

»The idea of merging the packaging of a mobile phone including accessories with the product description as well as a story on the product's versatile use into one unity is brilliant and proof of the passion and innovative thinking of the designer. The highly charming design showcases simple yet humorous drawings and a recyclable packaging case made of cardboard that makes a difference by avoiding the look of generic "me-too" mobile phone packaging designs, predominant in today's market.«

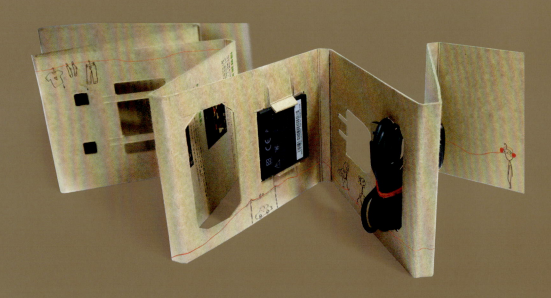

| Interface Design | Mobile & Apps | Game Design | Sound Design | **Red Dot: Junior Award**
Packaging Design | Designer Portraits |

university
Asia University,
Taichung City

design
Mi-Na Wei,
Ching-Chia Chiou,
Asia University,
Taichung City

→ designer portrait: p. 461

Red Dot: Best of the Best

STEREOTYPOLOGY/IE
[Book]

This book investigates the phenomenon that even today our ideas and views of people from other cultures and countries are still shaped by national stereotypes. The starting point of this cross-border exploration by a team of 35 design students from Augsburg in Germany and Falmouth in the UK were ten national stereotypical characteristics that are ascribed to people in both countries. Contrary to what might be expected, the students were asked to look for evidence of German stereotypes in England and English stereotypes in Germany, thus subverting the stereotype's function as an instrument of definition and demarcation. The 256 pages of the resulting bilingual "lab report" document the responses to the respective national "stereotypes" in a humorous and highly illustrational design that condenses the findings on these ubiquitous stereotypes into a collage comprising found materials and personal insights. Diagrams, photo spreads and illustrations are complemented by editorial texts and thus combine into a visually diverse presentation that turns the creative interpretation of this subject matter into an exciting read.

Statement by the jury

»The cooperation project STEREOTYPOLOGY/IE, which investigated the "foreign" national stereotypes in one's own country, does not only deal with an interesting sociological subject; above all it also fascinates with sophisticated, high-quality design implementation. Featuring an eye-catching green colour, the book boasts a myriad of distinctive ideas of how to visually represent the subject in a stimulating and convincing manner.«

Interface Design | Mobile & Apps | Game Design | Sound Design | **Red Dot: Junior Award**
Editorial | Designer Portraits

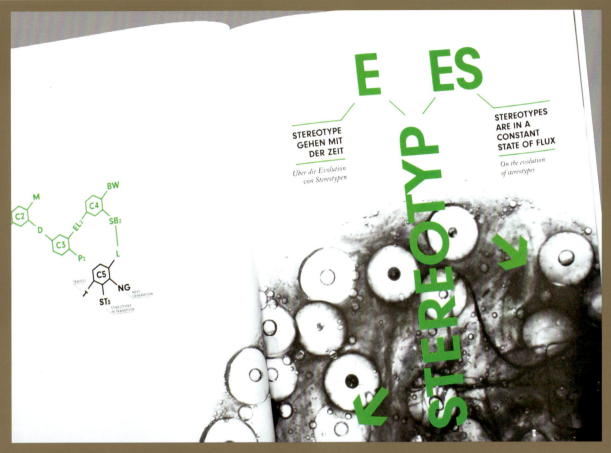

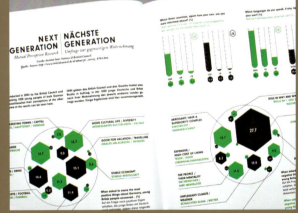

university
Augsburg University
of Applied Sciences
Falmouth University

supervising professor
Prof. Stefan Bufler,
Ashley Rudolph

design
Augsburg University
of Applied Sciences,
Fachwerkstatt Identity Design
Falmouth University,
BA (Hons)
Graphic Design

design team
Nadine Baur, Blandine Beer, Christina Beresik, Vivian Breithardt, Henry Brown, Bianca Bunsas, James Burbidge, Hannah Cottrell, Jed Dean, Josie Evans, Jessica Fink, Bradley Fletcher, Benedikt Frommer, Andrew Gabb, Henrike Großer, Owen Harvey, Ashley Kinnard, Alexander Kohler, Saul Logan, Michael Lieu, Michael Peacock, Michael Phillips, Rose Priddy, Yvonne Sauter, Helene Schönfeld, Frauke Schwenk, Daniela Stölzle, James Sutton, Kirsty Tavendale, Sara Thurner, Annkatrin Vierrether, Jessica Webb, Stefani Wiatowski, Nicole Wiedemann, Magdalena Winkler

→ designer portrait: p. 440

| Event Design | Information Design & Public Space | Corporate Films | TV, Film, Cinema & Animation | Online World |

Red Dot: Best of the Best

Rezepte für die Zukunft
Recipes for the Future

[Book]

Our consumer behaviour and dietary habits correlate to multifaceted environmental pollution and enormous greenhouse gas emissions. With the aim of raising awareness of the negative impact of today's diet on the environment and the climate, and showing that everybody can make a relevant contribution by taking targeted measures with regard to shopping and cooking, this book highlights the complex issue of diet, consumption and climate protection. Coming in an eye-catching large-size square format and featuring a clear typeface, distinctively visualised infographics and a unique picture language, this substantial publication reveals potential measures for reducing greenhouse gas emissions related to diet without giving an educational or frightening impression. A varied and seasonal recipe collection for the entire year literally spices up the content, suggesting in a visually distinctive and appealing manner that a balance between culinary pleasure and climate protection can be achieved through our choices.

Statement by the jury

»This comprehensive, clearly laid-out book is both a cookbook and a kind of life guide on how to follow a diet that is environmentally friendly. Alongside well-grounded facts and information, for instance on how many resources are consumed for the production of certain foodstuffs, the design represents a solution that is outstanding and highly convincing by means of visually appealing and easy-to-understand infographics.«

university
FH JOANNEUM –
University of Applied Sciences,
Graz

design
Susanne Pretterebner,
Graz

→ designer portrait: p. 459

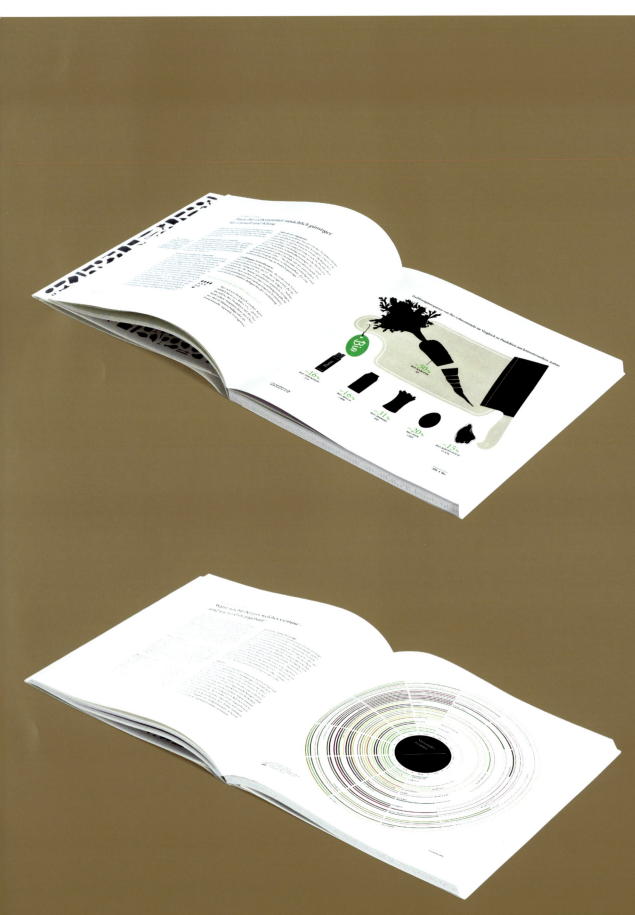

| Event Design | Information Design & Public Space | Corporate Films | TV, Film, Cinema & Animation | Online World |

Red Dot: Best of the Best

Type Capsule
[Book]

Type Capsule is an infographic book about typefaces based on a personal survey conducted by the designer. Fascinated by the fact that certain typefaces such as Garamond and Helvetica are more frequently used than others, as they are considered by many as timeless, and that these typefaces are obviously impervious to passing trends, the designer set out to investigate on this preference by asking 432 designers around the world what five typefaces they would select if they could put them into a type capsule for people to find and use in one hundred years. The 125 responses he received were the starting point for a highly interesting exploration comprising a lot of innovatively illustrated statistics in which, for instance, national typeface preferences are shown or the specific use of a typeface for a special content is communicated. This book focuses on the many different typefaces not only as its topic but also uses them as a design means to lend the book a clear and simple style. In addition, the book comes in a wooden slipcase in which the letters the designers were asked about are punched out.

Statement by the jury

»The design of this book captivates the reader's attention with its profound exploration of its topic and in particular with the way this has been implemented aesthetically. The layout features a typographic design of discreet colours and a great attention to detail that also reflects in the embossed wooden slipcase that complements and harmoniously rounds off the design.«

design
Jeong Ho Park,
Edina, Minnesota

→ designer portrait: p. 457

| Event Design | Information Design & Public Space | Corporate Films | TV, Film, Cinema & Animation | Online World |

Red Dot: Best of the Best

Origami for Environmental Conservation

[Editorial Design]

The work "Origami for Environmental Conservation" includes a selection of 20 structures of folded paper animals, combinations that are created based on the art of paper folding, an instruction manual on how to fold these papers, as well as an introduction and description of the 20 selected species. All the elements are further integrated into a folding paper book design that serves the function of both storage and exhibition. With its simple, child-oriented and easy-to-grasp design, this editorial publishing work gives both an insight into plus practical instructions on how to use the art of paper folding, and an overview of the paper animals that were inspired by the unique species in Taroko National Park in Taiwan. Children thus learn about these animals in a sustainable way and develop a sense of concern about the ecological environment of Taiwan. Accommodating the various elements and also made of paper, the box itself simultaneously serves as a backdrop against which the finished paper animals introduce the natural world of the country.

Statement by the jury

»This work represents an outstanding idea of how to playfully introduce children to the different animal species deserving protection in Taiwan: inviting children to fold 20 selected animals by themselves in origami art style, backed up by descriptions, children learn about and establish a relationship to these animals. The multifaceted set was designed with great love and convinces with a concept that is well thought out to the last detail.«

Interface Design Mobile & Apps Game Design Sound Design **Red Dot: Junior Award** Designer Portraits
Editorial & Corporate Publishing

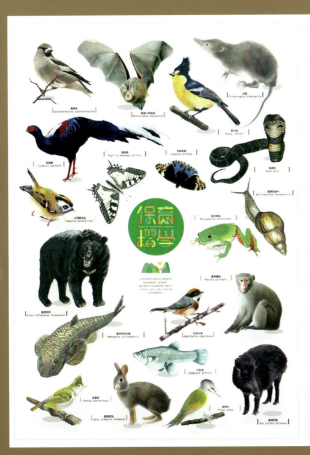

university
Shu-Te University,
Kaohsiung City

supervising professor
Cheng-Chang Chen

design
Shu-Te University,
Department of Visual
Communication Design,
Kaohsiung City

graphic design
Hsun-Yang Cho,
Tian-Yu Guo,
Ying-Ting Lyou,
Guan-Ling Lu,
Tai-Hsin Lin,
Yu-Tian Sun

→ designer portrait: p. 443

Red Dot: Best of the Best

sushi 14
[Catalogue]

The 14th issue of the "sushi" magazine is all about "Haltung" (German for "attitude" but also "position") since it is considered the basis for the development and realisation of creative ideas. It portrays people who possess such an attitude, propose original ideas and have something to say, people such as Juliane Rebentisch, Niklaus Troxler, Erik Kessels, Julius von Bismarck and more. The 300 pages of the magazine alternate between editorial contributions and photo spreads presenting the enormous creative potential of the best of the best and, above all, documenting the award-winning works in the ADC Talent Competition 2012. The spectrum of the individually created layout covers typographic, photographic and illustrational page designs, and thus turns the magazine into a true source of inspiration. Another outstanding feature is that readers literally have to adjust their point of view as the magazine rotates the pages through 360 degrees in layout orientation, making each article or contribution require a different reading position.

Statement by the jury

»The current issue 14 of "sushi" is not only fascinating in that it offers readers an overview of the creative spectrum and sheer richness of design approaches. It is outstanding with regard to the concept of how it visually presents its topic: readers too are asked to have "attitude" and change the "position" of the book little by little in order to read the individual book pages.«

Interface Design | Mobile & Apps | Game Design | Sound Design | **Red Dot: Junior Award** Editorial & Corporate Publishing | Designer Portraits

client
Art Directors Club für
Deutschland (ADC) e.V.,
Berlin

project management
Marlene Bücker

design
University of Art
and Design Offenbach

editor-in-chief
Prof. Klaus Hesse

art direction
Nikolas Brückmann,
Yuriy Matveev,
Sophia Preußner

photography
Kyung-Ho Peter Sun,
Heinrich Zimmermann

publisher
avedition GmbH,
Verlag für Architektur und Design

printing
Rasch Druckerei und Verlag
GmbH & Co. KG

→ designer portrait: p. 454

Red Dot: Best of the Best

foanetiks
[Book, Posters]

Recent studies show that 20 per cent of New Zealand adults do not have the literacy skills to meet the demands of everyday life. A contributing factor to this is the complexities and irregularities in letter and sound relationships within the English language. The project foanetiks is a typographic exploration into the chaos and the patterns of the English language. Its idea is to translate between English and phonetic spelling and to bridge this gap by helping learners to recognise correct pronunciation represented by inconsistent spelling. The single letters were modified in a way that readers may receive the required help for the requested pronunciation on the one hand and recognise the correct spelling on the other, as the modification is coloured slightly differently. The layout of this typographical work comes in a reduced and tidy design helping readers to overcome their difficulties step by step.

Statement by the jury

»foanetiks presents a fantastic solution to the difficulty facing the differences between the spelling in written and the pronunciation in spoken English: the differences in pronunciation of letters are indicated by way of different colour modifications, allowing readers to recognise these differences and see both variants at the same time. The spaciously laid-out pages visualise this idea in an outstandingly instructive manner.«

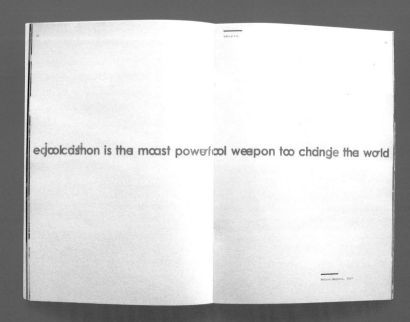

Interface Design | Mobile & Apps | Game Design | Sound Design | **Red Dot: Junior Award**
Typography | Designer Portraits

university
Massey University, Wellington

supervising professor
Anna Brown

design
Samantha Lewis, Massey University, Wellington

→ designer portrait: p. 452

Red Dot: Best of the Best

Jiji Thousand Banana Territory
[Illustration]

This illustration work visualises the historical features of the mountain banana industry in the township of Jiji in Nantou County, Taiwan, during the Japanese occupation with the aim of promoting this branch of industry and help revive the local industry today. For these purposes, it narrates four different tales of the abundant treasure of folk anecdotes related to the mountain bananas of Jiji, which have been transformed into skilfully designed illustrations. The individual tales, for example that the bananas approved by Japanese emperors were marked with the Chinese character for "thousand" which represented a seal of top quality for mountain bananas at that time, were realised using a wood printing technique by laboriously carving them with knives into woodblocks, an approach that symbolises humble yet steady progress. The four prints present the four tales separately but, when the illustrations are combined, they connect to form a mark that corresponds to the Chinese character for "thousand", symbolising the highest quality.

Statement by the jury

»In order to visualise the topic of the history of the banana industry in the township of Jiji in Taiwan, this work uses a historically appropriate handicraft. In both the way that the four meticulously carved pictures illustrate typical scenes from the past and that in combination they form a "character mark" that stood for quality back then, it represents a sophisticated implementation and outstanding stylistic achievement.«

Interface Design | Mobile & Apps | Game Design | Sound Design | **Red Dot: Junior Award** Illustrations | Designer Portraits

university
Asia University,
Taichung City

creative direction
Chun-Chun Hou

design
Yan-Yu Huang,
Yan-Ting Chen,
Ya-Chi Chiu,
Lee-Wa Lin,
Cheng-En Chang,
Asia University,
Taichung City

→ designer portrait: p. 442

Red Dot: Best of the Best

The Lonely Lives of Miserable Men
[Illustrated Book]

"The Lonely Lives of Miserable Men" represents the lives and accomplishments of lonely and forgotten individuals, such as Nikola Tesla, who helped shape the world we live in today. Tesla was responsible for powering the world with his alternating current, but is now relegated to the past without so much as a nod. This project employs the comic book format and sequential art to bring to light his life and achievements, and to communicate why his genius should be remembered today. The black-and-white ink drawings in this graphic novel tell the story of this electrical engineer, who was born in Croatia and emigrated to the USA, in detailed and elaborately crafted illustration. They invite readers to travel straight back in time to before the turn to the 20th century to experience and learn about Tesla's inventions and his life full of personal drawbacks, by opening up a world of images that are marked by compelling distinction and expressivity.

Statement by the jury

»History is not always fair – against this backdrop this book retraces the life and destiny of Nikola Tesla with ink drawings that reflect the aesthetic style prominent back in Tesla's lifetime at the turn of the last century. Both the idea for the content and the outstanding craftsmanship of the drawings are convincing.«

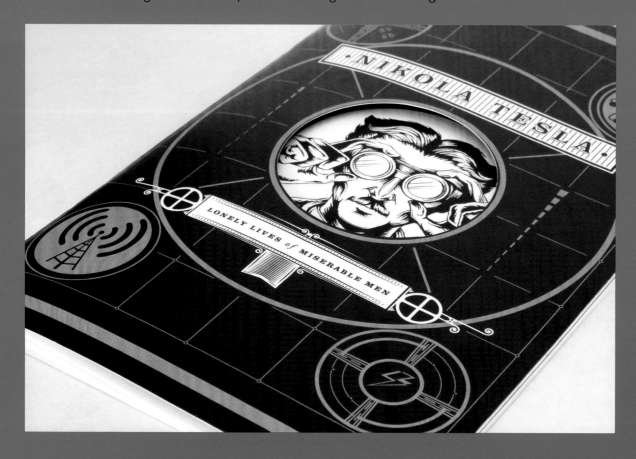

| Interface Design | Mobile & Apps | Game Design | Sound Design | **Red Dot: Junior Award**
Illustrations | Designer Portraits |

university
Massey University,
Wellington

supervising professor
Lee Jensen

design
Brodie Nel,
Joshua Thompson,
Massey University,
Wellington

→ designer portrait: p. 455

Red Dot: Best of the Best

Mechanisms of Evolution
[Animation]

Is it possible with the help of design to present complex scientific topics in a way that is easy to understand for everyone – even without previous knowledge – and thus facilitate learning? This animation film sets out to prove that design can support and thus promote a deeper understanding of a topic, and it does so by taking the example and explaining the mechanism of evolution. The film features clear and plain infographics as well as video and audio information to illustrate the subject and its complex interrelations step by step to make them easily comprehensible for laymen. The theory of evolution, which explains how the enormous variety of life could come into existence and how it was possible for primitive life forms to spawn the millions of different creatures that exist today, is illustrated through visualisations kept in a childlike style that is attention-grabbing and easy to grasp. Thus lending the illustrations a high appeal and entertainment value, the information is more likely to sink in playfully.

Statement by the jury

»The animation film "Mechanisms of Evolution" is convincing as it presents the complex and, in school, often less than inspiringly taught topic of evolution in a simplified manner, paired with a highly humorous design approach. The content was outstandingly well researched and staged with many details that make it not only easy to understand but also fun to watch and learn.«

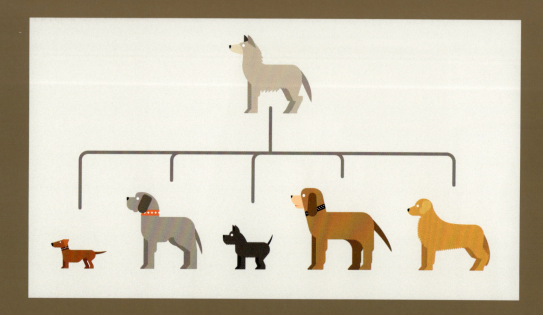

| Interface Design | Mobile & Apps | Game Design | Sound Design | **Red Dot: Junior Award**
TV, Film, Cinema & Animation | Designer Portraits |

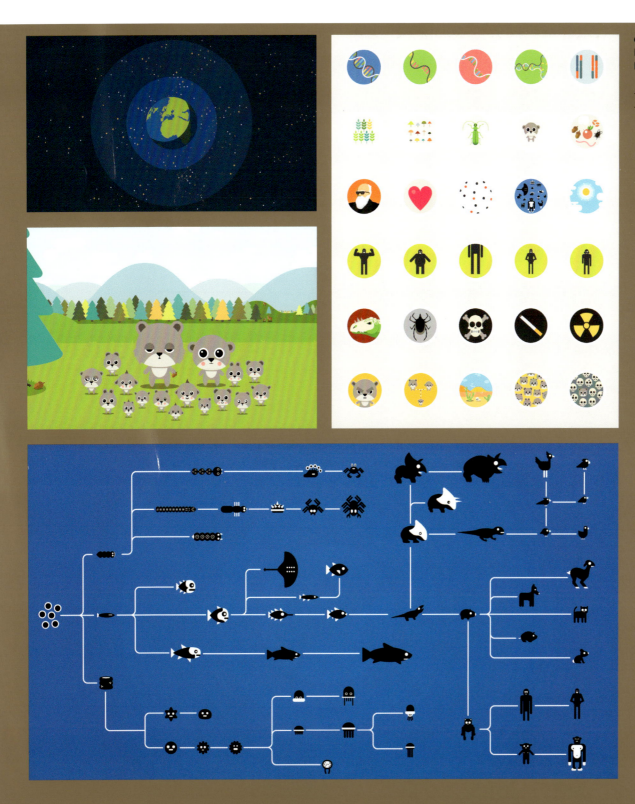

design
Philipp Dettmer,
Munich

→ clip on DVD
→ designer portrait: p. 444

319

Red Dot: Best of the Best

Education not Medication
[Infographic Campaign]

"Education not Medication" – more affectionately known as EdnotMed – is a graphic social media strategy working through a range of design mediums to promote the message that heart disease, a common deadly killer, is preventable, stating the cause as being a series of poor dietary and lifestyle choices. In particular, the aim is to also help educate young people about the remarkable benefits of living a healthy and more "vegetabally" abundant lifestyle. The strategy began as a series of short, humorous and informative infographic animations, which were designed to be shared through social media, elucidating on important facts and alternatives in an attractive and emotive manner. Since the release in late 2012, the EdnotMed Facebook page has amassed over 2,600 followers and is exponentially growing in numbers. This stimulatingly designed page acts as a hub for sharing useful and carefully executed information regarding food, environmental issues and other inspiration and general tips on well-being.

Statement by the jury

»This infographic campaign manages in a highly refreshing and inspiring manner to raise awareness of a health issue that otherwise is mainly communicated morally with a raised finger. With an appealing design and a mode of presentation that is both informative and entertaining, the campaign stages the topic as a lifestyle theme and thus successfully triggers interest and engagement.«

Interface Design | Mobile & Apps | Game Design | Sound Design | **Red Dot: Junior Award**
Online Advertising | Designer Portraits

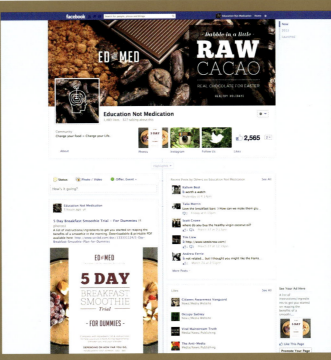

university
Massey University,
Wellington

supervising professor
Donald Preston

design
Graedon Parker,
Massey University,
Wellington

→ clip on DVD
→ designer portrait: p. 458

Red Dot: Best of the Best

Planto
[App]

Planto helps with nourishing and cultivating indoor plants. It is loaded with an RFID system, a solar power system and other detective systems that monitor and report on the temperature, humidity and further vital information required for plants. The device calculates the perfect requirements for each plant so that it is easy for users not only to always provide ideal conditions for their plants but also to get information quickly about irregularities and problems that may occur during the plants' growth. Furthermore, the device also connects with a smartphone application that also notifies users of possible problems and provides solutions at the same time. Planto is designed with a reduced appearance allowing intuitive user navigation. The app's symbols for temperature, humidity and sunlight feature at the bottom of the screen and, when touched, illustrate the corresponding information in an immediately comprehensible manner.

Statement by the jury

»The Planto system offers a unique possibility of providing plants with the best possible conditions at all times and users can be notified immediately, for example when the plants need water. Via a detective device, which is simply placed inside the pot, the plant "communicates" directly via the device or the app, informing users about its current status. The charming and simple design makes the application easy to use and self-explanatory.«

Interface Design   Mobile & Apps   Game Design   Sound Design   **Red Dot: Junior Award**
Mobile & Apps   Designer Portraits

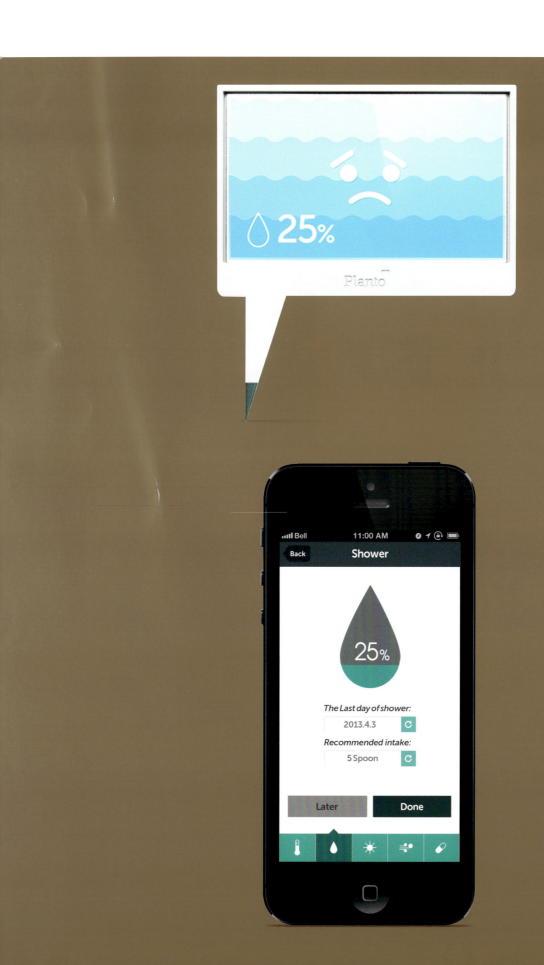

university
Hanyang University,
Ansan City,
Gyeonggi Province

design/concept/photography
Sol-E Lee,
Heeyeon Jung,
Hanyang University,
Ansan City,
Gyeonggi Province

→ designer portrait: p. 451

| Event Design | Information Design & Public Space | Corporate Films | TV, Film, Cinema & Animation | Online World |

SeaAra
[Corporate Design, Corporate Identity]

This stationery shows the new corporate identity design of SeaAra, a yachting and marine leisure company based in South Korea. The name consists of the words "sea" and "ara" – ara means sea in Korean. The logo is based on the name's first letter, which visualises the shape of a yacht or boat. It also represents the sun and water as well as yin and yang. The logo is a crucial design element as its positive and negative spaces create a key layout which ties everything together as a series. It also expands into various graphics and patterns.

client
SeaAra,
Seoul

design
Youngha Park,
New York

project management
Sang Rak Choi

printing
Ecard21,
Seoul

Floating Code
[Logotype]

People interpret their surroundings in different ways, with perception turning into thoughts and feelings and thus into brainwaves. These, in turn, are encoded as signs for communication and have to be decoded by the receiver. This corporate design, which can be used with different media, alludes to this process. The flowing lines and waves represent the connection between thoughts and feelings in flux and the symbols used for communication.

design
Po-Hua Lin,
Ren-Wei Pan,
Yung-Ching Chen,
Shih-Yu Huang,
Shan-Yao Yang,
Li-Ting Kao

→ designer portrait: p. 453

| Event Design | Information Design & Public Space | Corporate Films | TV, Film, Cinema & Animation | Online World |

Lügnern auf der Spur
How to Detect Liars
[Book]

The book "Lügnern auf der Spur" (how to detect liars) explores lies from different perspectives. Photographs of faces demonstrate which muscles are activated by different emotions and how to spot indications of a lie in facial expressions. Many readers will only notice after having read the book that the sweet smile on the cover is false and therefore indicative of a lie. The book's design concept is precise and consistent, thus bringing together the individual pages containing photographs, quotations, information, interviews and graphics in a uniform design.

university
School for Design Ravensburg

supervising professor
Georg Engels,
Jürgen Weltin

design
Janet Kofler,
Berlin

Volut

[Corporate Identity, Brand Design]

The subject of this work is the development of a bicycle brand. Guided by the core terms of added value, craftsmanship, identification, lifestyle and purism, the design for the bicycles and a range of corresponding advertising media were created. In this process, the use of old materials and technologies was combined with modern components and manufacturing methods. The bicycles consist of second hand as well as new parts and the catalogue, stationery and posters were created using a combination of letterpress, silkscreen and digital printing methods.

university
University of Applied Sciences Würzburg-Schweinfurt

design
Volut, Leipzig

creative direction/art direction
Conrad Gerlach,
Johannes Stacheder,
Aljoscha Subke

Event Design　　　　Information Design & 　　　Corporate Films　　　　TV, Film,　　　　　　　　Online World
　　　　　　　　　　Public Space　　　　　　　　　　　　　　　　　　Cinema & Animation

Yuan Ze University, Department of Information Communication

[Corporate Identity]

These logos were developed for the Department of Information Communication at Yuan Ze University. They consist of twelve individual elements in different colours, the design of which was inspired by the digital shapes of zeros and ones. Following the golden section, they were put together as a unit based on the ratio of 1:1.618 and arranged around a central point. The designs of the logos, some of which are animated, are based on studies of four different forms of visual expression which are to function as a trademark.

university
Yuan Ze University,
Department of Information
Communication,
Chung-Li,
Taoyuan County

design
Ming-Chieh Hsu,
Yu-Cheng Chen,
Chung-Li,
Taoyuan County

(2) rotational motion-moving rotationally.

(4) motionless dynamic logos-static/dynamic logos without animation or motion graphics.

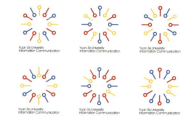

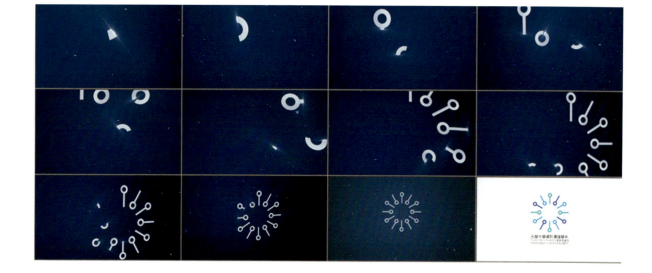

Sino-Finnish Centre, Tongji University

[Corporate Identity]

This corporate identity design was developed for the Sino-Finnish Centre, a cooperation of Tongji University in China and Aalto University in Finland. Lines in three different colours are woven together representing the centre's concept of "cross-disciplinary innovation and cooperation". The multiform logos emphasise the innovative concept. The colours of the Sino-Finnish Centre are red and blue – they are used consistently and demonstrate the centre's characteristics. The dynamic and smooth logo creates a strong visual impact and is easy to recognise.

client
Sino-Finnish Centre,
Tongji University,
Shanghai

university
Tongji University,
Shanghai

design
Dawang Sun,
College of Design
and Innovation,
Tongji University,
Shanghai

creative direction
Guoxin Wu

art direction
Dawang Sun

concept
Yongqi Lou

graphic design/illustration
Dawang Sun

text
Hui Pan

Buddha Spirit

[Corporate Design]

design
OKIN,
Zhang Yangsheng,
Shanghai

→ designer portrait: p. 463

The corporate design for the Buddha Spirit club communicates the values and teachings of Buddhism. The key element is the logo, the design of which is inspired by the Diamond Sutra. The leaf-shaped logo shows the outline of Buddha in the centre. The purpose of this reference is to enable observers to see themselves in it and grasp that all beings are Buddha. The four colours arranged around Buddha indicate four different spiritual states of being which the mind of a disciple goes through when practising Buddhist teachings.

Motion Theater
[Brand Identity]

university
IN.D Institute of Design
Düsseldorf

design
Caroline Grohs,
Düsseldorf

photography
John Davis

Interface Design | Mobile & Apps | Game Design | Sound Design | **Red Dot: Junior Award** Brand Design | Designer Portraits

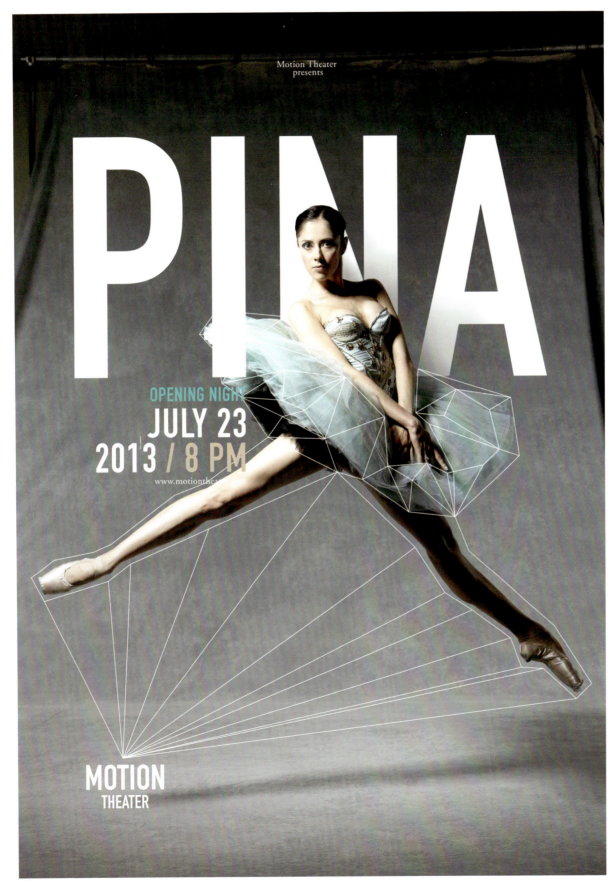

The focus of this work is the development of a corporate design for a dance theatre company. The design incorporates attributes of dance such as dynamics, elegance and sensuality. The logo combines the close connection of the performance style with the movements of the dancers. This results in constantly new forms and figures, which make the logo appear to be in motion at all times. The impression of dance as "movement in space" is further supported by the seemingly floating typography. Different variants of the logo are used on programme booklets, business cards, stationery, flyers, the website and apps.

| Event Design | Information Design & Public Space | Corporate Films | TV, Film, Cinema & Animation | Online World |

eastar air Rebranding
[Brand Design]

The corporate design for the airline "eastar air" comprises the development of the brand name, the logo and the attention-grabbing brand colours red orange, mint blue and yellow. The brand name represents the star in the east. The symbol of the airline has the shape of a star that consists of two triangles. Simple, graphical illustrations also characterise the advertising posters. The design of the stationery, tickets and lanyards as well as the web and mobile presence complete the corporate design.

client
eastar air,
Seoul

university
Sungkyunkwan University,
Seoul

design
Sungkyunkwan University,
Seoul

creative direction/art direction
Seungkwan Kang

graphic design
Jihyung Im

artwork
Eunsun Kim

Wolffstrunk
[Brand Design]

True to the motto "less is more", graphic reduction and precision characterise the corporate design of the private distillery from Extertal, which sells under the brand name "Wolffstrunk" (wolf drink) finest fruit schnaps and fruit liqueurs. The corporate design plays with the "wolf" metaphor – its graphically simplified image provides the basis for the visual identity of a range of media. The corporate design includes the design and concept of a composite mark, business stationery, bottle labels, posters and a brand book as well as a short website animation.

university
University of Applied Sciences Bielefeld

supervising professor
Margarethe Saxler,
Prof. Dr. Anna Zika

design
Karen Cuthbert,
Schloß Holte-Stukenbrock

| Event Design | Information Design & Public Space | Corporate Films | TV, Film, Cinema & Animation | Online World |

Jiji Mountain

[Gift Packaging]

This gift packaging design pays tribute to the region of Nantou County and its citizens, who did not lose their positive attitude after the devastating earthquake which had struck Taiwan in 1999. It presents illustrations of Jiji Mountain, for example, a place where mountain bananas grow, and the symbol for "one thousand", which stands for good quality. The box can be opened like a banana from top to bottom – inside, there are four packets of processed food made from mountain bananas. They can be stacked and put into a mountain-shaped box, which shows scenes of local life.

university
Asia University,
Taichung City

creative direction
Chun-Chun Hou

design
Yan-Yu Huang,
Yan-Ting Chen,
Ya-Chi Chiu,
Lee-Wa Lin,
Cheng-En Chang,
Asia University,
Taichung City

→ designer portrait: p. 442

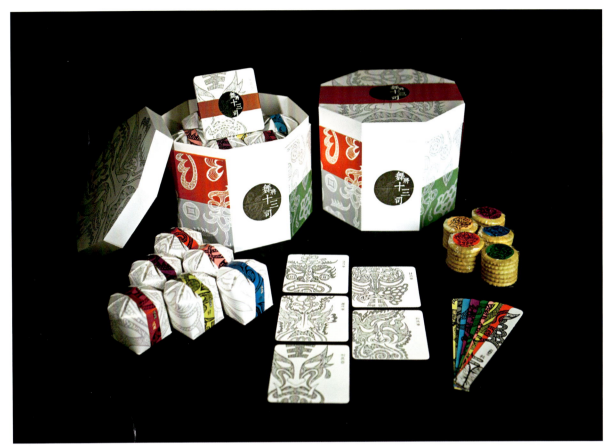
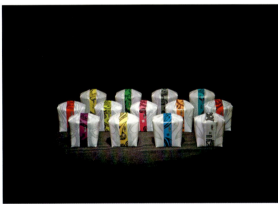

Eight Infernal Generals

[Gift Box]

Eight Infernal Generals is a special Taiwanese folk tradition, an important element of which are the "peace cakes". As symbols of the gods that protect the people, they play an important role and are to make the recipient of the blessing believe that they can imbibe peace by eating them. The design of the gift boxes aims to keep the memory of this tradition alive. It combines the main colours of red, green, white and black with Chinese cultural content in an attention-grabbing style. The design of each individual packaging is based on a collection of thirteen different mask features.

university
Asia University,
Taichung City

design
Ya-Li Huang,
Syue-Ru Chen,
Yu-Chi Chung,
Yu-Shu Sun,
Tien-Yuan Ku,
Chia-Hsuan Wu,
Hsiao-Ling Wu,
Asia University,
Taichung City

Chopping Food

[Packaging]

Its unusual design concept makes this packaging stand out. Not only does it show an illustration of the kitchen utensil contained in each box, it also features a colour image of a food with which it is used. The packaging of a knife, for instance, shows an onion. When opening the packaging, the illustration is separated in half which has the aim of evoking associations with cooking. An illustration on the inside of the packaging indicates the result of using the utensil; in the case of a knife, it is chopped onions.

university
Dongduk Women's University,
Seoul
Korean Bible University,
Seoul
Hansei University,
Gunpo

design
Yeji Jung,
Anyang City,
Gyeonggi Province
Hyosin Kim,
Seoul
Kyung Lee,
Anyang City,
Gyeonggi Province

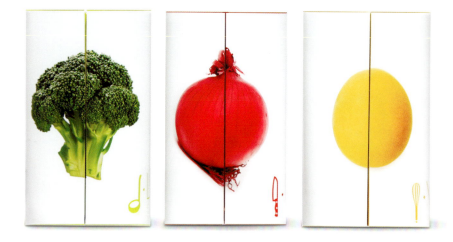

Mari – The interactive label
[Label Design]

The interactive bottle label of the Mari wine cocktail communicates the drink's refreshing effect. To highlight this effect, a sleeve is slid over the actual label which shows the graphical representation of a heart, an eye and a drop. By turning the sleeve, the graphics become animated, visualising, for instance, a heartbeat or the opening and closing of an eye. With the help of the interactive label, the design aims to position the brand and make the bottles sought-after collector's items.

design
Patrick Pichler,
Wolfgang Warzilek,
Vienna

A.Skate

[Advertising Campaign]

This is a campaign for the non-profit organisation A.Skate, the aim of which is to support autistic children through skateboarding in their efforts to improve social interaction. It is called "crazy enough to work". The campaign involves posters, paper coffee cup ring designs and direct mail to families with autistic children. The design combines handwritten typography with "home-video" style photography. These show scenes from skateboarding clinics, directing the viewer's attention to the people, shown in colour, standing out against the black-and-white background.

university
Massey University, Wellington

supervising professor
Euan Robertson

design
Logan Smith,
Massey University, Wellington

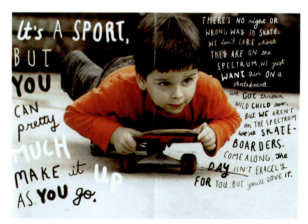

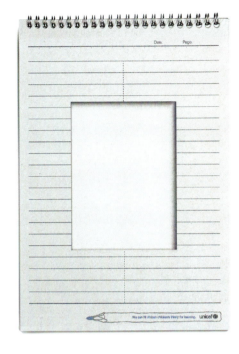

Lacking Note
[Print Advertising]

Lacking Note addresses the African educational environment, which is characterised by, among other things, a lack of teaching materials. In line with the insufficient educational opportunities, there is something missing from this writing pad, namely a punched-out area in the centre. After removing the last page, a list of everyday school items such as pencils and pencil sharpeners becomes visible. Such items can improve the learning environment of African children significantly and thus quench their thirst for learning.

university
Gachon University,
Incheon

design
Ju-Ho Han,
Da-Woon Jung,
Kyung-Chan Ahn,
Gachon University,
Incheon

→ designer portrait: p. 446

| Event Design | Information Design & Public Space | Corporate Films | TV, Film, Cinema & Animation | Online World |

Sample Copy – An Exploration of the Role of Copying in Design

[Book]

The core statement of this work is that new developments are made because good designers copy existing works with the intention of surpassing them. The design itself is also inspired by the topic of copying and uses carbonless copy paper, among other things. The photographs, taken with a blue filter, create the impression of being carbon copies. The 45-degree angle the title is positioned in on the cover is reminiscent of the position in which a "sample copy" stamp is normally placed. The book includes interviews with several designers on the subject of copying, complementing the full-page photographs.

university
Auckland University of Technology, Auckland

supervising professor
Dean Poole

design
Kate Cullinane, Auckland University of Technology, Auckland

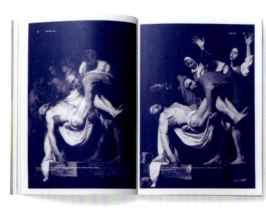

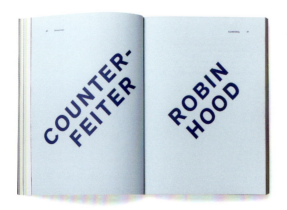

Seabiscuit vs. War Admiral

[Book]

The book "Seabiscuit vs. War Admiral" tells the story of what many consider to be one of the greatest horse races ever, which took place in Baltimore in 1938. The design focuses on the duel between these two exceptional horses. The opposing stables' jerseys represent the two horses and guide the reader through the whole book. Full-page illustrations provide a direct comparison of details such as, for example, performance and prize money. The text layout is inspired by the newspaper design from that time period featuring large expressive headlines and black-and-white photography.

design
Lina Louisa Fliedner, Düsseldorf

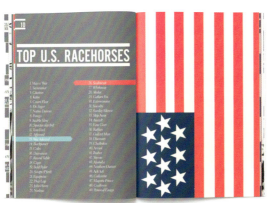

| Event Design | Information Design & Public Space | Corporate Films | TV, Film, Cinema & Animation | Online World |

Chinese Characters Big Bang

[Book]

university
China Central Academy of Fine Arts, Beijing

design
Dong Yuexi, Beijing

→ designer portrait: p. 445

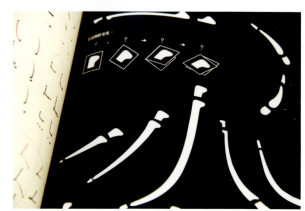

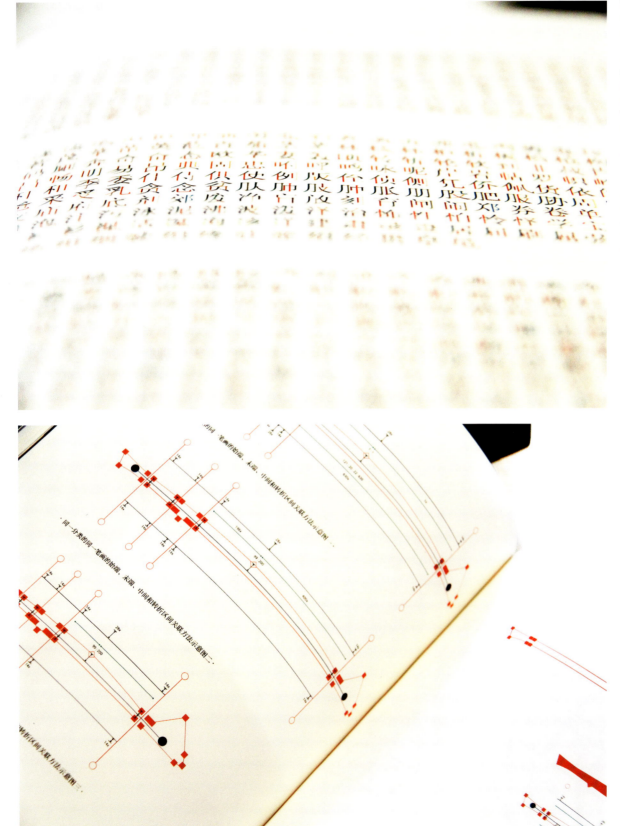

The book "Chinese Characters Big Bang" deals with Chinese characters and explores the question of how they can be converted into a digital form faster and more effectively than before. Its aim is to create new possibilities of producing a digital Chinese font using different calculation methods. The book stands out due to its elaborate cover design in black with golden embossing. It contains a mixture of full-page illustrations, pages with text only, and graphics. Its dominant colours are black and white; this bicolour look is interrupted by a few colour accents in red.

Seasonal Programme 13/14

The seasonal programme Jahresspielzeitheft lists the company's premieres, presents the actors and provides additional information about the Düsseldorfer Schauspielhaus (Düsseldorf Theatre) in a three-part book. The choice of different types of paper creates an interesting haptic experience and hierarchy. The design establishes a contrast between the austere typographical look with its clear layout and the creative freedom of the headings and images. The programme is mostly designed in black-and-white, only headings and individual keywords provide attention-grabbing accents in red.

client
Düsseldorfer Schauspielhaus, Düsseldorf

design
Sven Quadflieg, Cologne

project coordinator
Alexander Antunovic

photography
Sebastian Hoppe

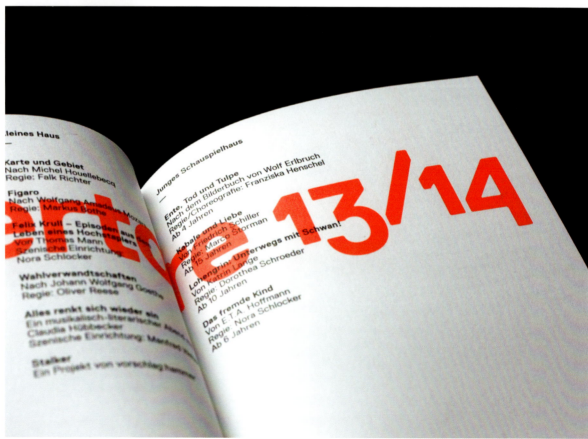

| Interface Design | Mobile & Apps | Game Design | Sound Design | **Red Dot: Junior Award**
Editorial | Designer Portraits |

Madagaskar – Look and Feel
[Book]

The book "Madagaskar – Look and Feel" approaches the island's great variety of flora and fauna in a minimalist way. The variety is represented by a simple sign, which varies in colour and form. The circular eyes of the lemurs living on Madagascar, in particular, were used as a template for the shape of the sign. The sign's variability illustrates the process of evolution, just as the flora and fauna of Madagascar have taken advantage of the environment on the island through mutation and assimilation.

university
IN.D Institute of Design Düsseldorf

design
Lisa Lufen, Cologne

| Event Design | Information Design & Public Space | Corporate Films | TV, Film, Cinema & Animation | Online World |

Wufeng Lin's Family Site Map

[Corporate Publishing]

This updated guidebook introduces the "Wufeng Lin Family Mansion and Garden", the residence of a Taiwanese family clan. Each of the pages with coloured illustrations describes the special features and the cultural richness of this residential complex. The design combines two- and three-dimensional elements and does not use simple orientation maps. Instead, sophisticatedly folded maps encourage the user to get actively involved in the exploration of the residence.

university
Asia University,
Taichung City

art direction
Chien Hua Cheng

design
Shao Shu Wen,
Zeng Yi Chun,
Lin Jia Yan,
Lin Meng Pei,
Yu Kun Ho,
Asia University,
Taichung City

Vertraulich
Confidential

[Book]

In lives of rapidly accelerating complexity, trust becomes a rare and desired thing. The principles that once protected our most confidential information provide the concept behind "Confidential". It employs the technique with which banks protect the content of their letters. Some of the text is hidden – locked between two pages – and can only be read by ripping them apart. Some words are superimposed and thus obliterated, with the next page revealing the solution.

design
Anna Gruchel,
Cologne

jwd

[Book]

university
Folkwang University
of the Arts,
Essen

design
Mareike Hundt,
Essen

Aphasia is a disorder characterised by loss of speech. This two-volume work, combined in a slipcase, approaches the inner experience of a person suffering from aphasia and a relative with artistic and typographic means. The title "jwd" (an abbreviation for "janz weit draußen", meaning "in the middle of nowhere") describes the emotional state of someone suffering from loss of speech. The seemingly endless design of the pages, which only contain small steps, illustrate the recovery process. The text, which appears slow, describes the thoughts and perceptions of a person suffering from aphasia.

FLOWER islAND
[Editorial Design]

university
Shu-Te University,
Kaohsiung City

supervising professor
Cheng-Chang Chen

design
Shu-Te University,
Department of Visual
Communication Design,
Kaohsiung City

graphic design
Che-Wei Hsu,
Su-Huei Chen,
Yi-Ting Dong,
Yu-Zheng Lin,
Xiao-Han Lai,
Szu-Jung Ho

→ designer portrait: p. 450

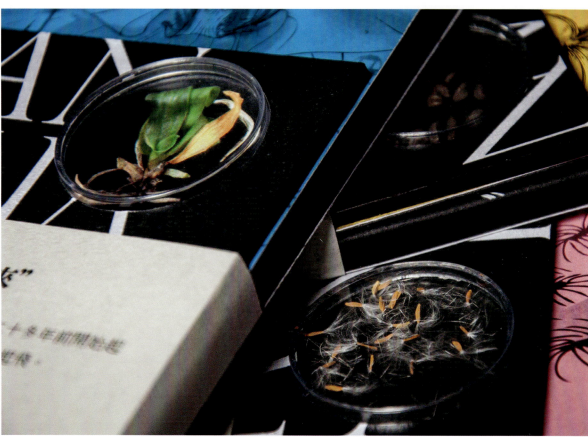

| Interface Design | Mobile & Apps | Game Design | Sound Design | **Red Dot: Junior Award**
Editorial | Designer Portraits |

The book FLOWER islAND deals with the origin and evolution of Taiwanese plants. It is based on the assumption that their development from growing roots to spreading and blossoming is affected by events in the past. Thus, individual plants have special meanings: morning glory represents diligence, dandelion being generous and moth orchid economic success. The three-volume work is characterised by its elaborate and comprehensive design. It consists of individual slipcases with a paper band wrapped around them as well as books and posters. The texts are combined with full-page photographs and illustrations, partly in black-and-white and partly in colour.

Sind wir nicht alle ein bisschen Bio?
Aren't we all a little bit organic?
[Book]

university
FH JOANNEUM –
University of Applied Sciences,
Graz

design
Ricarda Schweigler,
Graz

printing
Classic Druck Graz

letterpress
The Infinitive Factory

bookbinding
Buchbinderei Gutmann

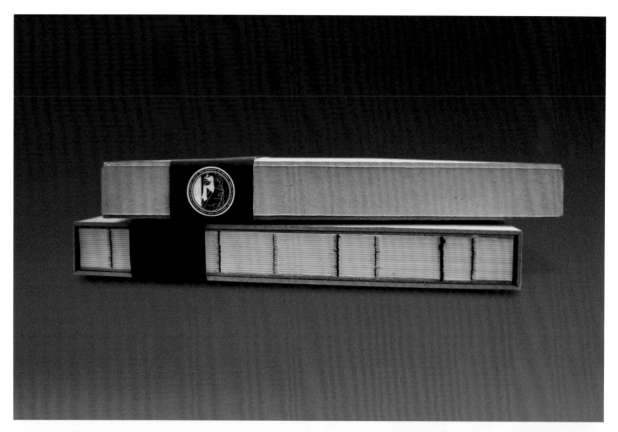

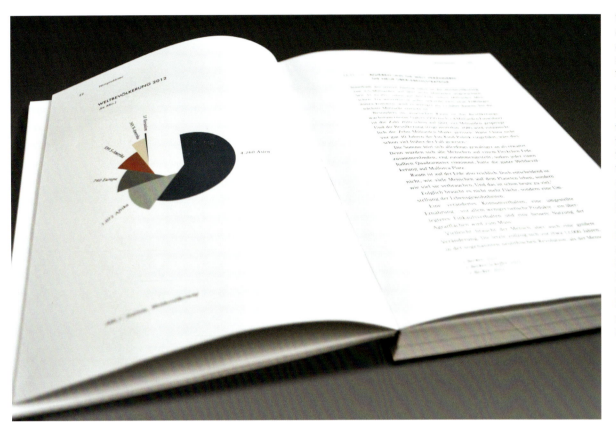

When it comes to organic produce, there is a wealth of terms as well as quality certificates and seals creating more confusion than transparency among consumers. This book, entitled "Sind wir nicht alle ein bisschen Bio?" (Aren't we all a little bit organic?), tries to counter this. It organises the vast amount of information and examines the origins of the organic trend as well as its development and role in marketing and advertising. In addition, it promotes a responsible use of resources. The design follows the book's content. The cover of the stitch-bound book is designed in plain grey. The accompanying slipcase has the same cover design but is embossed. The book's text is complemented with numerous illustrations in colour and black-and-white.

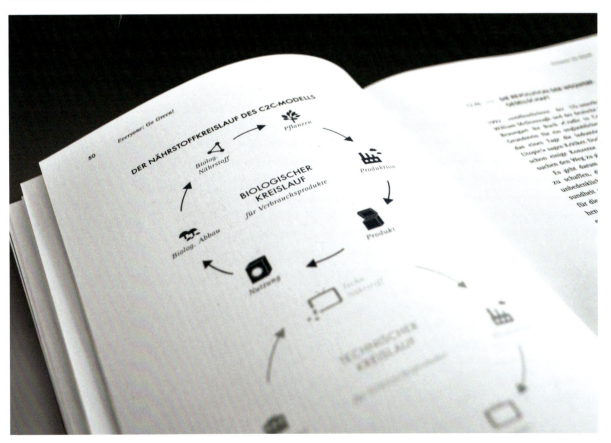

KOMMA X
[Magazine]

university
University of Applied Sciences Mannheim

design
komma Mannheim,
University of Applied Sciences Mannheim

**editor-in-chief/
creative direction**
Dennis Jakoby

art direction
Sascha May,
Sebastian Schellenberger,
Sven Wagenbach

photography
Heidi Rondak

illustration
Sascha May

editor/design
Mauro Simone

The tenth issue of komma magazine, published by Mannheim University, deals with the topic of identity and the effect that a designer's personality has on his or her work. The works presented reflect different ways of experimenting, breaking new ground, deliberately breaking the rules and thinking outside the box. The booklet in black-and-white with red colour accents provides space for texts, graphics and photographs.

Event Design | Information Design & Public Space | Corporate Films | TV, Film, Cinema & Animation | Online World

Sunset
[Poster]

"Sunset" is a poster that draws attention to the far-reaching effects of the nuclear disaster of Fukushima. These effects do not only concern people who are directly affected by the incident. The poster is divided into two halves. The lower half looks like it has been submerged in water. This in part also applies to the red circle, the symbol of Japan, in the middle of the poster as well as the roofline of the Fukushima houses along the bottom. The design thus expresses that the disaster has spread.

university
Asia University,
Taichung City

design
Chen-Ping Chen,
Shun-Ming Yang,
Asia University,
Taichung City

Interface Design | Mobile & Apps | Game Design | Sound Design | **Red Dot: Junior Award** Posters | Designer Portraits

Macht & Design, Kunst & Design
Power & Design, Art & Design
[Event Posters]

In order to depict the assumption that the power of religion, political parties and brands became manifested through design, the poster for "Macht & Design" (power & design) shows a collage of strong symbols. Their central arrangement underscores the influence of the ideas behind them. The poster "Kunst & Design" (art & design) shows a collage of famous items from art and design. It underlines not only the question as to what their differences and similarities are, but also points out that art needs designed objects and communication in order to be successful in the economy of attention.

university
Folkwang University of the Arts, Campus Wuppertal

text
Dr. Bernhard Uske

design
Andreas Golde,
Thomas Kühnen,
Wuppertal

Rentnerschwemme
A Glut of Retirees

[Poster]

This poster addresses the newly created word "Rentnerschwemme" (a glut of retirees), which polemically alludes to the increasing age of the population. It shows an illustration of angry pensioners. The contrast between the blue illustration and the red writing captivates the viewer's attention. The individual letters are printed in a font that looks like handwriting and are spread across the whole poster. Thus at first glance it does not become apparent that the letters form a word – this requires closer attention and thus examination of the content.

design
Lin Gong

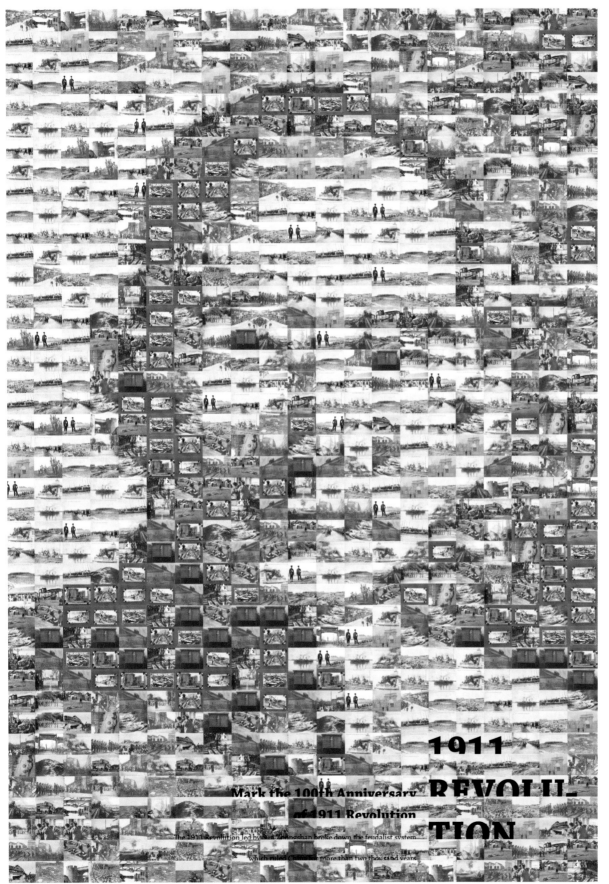

1911 Revolution
[Poster]

This black-and-white poster is reminiscent of the 100th anniversary of the 1911 Chinese revolution. Under the leadership of Sun Yat-sen, the feudal system, which had ruled China for more than two thousand years, was overthrown. The poster is composed of numerous old photographs and looks like a mosaic. The individual photos are arranged according to brightness to form Sun Yat-sen's portrait. While reflecting historical events, the design also demonstrates the cruelty of war. The poster is printed on transparent film.

client
Wuhan Art Museum,
Wuhan

university
Tongji University,
Shanghai

design
Dawang Sun, College of
Design and Innovation,
Tongji University,
Shanghai

creative direction/concept
Dawang Sun

graphic design
Dawang Sun

text/image editing
Hui Pan

project management
Hui Pan

| Event Design | Information Design & Public Space | Corporate Films | TV, Film, Cinema & Animation | Online World |

FREEDOM OF SPEECH
[Poster]

university
Shu-Te University,
Kaohsiung City

supervising professor
Chein-Feng Chang

design
Shu-Te University,
Department of Visual
Communication Design,
Kaohsiung City

graphic design
Pei-Ling Ou

→ designer portrait: p. 456

| Interface Design | Mobile & Apps | Game Design | Sound Design | **Red Dot: Junior Award**
Posters | Designer Portraits |

"I disapprove of what you say, but I will defend to the death your right to say it." This famous sentence at the bottom aptly summarises the intention of this poster. It calls attention to the right to freedom of opinion and expression according to Article 19 of the Universal Declaration of Human Rights. The poster, designed in yellow and black, depicts this objective using a large microphone. Inside the microphone head, which looks like a cage, sits a bird.

Event Design | Information Design & Public Space | Corporate Films | TV, Film, Cinema & Animation | Online World

VISUAL ARK
[Poster]

university
Shu-Te University,
Kaohsiung City

supervising professor
Yueh-Ying Chen

design
Shu-Te University,
Department of Visual
Communication Design,
Kaohsiung City

graphic design
Mu-Huai Hsueh,
Tze-Yen Juang,
Ching-Wen Chang,
Bing-Ru Yang,
Cheng-Yang Chen

→ designer portrait: p. 448

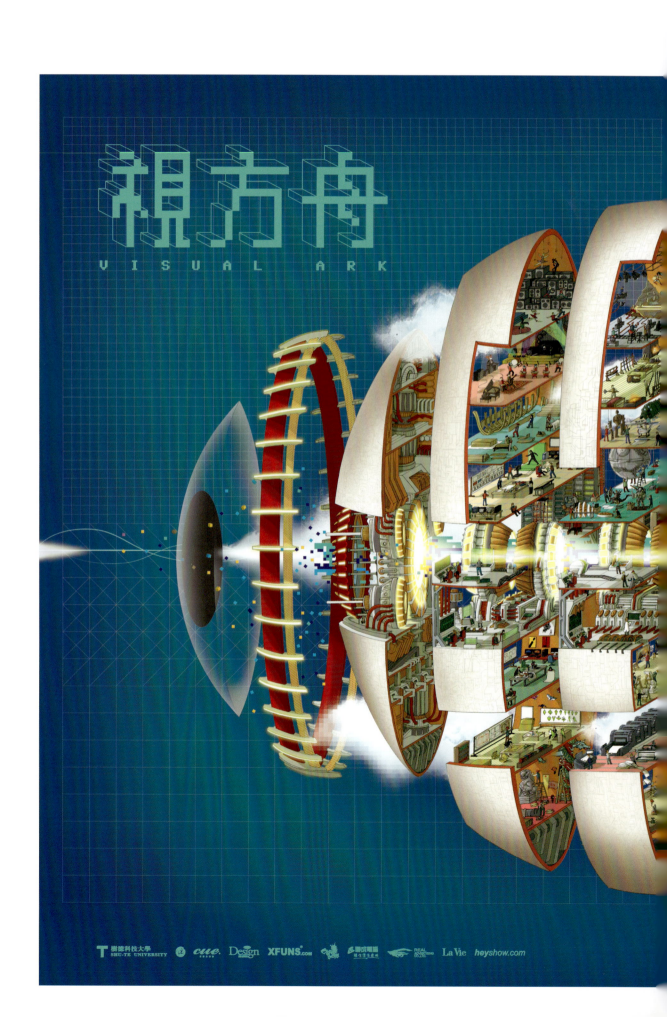

| Interface Design | Mobile & Apps | Game Design | Sound Design | **Red Dot: Junior Award** Posters | Designer Portraits |

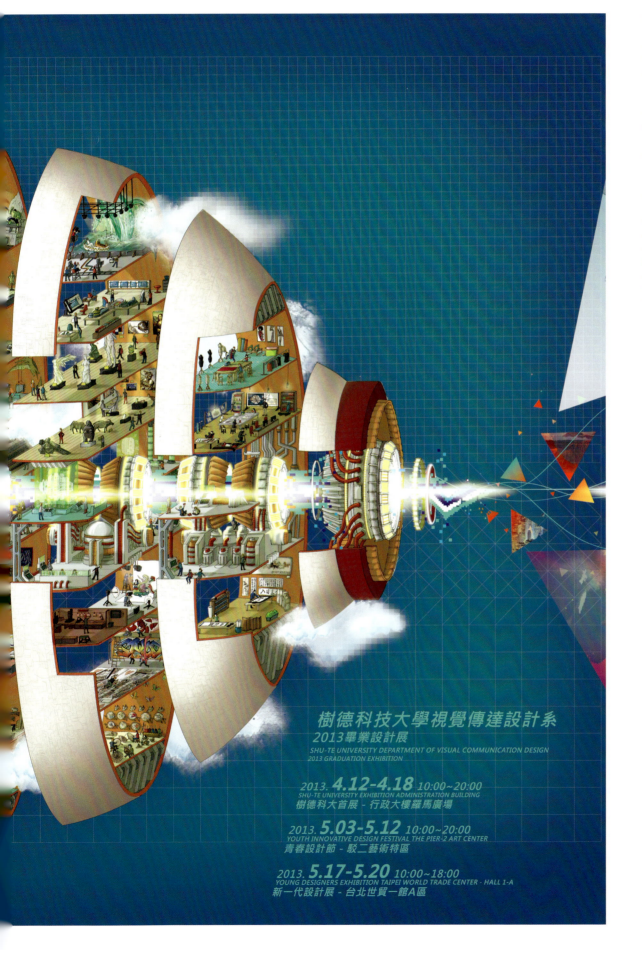

This poster shows Visual Ark, an eye-shaped object with a world of design options opening up behind the iris and the pupil. The colour illustration depicts this world as a cluster of spaces. Each space is a place where creativity can unfold, therefore offering the possibility of creating new styles of visual effects with a wide range of different materials. One can make out a museum as well as a tailor's workshop, a painting room, a printing work and a wood workshop. The many fine details of the illustration are made visible with the help of a magnifying glass. The interaction between the peripheral magnifying glass and the poster is used to represent the meanings of "observation" and "searching".

i-ADDICTION

[Poster]

university
National Yunlin University of Science and Technology, Douliou City, Yunlin County

design
Jin-An Chung,
Jun-Kai Lin,
Taipei City

| Interface Design | Mobile & Apps | Game Design | Sound Design | **Red Dot: Junior Award** Posters | Designer Portraits |

With the advancement of technology, addictions to electronic devices increase. Both posters deal with this issue, showing children in one poster and adults in the other, both depicted in the form of colour illustrations as prisoners of the three Cs – computer, communication and consumer electronics. And even though they are actually close to each other, each of them lives in his or her own, electronic world. The slogan "i-ADDICTION" emphasises this, on the one hand it refers to the widely used iPhone, while on the other hand it means "I have become addicted to my iPhone".

| Event Design | Information Design & Public Space | Corporate Films | TV, Film, Cinema & Animation | Online World |

Glamour of Words – Pictograph Essence of Chinese Characters

[Book]

The key elements of Chinese characters are form, tone and meaning. This book is designed to help people who are learning Chinese characters. It is based on the assumption that learning becomes easier when the student knows about the development of the characters from their original pictures to their contemporary forms. The design of this square-shaped book features folding pages. The user can see the original images of the Chinese characters through the holes cut into the pages and thus gets an understanding of the meaning behind the characters.

client
National Taiwan Normal University, Taipei

design
China University of Technology, Taipei

creative direction
Shih-Lun Chen

design team
Jia-Hong Lin,
Yu-Ru Cho,
Siao-Huei Tang

→ designer portrait: p. 441

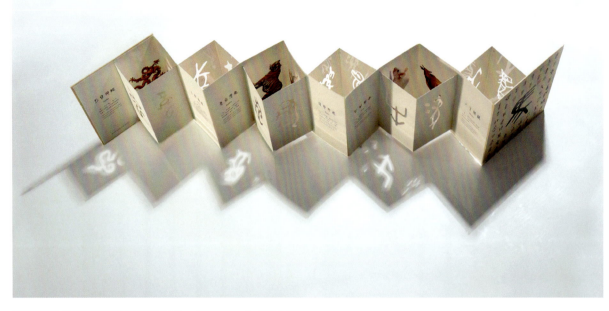

Interface Design | Mobile & Apps | Game Design | Sound Design | **Red Dot: Junior Award** Typography | Designer Portraits

1980 - 2012, 서울   나이들지않는 도시

IS ALWAYS UNDER CONSTRUCTION. THE CITY NEVER GETS OLD, HAS NO MORE MEMORIES, PLACES TO REMEMBER.

1980 - 2012, SEOUL   THE AGELESS CITY

The Ageless City – Seoul

[Typographic Poster]

Seoul City has a long history but more than 75 per cent of its architecture has been built after 1980. These posters address this situation. "The ageless city, Seoul" is a typeface design that describes the change in architecture of five representative landmarks from 1980 to 2012. Each letter shows the style of architecture at a specific time: for instance, the characters M, A, H, P, R and N describe the change in architecture of Seoul station. All letters have been selected for this design based on the connection between their shape and that of the specific building, and the architectural style they represent.

university
Ewha Womans University, Seoul

design
Sookwung Lee

| Event Design | Information Design & Public Space | Corporate Films | TV, Film, Cinema & Animation | Online World |

Eight Infernal Generals

[Illustration]

This colour illustration depicts masks with traditional patterns as they are worn by the Eight Infernal Generals, who are part of a special Taiwanese folk tradition. According to folk belief, the Eight Infernal Generals fight all evil forces, sins and plagues and bring a blessing instead. The dominant colours of this illustration are red and blue. The special symbols on the mask were drawn in fine lines. The black ink used pays homage to Chinese drawing traditions and conveys power.

university
Asia University,
Taichung City

design
Ya-Li Huang,
Syue-Ru Chen,
Yu-Chi Chung,
Yu-Shu Sun,
Tien-Yuan Ku,
Chia-Hsuan Wu,
Hsiao-Ling Wu,
Asia University,
Taichung City

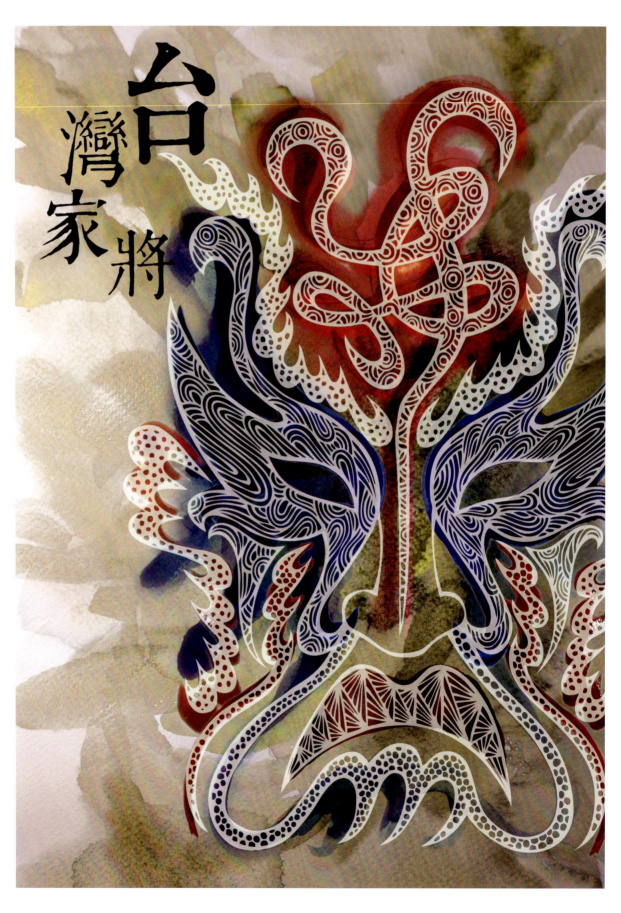

Die Schattenwelt des Gio Medina
The Shadow World of Gio Medina
[Picture Book]

This crime thriller short-story tells the reader about a Sicilian in New York in the 1920s. Besides the illustrations, the experimental use of light is one of the key design elements. The Mafia is a shadow society, and likewise, the main character is also a figure that exists in the shadows. All objects of the book were illustrated by hand, placed in an extreme perspective and then photographed. The interplay of light and unusual perspectives as well as the material characteristics of the paper create a consistent and captivating atmosphere.

university
School for Design Ravensburg

supervising professor
Georg Engels,
Jürgen Weltin

design
Claudia Mikosch,
Weingarten

HATCH UP
[Postcard Illustration]

university
Shu-Te University,
Kaohsiung City

design
Shu-Te University,
Kaohsiung City
Chihlee Institute of Technology,
New Taipei City

creative direction
Aaron Yin

art direction
Chun-Wen Chao,
Kai-Li Wu

concept
Jui-Chieh Hung,
Kai-Li Wu,
Chun-Wen Chao

graphic design
Kai-Li Wu

photography
Jui-Chieh Hung

illustration
Jui-Chieh Hung,
Kai-Li Wu

These illustrations, dealing with the issue of environmental protection, are inspired by the rubbish that is thrown away every day. Initially, the design depicts untouched nature using coloured pictures painted by hand. Some of the individual illustrations are combined to form a unit, thus telling a story about two creatures that live a secluded life in a cave, plant trees and recycle resources that keep on being dropped into their surroundings as rubbish. Their adventure begins when they accidentally come into contact with the human world, which is very different from theirs. The aim of the work is to show how important a healthy environment is for everybody.

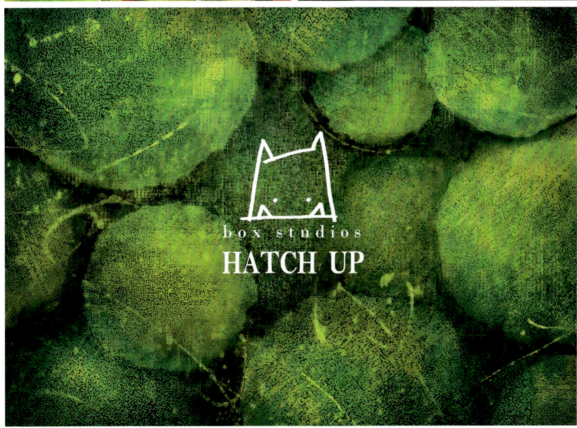

Embrace Butterfly
[Illustration]

university
Shu-Te University,
Kaohsiung City

supervising professor
Yu-Lung Yang,
Ti-Wan Kung,
Chein-Feng Chang

design
Shu-Te University,
Department of
Visual Communication Design,
Kaohsiung City

graphic design
Baihao Qiu,
Weiming Lai,
Chun-Yat Zhao

→ designer portrait: p. 460

Taiwan was once known as the butterfly kingdom. However, as time progressed and society advanced, over-cultivation has endangered the living environment of those butterflies. Destructive human behaviour has caused the near extinction of these insects. This book aims to represent the ideas of respecting life, being concerned about the environment and embracing the "butterfly culture" in Taiwan. It tells its story with the help of colour illustrations, which stand out due to their numerous elaborate details. The layout combines a page of text and a full-page illustration for each double page. The design of the text page is very restrained due to its large amount of white space and does not distract attention from the illustration.

Cardinal Vices

[Illustration]

university
Shu-Te University,
Kaohsiung City

supervising professor
Ma-Yi Yang,
Ti-Wan Kung

design
Shu-Te University,
Department of Visual
Communication Design,
Kaohsiung City

graphic design
Yan-Yi Kuo,
Hong-Yi Shih,
Yu-Shen Pan,
Yu-Shu Cheng,
Fu-Ciang Yang,
Sian-Jhen Zeng

→ designer portrait: p. 462

The illustration Cardinal Vices stands out with its unusual format in the style of a panorama image. And thus, similar to a panorama image being characterised by a wide viewing angle, this illustration paints a detailed picture of current events in Taiwan's society. The main topics are wine, sex, avarice and temper. They are represented by interesting characters in a fresh style. The colour scheme is dominated by pastel hues such as light blue, light green, purple and pink, which creates a friendly impression and a contrast to the content. The illustration captures the daily life of ordinary people in Taiwan and wants to get viewers involved in this virtual world with empathy and understanding.

Yonghe Soy Milk – River City Soul

[Illustration]

design
Hsien-Chu Kuo,
New Taipei City

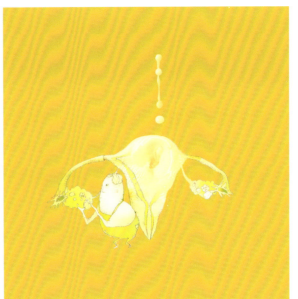

Yonghe soy milk is a familiar and widely used food in the Yonghe district. The illustrations clearly portray the drink's health promoting effect. The images present individual organs such as the lungs, the stomach, the intestines and the ovaries. The soy milk is depicted as it flows into individual organs where it unfolds its beneficial effect. It is supported by industrious "workers", who efficiently use the nutrients contained in the soy milk. Isoflavone, for instance, is mentioned, which plays an important role in lung cancer prevention.

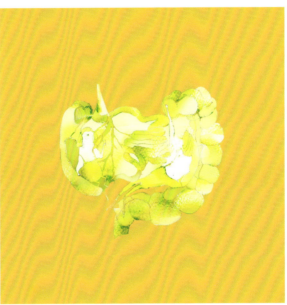

| Event Design | Information Design & Public Space | Corporate Films | TV, Film, Cinema & Animation | Online World |

Graphic Film Transcription

[Infographic]

The Grafische Filmtranskription (graphical transcription of film), executed in a poster and book format, is a system for the visual representation of a film's structure. The film is deconstructed into its component parts and then put together again into a kind of infographics. Film minutes thus become centimetres. Individual, coloured surfaces, symbols and writing together form an abstract representation of the film, which makes the structure of the content as well as the technical construction visible. Thus, elements come to the fore that are mostly perceived unconsciously during a single viewing.

design
Christoph Lohse,
Hamburg

→ clip on DVD

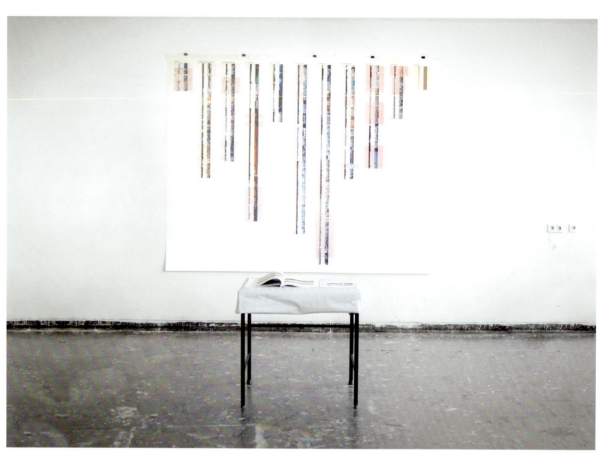

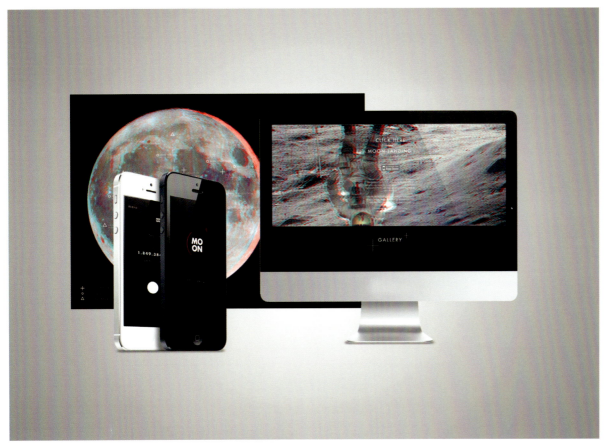

Moonlanding
[Multimedia Concept]

"Moonlanding" is a multimedia concept with which anyone can relive the historic event. First, an introductory video in 3D is shown to arouse interest. Besides moon posters and a moon map, the app forms the heart of this concept. It provides not only news about the exploration of the moon, but allows its phases to be defined and to measure the current distance from oneself to it. This multimedia concept is an opportunity to awaken people's interest in events that should never be forgotten. It is transferable to any historic event.

university
IN.D Institute of Design
Düsseldorf

design
Jennifer Laura Signon,
Düsseldorf

→ clip on DVD

| Event Design | Information Design & Public Space | Corporate Films | TV, Film, Cinema & Animation | Online World |

JK5
[Interactive Chalkboard Walls]

client
HOAS Foundation for Student Housing in the Helsinki Region

design
Ilari Laitinen,
Enni Koistinen

**creative direction/
art direction**
Ilari Laitinen,
Enni Koistinen

**concept/
final artwork**
Ilari Laitinen,
Enni Koistinen

strategic planning
Ilari Laitinen

photography
Antti Ahtiluoto

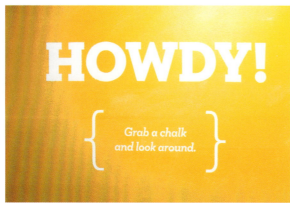

The aim of the project was to turn a dilapidated building, which offers rooms for foreign students, into an appealing home. To achieve this, communal areas were re-designed. With colourful chalkboard paint and bold typography, the interior was turned into part of the architecture and converted into a vibrant living space. The hallways were painted from floor to ceiling, turning them into chalkboards. Instead of forbidding people to write on the walls, the students now use them as an interactive communication surface.

Event Design | Information Design & Public Space | Corporate Films | TV, Film, Cinema & Animation | Online World

The Photographer
[Animation]

university
National Yunlin University of Science and Technology, Douliou City, Yunlin County

design
Lung-Kai Hsu,
National Yunlin University of Science and Technology, Douliou City, Yunlin County

graphic design/animation
Lung-Kai Hsu

film production/editor
Lung-Kai Hsu

music/sound design
Ying-Chih Chen,
Chia-Wei Chen

→ clip on DVD

| Interface Design | Mobile & Apps | Game Design | Sound Design | **Red Dot: Junior Award** TV, Film, Cinema & Animation | Designer Portraits |

Regretful things always happen in life and people often think afterwards "What if I hadn't done this?" and imagine a different ending. It is exactly these kinds of thoughts the animated cartoon The Photographer is about. The main character is accidentally reminded of an event in the past which had a negative outcome due to the decisions he had made. At the heart of this film there is the search for alternatives; what, for example, a decision would look like, if one could travel back in time and view things from a different perspective. Regret about wrong decisions could thus be avoided.

Burglar Sitter
[Animation]

university
Ming Chuan University,
Taoyuan County

design
Ming Chuan University,
Taoyuan County

concept
Chan Hui Ying

music/sound design
Loh Juei Wen,
Fang Lee

animation
Wu Bo Syun

lighting design
Khor Cheng Kee

post-production
Siau Yung Bing

technical direction
Lee Chuan Yueh

→ clip on DVD

| Interface Design | Mobile & Apps | Game Design | Sound Design | **Red Dot: Junior Award**
TV, Film, Cinema & Animation | Designer Portraits |

Burglar Sitter is a fresh film with 3D technology. The aim of this animation is to bring children closer to their parents through the warm and interesting story. The film is dominated by wooden materials and facet shapes. Animals, shapes and colours are fundamental learning materials for children. The scenes and characters are designed based on this principle – pigs are the main characters, for example. The animation plays with opposites; indoors, the atmosphere is warm and safe, in contrast to the cold outside environment which represents danger.

| Event Design | Information Design & Public Space | Corporate Films | TV, Film, Cinema & Animation | Online World |

Käferkunde
The Study of Beetles
[App]

client/publisher
FOVEA,
Göttingen

design
Nadine Weiberg,
Alfeld

Interface Design | Mobile & Apps | Game Design | Sound Design | **Red Dot: Junior Award** Mobile & Apps | Designer Portraits

Worldwide there are more than 350,000 different species of beetles. Many of them have to be correctly identified by foresters. "Käferkunde" (the study of beetles) is a very appealing and attractively designed app which allows users to learn about beetles, look them up and identify them via filter function using characteristics such as size and colour. Users can enter the beetles they encounter via photo function and GPS into an integrated interactive map and thus show others which beetles they have already identified correctly.

HAPTICUS – Sensibilisierung für den Tastsinn
HAPTICUS – Sensitisation to the Sense of Touch
[Game]

university
University of Applied Sciences Düsseldorf

design
Anne-Katrin Reinl, Hannover

→ clip on DVD

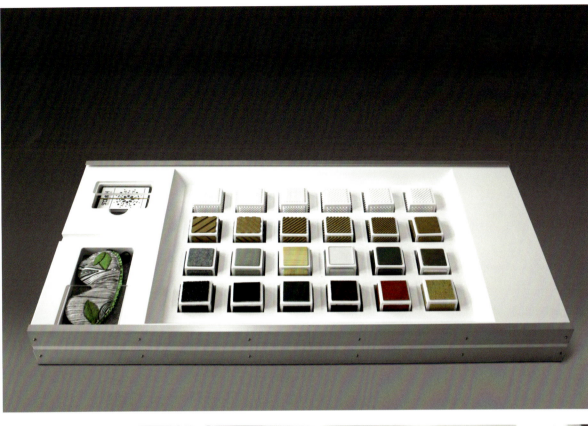

The objective of this game is to make players more aware of the unconscious processes and conscious for the sense of touch to develop more sensitivity for this sense. To achieve this, players touch different surfaces with their finger tips. The game contains 24 cubes which simulate the four types of tactile perception: pressure, temperature, vibration and pain. There are six levels in each category and also three different playing levels, which increase in difficulty. Instruction cards and an eye-mask complete the tactile game.

INTERNATIONAL YEARBOOK COMMUNICATION DESIGN 2013/2014

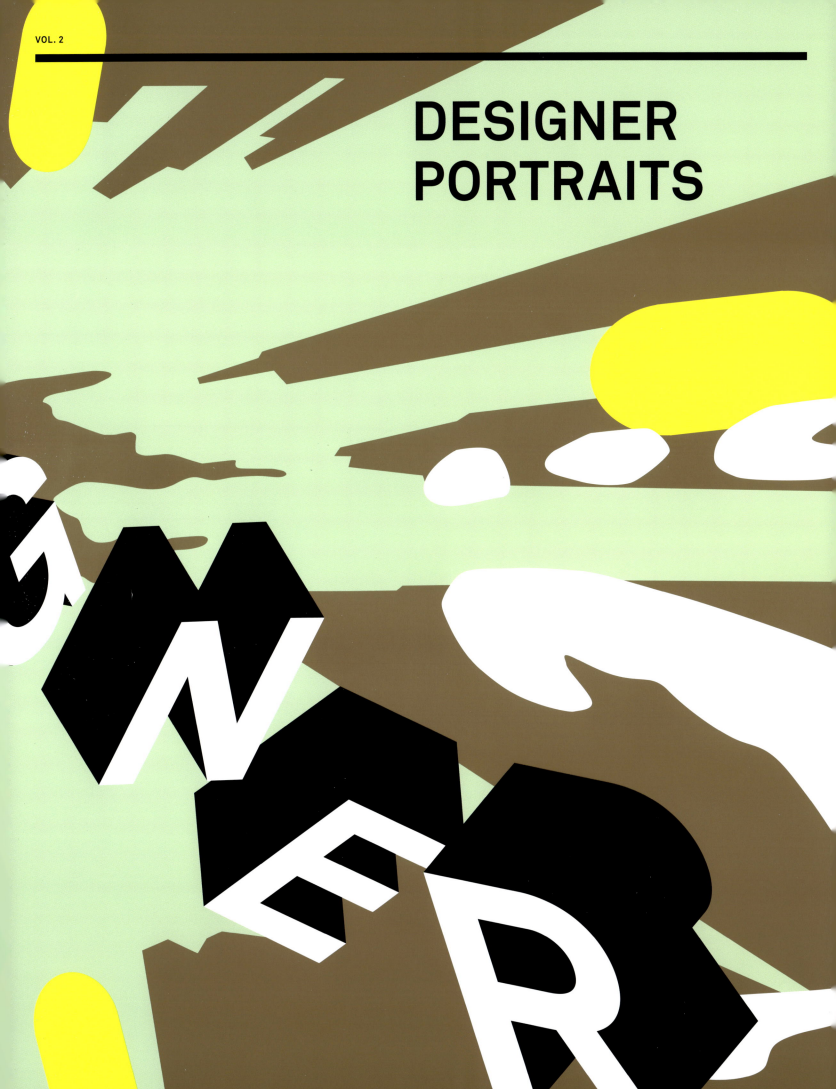

ACHTA DESIGN
SARA BÖHMER, ACHIM BÖHMER
— design brand value.

Red Dot
→ Online World: p. 152

Sara and Achim Böhmer both graduated with distinction when they completed their degree in communication design at the Folkwang University in Essen. Sara Böhmer received her first Red Dot Award while she was still a student for her first book project. Achim Böhmer worked for established branding agencies as well as independently in his own Logo project agency, and developed brand concepts for, amongst others, Allianz, WestLB, DSM and Wilo. Sara and Achim Böhmer have published joint books such as "Retrodesign stylelab" and "Formstrahl". In 2008, they founded the achta design agency for brand strategy, brand development and corporate design with a particular focus on well-designed web concepts suited to CI.

What do you understand by good communication design?
Good communication design is always rooted in a smart, understandable concept that brings people together, sets communication in motion and gives undertakings wings.

Why did you become a communication designer?
As a communication designer you can support institutions and companies in the long-term with meaningful brand strategies and brand developments. Intelligent design concepts can provide order for contents, communicate issues more clearly and convey emotions.

What does the future of communication design look like?
Due to the mobile web there are ever more effective communication channels. We believe this is a fantastic opportunity to create interactivity with a brand in a new way.

BBDO PROXIMITY BERLIN
TON HOLLANDER
— Every client gets what he deserves.

Red Dot: Best of the Best
→ TV, Film, Cinema & Animation: p. 118-119

Red Dot
→ Sound Design: p. 288

Ton Hollander, born in Hengelo (Gld) in the Netherlands, studied graphic design in Utrecht and Eindhoven. After working for various design agencies in the Netherlands, he moved to BBDO in Düsseldorf in 2000, then on to Hamburg in 2004 to reinforce the founding team of Kempertrautmann. In 2006, he returned to Düsseldorf where he took over responsibility for the BBDO Team smart as creative director.

Today, he looks after this client from the Berlin office as executive creative director. He has been awarded prizes at numerous national and international competitions, including the Cannes Lions, ADC Germany, D&AD, ADC Europe, ADC New York, Eurobest, Clio Awards, New York Festivals, Red Dot Award, One Show, LIAA London, Andy Awards and Euro Effie Awards.

What do you understand by good communication design?
Good communication design moves the viewer to get to grips with the content and it visually conveys a message.

Which of your projects has been the biggest challenge for you so far?
The development of the car2go brand. Creating a brand from scratch without the benefit of a background – from the development of the name, the corporate identity and the car design via the brand story and philosophy right through to translating it for the real and virtual world.

BBDO PROXIMITY BERLIN
DANIEL SCHWEINZER, LUKAS LISKE

Red Dot: Best of the Best
→ Sound Design: p. 286-287

Red Dot
→ Event Design: p. 53

Daniel Schweinzer (creative director/art) and Lukas Liske (creative director/text) have worked together as a creative team since 2009. In 2011, they moved from Ogilvy & Mather (Frankfurt) to BBDO Proximity in Berlin. In the last four years, they have won awards, including 16 Cannes Lions, for works such as "Tree Concert" (BUND), smart "Offroad", "smart EBALL", "Cinema Rear View Mirror" (Europcar).

What do you understand by good communication design?
Good communication design doesn't only look good. It touches, surprises, fascinates people – at a content level. If that works, you have already achieved a good deal.

Which of your projects has been the biggest challenge for you so far?
With Tree Concert, we really entered virgin territory. How do you construct an instrument for a tree? When exactly do chestnuts fall? And how does all of that turn into an experience that one can tell others about? We probably never before learnt so much from a project. Nor had so much fun.

What inspires you?
Inspiration can come from anywhere. It's best when it comes from areas other than advertising. That makes it much easier to create something fresh, previously unseen – rather than produce the next manifestation of a pre-existing idea.

BIBOBOX STUDIO, DALIAN NATIONALITIES UNIVERSITY
BO LIU
— Design the best for children with love and kindness.

Red Dot
→ Game Design: p. 280-281

Bo Liu, born in China in 1978, has been working in design for over a decade. In 2009, he founded BiBoBox Studio, which focuses on developing interactive educational products for children and has published over a hundred children's books. Bo Liu and his teammates have received numerous international awards including the 2012 Apple Design Award and the 8th Golden Dragon Award (Best Original Comic for Kids). BiBoBox consists of education experts, interactive designers, professional artists and developers and is currently developing a series of products about traditional Chinese learning and understanding.

What do you understand by good communication design?
Good communication design is able to concern itself with and address current social issue.

What are the qualities a successful communication designer must have?
A successful communication designer not only should have good design sense, ideas, motivation and technique, but also pay great care and attention to culture and humanity.

Which of your projects has been the biggest challenge for you so far?
The launch of the Hanzi Study project. The biggest challenge was to merge traditional Chinese character symbols with interactive technologies.

What inspires you?
Most of my design projects are for children. They are my greatest source of inspiration.

CADERADESIGN
TOM CADERA

Red Dot: Best of the Best
→ Interface Design: p. 196–197

Tom Cadera, born in the Bavarian town of Ochsenfurt, studied industrial design at the Braunschweig University of Art (HBK Braunschweig). While he was doing so, he already started working for companies operating in the fields of medical and mechanical engineering. He founded the CaderaDesign agency, which has been developing and designing intermedial projects since 1992 and is specialised in industrial design and user interface design, including apps. Between 1997 and 2008, Tom Cadera also worked as lecturer at the Furtwangen University (HFU). The CaderaDesign team consists of industrial designers, communication designers, media designers, usability engineers, IT specialists and design engineers.

What do you understand by good communication design?
Good communication design is when the user can find his/her way around quickly, securely and intuitively and, on top of that, feels good while doing so.

What are the qualities a good
communication designer must have?
Creativity, tenacity, a solution-focused approach, but also patience, good people skills and empathy.

What else would you like to learn?
Meditating.

What does the future of communication design look like?
Not quite as flat as many believe.

CRYTEK
CHRIS AUTY, MAGNUS LARBRANT
— Envision. Enable. Achieve.

Red Dot: Grand Prix
→ Game Design: p. 276-277

Crytek is an independent company at the forefront of the interactive entertainment industry, which is dedicated to pushing the boundaries of gaming by creating standout experiences. The company's headquarters are in Frankfurt/Main, with additional studios in Kiev, Budapest, Sofia, Seoul, Nottingham, Shanghai, Istanbul and Austin.

Chris Auty is a design veteran of the games industry having worked on a variety of titles including Crysis, Far Cry, Counter-Strike and James Bond. Over the past ten years, he has worked at Crytek in Frankfurt as game design director on a variety of projects. Magnus Larbrant has also worked on Crytek's award-winning games for over a decade, acting as senior art director on Crysis 3.

What do you understand by good communication design?
Within gaming, it's not just about producing art or level design – we're making a game, we're making an experience. The job, then, is to come up with a way to provide that for the players. You need to invite them into this world and give them not just a visual PowerPoint, but shape everything accordingly to create that experience.

Which of your projects has been the biggest challenge for you so far?
In terms of visual style, Crysis 3. The challenge had to do with maintaining the vision. We were trying to really establish something new and come up with a visual language that flowed through the whole project – from concept to 3D, marketing, screenshots, story; everything had to follow a single line.

DAEDALIC ENTERTAINMENT
JAN MÜLLER-MICHAELIS
— He who bites off more than he can chew still gets enough to eat.

Red Dot: Best of the Best
→ Game Design: p. 278-279

Jan Müller-Michaelis was born in Hamburg in 1977, where he studied media technology at the University of Applied Sciences. As part of his diploma thesis on non-linear narrative in computer games, he developed the point-and-click adventure "Edna and Harvey: The Breakout", using his own graphics, scripting and game design. He and Carsten Fichtelmann are the co-founders of Daedalic Entertainment, a fast-growing German indie developer, which designs games with strong narrative and compelling characters. Jan Müller-Michaelis worked as creative director on numerous titles such as "A New Beginning", "Harvey's New Eyes" and the final part of Deponia trilogy "Goodbye Deponia", which is to be released later this year.

What are the qualities a successful communication designer must have?
On one hand, he is a psychologist who knows exactly what the expectations of his audience are and can arouse specific reactions and particularly emotions. On the other, there must be no working link between the two sides of his brain, so that he can surprise himself; because, only by doing that, can he surprise others.

What inspires you?
Problems and how people get round them.

What kind of project would you like to realise?
I would like to design the first game based on musicals. By that I mean create an interactive musical you can play with.

DENKWERK
GREGOR KUSCHMIRZ, CHRISTIAN WARSTAT
— Think laterally. Act with focus.

Red Dot: Best of the Best
→ Corporate Films: p. 96-97

Founded in 1998, denkwerk is an interactive agency with 170 employees in Cologne and Berlin, which develops digital products, innovative strategies and sustainable solutions for clients such as BMW, Condor, Deutsche Post, RWE or Nokia.

Gregor Kuschmirz studied communication design in Munich, as well as film and TV design at the Filmakademie Ludwigsburg, was a fellow at Benetton's research centre FABRICA and subsequently taught at the Germany University in Cairo. He worked for FOX in Rome before becoming motion director at denkwerk in 2011.

Christian Warstat studied communication with an emphasis on film and illustration at Aachen University of Applied Sciences, which included a period at RMIT in Melbourne. He worked as an intern in motion design at denkwerk in 2012/2013.

What do you understand by good communication design?
Good communication design is one that makes us look twice and prompts us to get to grips with the contents.

What are the qualities a successful communication designer must have?
He/she must be a good storyteller and be able to imagine the world in the same way as others perceive it.

Which of your projects has been the biggest challenge for you so far?
It is impossible to link the challenge to a single project. Instead, it consists in maintaining one's own standards in day-to-day work.

DESIGNCONCEPTS
— Design is strategy.

Red Dot
→ Online World: p. 153

designconcepts, founded over 20 years ago by Ulrich Nocke and Ulrike Claeys, considers itself to be a guarantor of effective and efficient communication solutions and stands for strategic design, excellent design quality and technical perfection. The approach of the agency, which today employs 12 designers, could be summed up as consisting of holistic thinking and work, based on close, long-term partnerships with its clients. Its network of experts offers comprehensive communication solutions for the entire digital and analogue world – out of conviction and passion, from the depths of the Black Forest.

What do you understand by good communication design?
Good communication design asks the question: "Who is speaking to whom about what?" and then says: "I'm talking to you!"

What are the qualities a successful communication designer must have?
Honesty, passion, expertise and attitude. In this respect, success only comes to those with attitude.

With whom would you like to work?
We are delighted by the interplay between communication and space. We would be very tempted to explore this field in cooperation with a good architect or scenographer.

What inspires you?
The Black Forest. The spurned emblem of the unadulterated enjoyment of nature.

DRAFTFCB DEUTSCHLAND
— Work that makes us proud.

Red Dot: Best of the Best
→ Information Design & Public Space: p. 76-77
→ TV, Film, Cinema & Animation: p. 122-123

Red Dot
→ TV, Film, Cinema & Animation: p. 130-131
→ Mobile & Apps: p. 252

Draftfcb Deutschland was founded in Hamburg in 1876 under the name of Centrales Annoncen Büro William Wilkens, which makes it Germany's first advertising agency. The Hamburg site is behind many interdisciplinary, international and national campaigns for, amongst others, D.A.S., Golden Toast, Philharmoniker Hamburg, Peter Kölln, Lieken Urkorn, Lindt and Beiersdorf. It is the lead agency worldwide for brands such as NIVEA, Hansaplast and Labello.

Draftfcb Deutschland is among Germany's Top Ten most efficient agencies. The Draftfcb network today includes 150 agencies in 90 countries with more than 9,000 employees worldwide and is part of the Interpublic Group of Companies (NYSE: IPG).

What do you understand by good communication design?
The basis for good communication design is always a good idea. Without it, design would be mere decoration. Design therefore always has to play a subordinate role with regard to the message. However, design is the first way in which an idea is perceived. That decides whether a viewer takes an interest in the message. Good communication design translates this message in a visually surprising way.

What are the qualities a successful communication designer must have?
Courage to follow new paths. Assertiveness to champion them. Patience to stay enthusiastic despite setbacks. Flexibility to find the perfect solution for very different and varied tasks.

Designer Portraits

EIGHT INC.
TIM KOBE

Red Dot: Best of the Best
→ Event Design: p. 22-23

Tim Kobe graduated in environmental design in 1982 from the Art Center College of Design, Pasadena. He worked with Herb Rosenthal, Murray Gelberg and The Burdick Group before becoming a founding partner of West Office Design Associates in 1987. In 1989, he set up the globally recognised strategic design firm Eight Inc. and became its CEO. The studio today has offices in San Francisco, New York, Honolulu, Tokyo, London, Singapore and Beijing, working with companies such as Apple, Virgin Atlantic Airways, Nike, Coca-Cola, Knoll and Citibank. Tim Kobe has lectured at renowned international institutes and universities and, amongst others, serves on the Board of Directors for the Grabhorn Institute in San Francisco.

What do you understand by good communication design?
Any design must have qualities that are relevant to the end user, be distinctive from others and connect on an emotional level.

Which of your projects has been the biggest challenge for you so far?
The most challenging projects are ones where there is a need for large companies to do things in new ways. Behaviour change within large companies is really the most difficult thing to achieve.

With whom would you like to work?
We worked with Steve Jobs for many years and still work with the world's most visible and best-loved brands. For us, any leader who appreciates the value of design and the power of meaningful outcomes is a person we admire.

FABRIQUE [BRANDS, DESIGN & INTERACTION]
RONNIE BESSELING
— Stay curious!

Red Dot: Best of the Best
→ Online World: p. 146-147

Red Dot
→ Online World: p. 181

Ronnie Besseling studied at the Academy for Art Direction and Design in Amsterdam and afterwards began working as a conceptual designer for JWT Amsterdam. At the same time, he was active as member of the board of Jonge Honden, the platform for young Dutch creatives, inspiring young and enthusiastic people at the start of their creative career. Today, he is creative director at Fabrique [brands, design & interaction] in Amsterdam and, always searching for challenging online concepts, has worked as designer and creative director for clients such as 9292 travel information, Adobe, Arco, SNS Reaal, Viktor&Rolf, Artis Amsterdam Zoo and xwashere.

What do you understand by good communication design?
I don't just want to make interesting, beautiful things. I want to change the world with my talent, in any event a little bit, by getting people to think, for example.

What are the qualities a successful communication designer must have?
The most important thing is to look at the world in a naive and fresh way each day. Clients are often locked into the world of their product or service. That's when you have to ask questions to make them think about things anew.

What inspires you?
For me, the most inspiring thing is meeting new people. Preferably mad people. The story behind people, discovering what their take on the world is. When I need inspiration, I prefer to hit the street rather than visit a museum.

GESSAGA HINDERMANN
JÉRÔME GESSAGA,
CHRISTOF HINDERMANN
— By means of simple phenomena, curiosity should once again find a place in our everyday lives.

Red Dot
→ Event Design: p. 42-43

Jérôme Gessaga trained as a cabinet maker and architectural draughtsman before qualifying at the Basel School of Design in interior design and product design. Together with Christof Hindermann he founded a joint agency in 2000.

Christof Hindermann also studied for a diploma at the Basel School of Design after completing Samedan commercial college in Switzerland. Prior to setting up the agency with Jérôme Gessaga, he had spent an exchange semester at the Cooper Union School of Art in New York, followed by work as a junior designer for Interbrand Zintzmeyer & Lux AG, Zurich. Both Jérôme Gessaga and Christof Hindermann also work as lecturers at different institutes and universities.

What do you understand by good communication design?
Creating clarity and direction aesthetically and subtly in a way that still triggers an emotional reaction with the observer.

What are the qualities a good communication designer must have?
Empathy is key to speaking the same language as the customer. That gives one the opportunity to extend his or her vocabulary by a chapter or two.

Which of your projects has been the biggest challenge for you so far?
The biggest challenge are customers who won't budge from what is currently trendy. Designing something new under those circumstances has a lot to do with communication.

GRASS JELLY STUDIO
MUH CHEN
— Learning by doing.
Go! Do it!

Red Dot
→ Corporate Films: p. 106-107
→ TV, Film, Cinema & Animation: p. 132

Muh Chen has directed national television commercial campaigns, music videos and short films. He founded the Taipei production studio Grass Jelly in 2005, which provides thorough visual production services from directing to CG, VFX and live-action. Grass Jelly has become one of the best visual production companies in Asia attracting widespread media attention, also from large brands. In 2013, a Pepsi television commercial featuring Momo Wu built up impressive brand awareness. Its music video version broke a record for music videos in Chinese-speaking Asia with a 100 million click-through-rate over an Internet media platform. Grass Jelly's work has won or been nominated for numerous international awards, including the Red Dot Design Award, iF design award, MTV Europe Music Awards, MTV Video Music Awards Japan, KKBOX Music Awards (Hong Kong) and Golden Melody Awards (Taiwan).

What do you understand by good communication design?
Good communication design allows the audience to get the idea behind the image, not just the technique presented.

What kind of project would you like to realise?
A film that can present the spirit of the East and achieve worldwide recognition at the same time.

What does the future of communication design look like?
In the future, communication will focus on interacting with audiences and be customised to individual needs.

Designer Portraits

HID HUMAN INTERFACE DESIGN
— Inspiring interaction.

Red Dot
→ Interface Design: p. 208-209

Human Interface Design is a design agency specialising in the user-centred design of high-quality interfaces for technical products, software systems and interactive media – essentially: user experience design. The 20-strong, multi-disciplinary team has been making technology comprehensible and usable for consumers for more than 15 years, developing products and service systems that are functionally strong and emotionally appealing in the realms of UX/UI design, interaction design, design anthropology, design strategy, user experience research, service design, interactive prototyping, graphical user interfaces, natural user interfaces, usability engineering and evaluation.

What are the qualities a successful communication designer must have?
As a user experience designer you need empathy to understand how people tick when they handle interactive systems – to know what their desires and fears are in doing so.

With whom would you like to work?
With a cultural or social organisation in order to be of high value by putting our expertise at the service of an even wider community in a social context.

What kind of project would you like to realise?
Breaking down nuclear waste into oxygen, pure water and love without leaving a trace.

What else would you like to learn?
How to bring about politically sustainable decisions and societal change with design solutions.

Designer Portraits

HOSOYA SCHAEFER ARCHITECTS
— Understand, communicate, change for the better.

Red Dot: Grand Prix
→ Interface Design: p. 190-191

Hosoya Schaefer Architects AG is a Zurich-based office for architecture, urban design and research founded by Hiromi Hosoya and Markus Schaefer in 2003. The firm works on a wide spectrum of projects such as the 230-ha masterplan for Ljubljana, mobility research for Autostadt/Volkswagen, hotel alterations, private houses or a train station in Toronto. The firm won first prizes for both the Engadin Airport and the train station area in St. Moritz. It has worked on a study for the metropolitan region of Zurich and several urban design projects in the same perimeter. Its communication design work is driven by research and revolves around understanding (urban) systems.

What are the qualities a successful communication designer must have?
Curiosity in order to ask questions, the desire to communicate and to be understood; and patience to make a design beautiful.

Which of your projects has been the biggest challenge for you so far?
Every project is challenging in its own ways: technical ability makes it possible to focus on content, strong content makes it possible to experiment with technology and design. Where both come together innovation can occur.

Where and how do you gather information on trends?
We are driven by content, not by trends; by questions, not by statements.

SCOTTIE CHIH-CHIEH HUANG & BIO LAB + SDAID
— Dream harder, find your passion and approach your goal step by step.

Red Dot
→ TV, Film, Cinema & Animation: p. 138-139

Scottie Chih-Chieh Huang is an artist, designer and assistant professor at the Department of Industrial Design of the College of Architecture & Design at Chung Hua University, where he directs the Biologically Inspired Objects (BIO) Laboratory and the SDAID (Studio of Digital Art and Innovative Design). Together, he and his team have presented their visions of "future living" by inventing a series of interactive installations. Huang's research has been featured in many international magazines. His art/design works have been shown at the Avignon Off Festival 2013, Holland Animation Film Festival 2013, SIGGRAPH Asia 2012 art gallery, LEONARDO/SIGGRAPH 2009 art exhibition, Digital Art Festival Taipei 2008 and Prague Quadrennial 2003, to name but a few.

What do you understand by good communication design?
A good communication channel between design products and users.

Why did you become a communication designer?
I believe a good design can change the world and even make it better than before.

What else would you like to learn?
The combination of traditional crafts and digital technology.

What does the future of communication design look like?
The future of communication design must care about the role of marketing and design.

INTERAKTIONSBYRÅN
EMMA ROZADA, JOEL ROZADA, HANNE MARTE HOLMØY
— Great design inspires great designers.

Red Dot: Best of the Best
→ Interface Design: p. 202–203

Based in Göteborg, Sweden, Interaktionsbyrån is one of the leading interactive design agencies in the automotive industry. Since it was founded in 2007, the agency has become a trusted supplier of user experience design for a large number of automotive brands in Europe, Asia and the USA, with clients like Volvo Cars, Volvo Trucks, Fiat, Range Rover, Land Rover, Jaguar, Koenigsegg, Opel, Lada, AvtoVAZ and SAAB. Interaktionsbyrån is a strategic design partner that helps its clients to innovate using a holistic user experience approach. The aim of its work is to deliver products that empower people in their private, professional and everyday lives.

What are the qualities a successful communication designer must have?
You must know how to design products that are pleasurable to use, easy to understand and effective to implement and, of course, be passionate about what you do. But you also need a deep understanding of business logic and politics in large organisations. The tricky part is not just to have great ideas, but to get them into the final product.

Why did you become a communication designer?
We are all product designers, but the digital world inspires us. Just look at the power of digital products e.g. in the Arab spring. They completely change how we live, work and communicate.

What inspires you?
A great design is often a reflection of the team behind it. To build and work with such a team is very inspiring.

INTERBRAND
BORJA BORRERO, CARLOS MAGRO MARTÍNEZ-ILLESCAS
— Brands have the power to change the world.

Red Dot: Best of the Best
→ Corporate Films: p. 94-95

Red Dot
→ Information Design & Public Space: p. 88

Borja Borrero studied advertising in Madrid (BA) and communication design in New York (MA). He worked for Lintas, Vitruvio/Leo Burnett and FutureBrand before joining Interbrand Spain in 2004 as founding member and executive creative director.

Carlos Magro Martínez-Illescas has worked for global advertising agencies such as Leo Burnett and Euro RSCG and is currently design director at global brand consultancy Interbrand.

What do you understand by good communication design?
It is the creation of a compelling idea rooted in a human truth that expresses the brand's unique point of view.

What are the qualities a successful communication designer must have?
A successful communication designer must understand the client's business, objectives of the communication and, most importantly, embrace free thinking and failure.

What does the future of communication design look like?
Fluid and flexible, yet quite simple and compelling. Right here right now, on the go.

Designer Portraits

JNS COMMUNICATIONS
— Visionary and positive communication design.

Red Dot
→ Mobile & Apps: p. 242-243

JNS communications, a design company founded in 1995, has been creating new and challenging designs for a considerable time. The team has invested its continuous efforts and research into producing works of perfect functionality, taking into consideration the aesthetic purpose of designs as well as the sophisticated strategy and characteristics of each media. JNS communications provides the service most needed by customers in advance of any situation, as well as positive and innovative efforts.

What do you understand by good communication design?
It is simple and conveys meanings easily.

What are the qualities a successful communication designer must have?
He needs to understand the assigned mission quickly and exactly.

What kind of project would you like to realise?
A project for a completely new type of communication.

Where and how do you gather information on trends?
We gather information through lots of reading, conversations with people and the Internet.

What does the future of communication design look like?
It may be a design, which helps people understand each other.

KIA DESIGN TEAM / UNIVERSAL EVERYTHING
KARSTEN THOMS, MATT PYKE
— We're all unique!

Red Dot: Best of the Best
→ Corporate Films: p. 92-93

Karsten Thoms initially worked as a freelancer for various design agencies. From 1996 to 2006, he was design and brand strategist at Volkswagen Group, but also worked as a visiting lecturer on design concepts and development at the University Duisburg-Essen between 2001 and 2002. Since 2007, he has been design strategy manager at Kia Motors and also works as curator inside the Hyundai Motor Group.

Matt Pyke is creative director at Universal Everything working at the crossover between art and design for clients including Audi, Coldplay, Chanel and the London 2012 Olympics. His works have been shown in galleries such as the V&A Museum in London, MOMA in New York, Framed in Tokyo and the digital art museum La Gaîté Lyrique in Paris.

What do you understand by good communication design?
Good communication design tells a story that evokes feelings, touches you instantly and expresses a vision without needing an explanation.

Which of your projects has been the biggest challenge for you so far?
The Mobius Loop project was the most challenging one. First of all, it was an experience with new media, but even more exciting was to work in a really multi-cultural team. Within this global context, the challenge was to communicate the company values in a different way that creates empathy and commitment beyond the cultural mind-set.

KIRCHERBURKHARDT
JEREMY BISHOP, HENNING GROTE, ANDREA ROHNER, MORITZ MAURER

Red Dot: Best of the Best
→ Mobile & Apps: p. 230-231

Red Dot
→ Online World: p. 156-157

Henning Grote has worked as creative director of concepts for KircherBurkhardt (KB) since 2012.

Andrea Rohner, who studied graphic design and product design, began working for KB as a freelancer and, in 2006, joined the agency's staff as senior art director.

Moritz Maurer studied media design in Ravensburg, qualifying in 2006. He went on to work for Publicis in Hamburg, DDB Tribal Hamburg/Berlin and Aimaq von Lobenstein, before moving to Berlin as a freelance art/creative director in 2011.

Jeremy Bishop, born in California, is an IT graduate who has been employed by KB as information architect since 2011.

What do you understand by good communication design?
Good communication design may surprise, irritate, delight or simply be fun, but what it may never do is get in the way of the message or the intention of the user.

What are the qualities a successful communication designer must have?
Warhol once said: "It's not what you are that counts, it's what they think you are."

What kind of project would you like to realise?
One in which augmented reality is used meaningfully.

What does the future of communication design look like?
With many more possibilities for physical and digital interaction, huge steps will be made towards designing intuitive experiences.

KMS BLACKSPACE
MICHAEL KELLER
— Experience is the easiest form of understanding.

Red Dot
→ Event Design: p. 26
→ Event Design: p. 27
→ Event Design: p. 30
→ Event Design: p. 31
→ Online World: p. 185
→ Corporate Films: p. 110–111

Michael Keller, born in 1963, studied at the Parsons School for Design in New York where he received the renowned Cooper Union scholarship. He is managing partner at KMS BLACKSPACE in Munich. Michael Keller's work is a synonym for magnitude and inspiration and moves people in Munich, London, New York, Shanghai and Seoul. He has given numerous brands, companies and cultural events meaning and identity, and his work for Audi, Vodafone, Heidelberger Druckmaschinen and the World Trade Center has received international recognition. He had his own exhibition about his work in the „Neue Sammlung" (Schaustelle/Pinakothek der Moderne) in Munich.

What do you understand by good communication design?
Good design is the result of thought taking shape. And good communication is communication one can touch and understand.

Why did you become a communication designer?
Because it is the profession with the greatest range, the greatest potential. Every day, every encounter challenges me anew in my function as designer.

What inspires you?
Creating a theme for which I have no pre-existing image in mind. The new. The unknown.

What kind of project would you like to realise?
Turning Germany into the most sustainable country in the world and, in doing so, make a political promise become a reality through coherent touchpoints.

Designer Portraits

KNSK
EVONIK TEAM
— We are the team for complex tasks.

Red Dot: Best of the Best
→ TV, Film, Cinema & Animation: p. 120-121

In 2006, a number of accomplished designers, copywriters and consultants in Hamburg came together as the Evonik Team in order to develop and launch this brand. In the autumn of 2007, it was ready: accompanied by a good deal of advertising in print, TV, Internet and on posters, Evonik went public. Since then the Evonik Team has been working from the fourth floor of the KNSK advertising agency right on Hamburg's Außenalster lake. The scope of their work ranges from trade show exhibits and stock exchange communications right through to the BVB sport sponsorship campaign.

What do you understand by good communication design?
Communication design is the art of presentation. Our job as advertisers is therefore to make the packaging so inviting that the viewer is happy to accept the enclosed advertising message. Almost as if it were just what he had always wanted.

What are the qualities a successful communication designer must have?
Good communication designers are interpreters. They have to master the language of the client just as much as that of the target group. After all, their task is to translate the client's message for this audience – and do so as alluringly as possible.

Why did you become a communication designer?
We want our work to entertain other people as much as possible. We are entertainers whose stage is the billboard or the commercial break.

Designer Portraits

  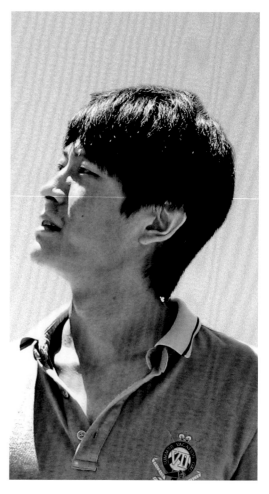

KOKUYO DESIGN TEAM
WATARU SATO, NAOKI SAWADA, RUI WANG
— Design needs to be unique and easy to understand.

Red Dot
→ Event Design: p. 66-67

Wataru Sato, born in Japan in 1979, graduated from the Tokyo Institute of Technology in 2003 with a master's degree in architecture and joined KOKUYO FURNITURE Co., Ltd., where he has been chief interior designer in the space solution planning division in 2013. He has received numerous awards at home and abroad for his work.

Naoki Sawada, born in Japan, joined Kokuyo Furniture Commerce And Trading (Shanghai) Co., Ltd. in 2005 and became interior designer in the design and project department design division in 2013.

Rui Wang, born in China in 1981, graduated from the art department of Nihon University, Japan, in 2008 as an architect and has worked at Urban Design System Co. Ltd. in the architectural design division as a planner ever since.

What do you understand by good communication design?
Wataru Sato: The major issue of communication design is that it has to be "easy to be understood". This is vital to achieve empathy with the client. The design should also have its own unique character. Target groups will be attracted by the discovery of a unique design. This gives the design the potential to involve them fully and to spread widely. Finally, good communication design must have "connotation". Design is not only about innovation and creativity. If the design forces the essence of the object, it should touch others and have an impact on society.

What inspires you?
Wataru Sato: It is very important to feel a little "discomfort" in everyday life. Because there is always the potential to make a small discovery leading to a new design.

Designer Portraits

LOTS
— Tomorrow's innovations start with people.

Red Dot
→ Interface Design: p. 200-201

For a decade now, Lots has supported its customers through the creation of innovative solutions for interfaces, systems, products and services by always basing them on people's needs and dreams – knowing that this is what works. This is the studio's way of achieving sustainable and unique solutions – and better business. Lots supports major international corporations as well as organisations and societal projects in developing true innovations always based on the reality of the users.

What do you understand by good communication design?
Product, system or service interfaces are a company's prime brand carriers and say more about the brand than a thousand words. The different interfaces confirm the brand promise to customers and users. This may seem obvious, but marketing communication often says one thing and the actual offering says something else. At Lots, we focus on the offering and ensure that we strengthen the brand promise by using all the interfaces, throughout the offering.

What are the qualities a successful communication designer must have?
A successful communication designer must have an understanding of people, driving forces, businesses and brands. The designer should also be able to apply a holistic view, dig into and analyse complex and conflicting data, and always be curious and ask questions. These are the prerequisite skills and qualities for anyone who strives to create ground-breaking innovations and generate value for people and business.

LZF
MARIVI CALVO, SANDRO TOTHILL
— Wood touched by light.

Red Dot
→ Sound Design: p. 290

LZF is a company producing handmade, wood-veneer lighting. It was set up in 1995 by a team of communication designers. To launch the new brand, the owners, Marivi Calvo and Sandro Tothill, implemented communication and graphic design campaigns and memorable events which caught people's attention.

In 2007, Emilio Lekuona joined the team and, together with Marivi Calvo, developed a specific form and look for the campaigns using a theme which united events and products as well as creating a timeline which told a story. The latest theme is High Fidelity. Basing it on jazz and cover art from the 50s and 60s, LZF collaborated with the musician and producer Etienne Stehelin II to give each light in the collection its own accompanying song.

What do you understand by good communication design?
Good communication design is like a train that takes you to your destination. It also gives you a key that lets you access the product and explore it in your own way.

What are the qualities a successful communication designer must have?
Basically there are three: a) Designers must be honest with what they propose and sincere about the product and/or the brand. b) They must be able to create a campaign that transmits the values of the company and brand in a way that positively benefits anyone who comes in contact with it. c) Finally, a communication designer must understand the product and brand and also comprehend and realise the expectations aroused by them.

MELTING ELEMENTS
BORIS JUHL
— The art of making complicated things look easy.

Red Dot: Best of the Best
→ Mobile & Apps: p. 236-237

Boris Juhl, born in 1985, completed his degree in 2010 with a Master of Information Management and Corporate Communication and today works as an interface designer and user experience concept developer. Amongst other things, he designs user surfaces to make everyday life easier both in the private and the professional sphere. As creative director since 2011, he has visually and conceptually put his mark on all the mobile apps, websites and campaigns of Hamburg agency melting elements. The agency's work has won several awards including the German prize for economic communications, the Deutscher Preis für Wirtschaftskommunikation, on two separate occasions, the iF communication design award and the Red Dot: Best of the Best.

What do you understand by good communication design?
Good communication design touches a nerve with the viewer, ties him into the message and leaves behind a visual impression that is also recognisable in other media.

With whom would you like to work?
Dieter Rams. His inspired reduction of analogue control elements transferred to frequently intricate digital interfaces is absolutely worth striving for.

What kind of project would you like to realise?
My dream is one day to develop a completely new control system for a car. I believe that modern navigation and entertainment systems could be much more intuitive – despite the ever increasing number of new functions.

Designer Portraits

MOMKAI
— We design and develop innovative digital projects that truly inspire, inform and interact.

Red Dot: Grand Prix
→ Online World: p. 142-143

Red Dot: Best of the Best
→ Interface Design: p. 194-195

Red Dot
→ Online World: p. 154

Momkai is an independent, digital creative agency founded in November 2002. It combines clear design with solid technical realisation to create projects that truly inspire, inform and interact. Its designers could talk for hours about user interface design – why a shape should move a pixel to the right or the beauty of a clear line of code –, but they prefer to create projects rather than spend a long time describing them to partners and clients.

What do you understand by good communication design?
Good communication design is the ability to strike a balance between aesthetics and functionality.

Why did you become a communication designer?
At Momkai, we were not only motivated by the idea of making something that looks aesthetically pleasing. We wanted to add a layer of depth and functionality to our work, which is why we operate in the field of communication design.

What inspires you?
We think inspiration is a subconscious thing that occurs while you carry out your daily tasks. If you break inspiration down to its essence, daily interactions and experiences are at the heart of it.

What does the future of communication design look like?
The lines between seeing something in a digital environment and seeing it in your natural environment will continue to blur until those lines eventually become non-existent.

Designer Portraits

N!03 [ENNEZEROTRE]
— Creating narrative environments.

Red Dot: Grand Prix
→ Event Design: p. 18–19

Milan-based N!03 is a multimedia production studio founded in 2003 the aim of which is to function as an image-based research laboratory with a particular focus on the design of interactive and "total" video environments. It acts as a workplace, which investigates the design possibilities inherent in moving images, sound and space/architecture in order to come up with new opportunities to communicate and interact with the audience. The studio's methodology uses storytelling and narrative development as core elements and translates key messages into visual and conceptual metaphors to be used throughout the exhibition pathway. In 2011, N!03 won the Compasso d'Oro in the category Exhibition Design.

Which of your projects has been the biggest challenge for you so far?
In "The Soul of Rubber", the challenge was to find a balance between content and space through a process of extreme abstraction and synthesis.

What inspires you?
More than an inspiration, we try to follow a process that starts with content and ends with an audience.

What does the future of communication design look like?
We think that in the future we will be witnesses of a huge cross-media network creation in which cultural sites, such as museums and exhibitions, will represent the emerged part.

NATIONAL MUSEUM OF MODERN AND CONTEMPORARY ART, KOREA - DESIGN TEAM
— Back to basics – in terms of always considering the purpose of a project.

Red Dot
→ Event Design: p. 45

The design team of the National Museum of Modern and Contemporary Art, Korea (MMCA) consists of specialists in all design areas including space, graphic and product design, etc. The design team is charged with design-related works for exhibitions and audience services. For exhibition design projects, the staff specialists design the overall image according to the theme of an exhibit, make a title for the exhibit, structure the space and produce the graphic design as well as other promotional materials for communication with audiences using visual language. In addition, the design team is charged with designs for advertisements, events and cultural products to establish the identity of the National Museum and convey the image of MMCA to the people of Korea and across the world.

What are the qualities a successful communication designer must have?
In order to be a good designer, you should be able to project the feelings portrayed by an inanimate object and should not miss the purpose of the design.

What inspires you?
Natural phenomena are the teachers that provide endless inspiration and ideas.

What does the future of communication design look like?
As the industry develops and each area becomes specialised, not only design but all areas will come to understand why communication is important. Communication design helps to render the process of communication more convenient and smoother.

NINEFIVE
— Inspiration is given. Creativity is earned. Creativity is a craft honed by always delving deeper.

Red Dot
→ Mobile & Apps: p. 250
→ Mobile & Apps: p. 262-263

NINEFIVE, founded in 2011, is a focused team of digital media professionals with an uncanny knack for inspired design. As a full-service creative direction and interactive design studio, it helps brands connect with consumers by building engaging and interactive worlds via UX research, UI planning, conceptualisation, GUI design, as well as rich 2D/3D visualisations for web, applications, videos and installations. The studio has produced award-winning digital campaigns for clients including Samsung Electronics, LG Electronics and Samsung Semiconductors.

What do you understand by good communication design?
We believe good communication design starts from the perspective of the user. Sometimes a brilliantly thought-out design on paper can turn out to be unusable in the real world. We attempt to meld these two tensions of communication design – complex logical systems versus intuitive emotive experiences – and hopefully create just that – good communication design.

Which of your projects has been the biggest challenge for you so far?
Every project has its own set of challenges, but some come with unique circumstances that require a whole new paradigm of thinking.

What inspires you?
Inspiration is everywhere, wherever you look. To be aware of both space and time, as we go about our daily lives, is to seize the moment, in order to appreciate and take note of beautiful details.

MORIYUKI OCHIAI
— Create vivacious and lively beauty.

Red Dot
→ Event Design: p. 70-71

Moriyuki Ochiai, born in Tokyo, Japan, in 1973, is an architect and designer. In 2008, he established his own studio, Moriyuki Ochiai Architects that is active in architectural, landscape, interior, furniture and industrial design. The studio's work is inspired by the vivacious beauty of nature and life, and by the sensitivity with which the Japanese respond to their unique culture.

It has received numerous awards including the iF communication design award, German Design Award, Interior Design Best of Year Award (USA), SBID International Design Award (UK), International Architecture Award (USA), Design for Asia Award (Hong Kong) and Japan Commercial Environmental Design Award.

What do you understand by good communication design?
A design that appeals deeply to all five human senses.

Why did you become a communication designer?
I want to give people dreams and make them feel passionate, as well as generally to improve people's lives.

With whom would you like to work?
Neuroscientists and musicians, because together we have the potential to create something that responds to the consciousness of people and not only consists of forms.

Where and how do you gather information on trends?
I travel to many different countries and observe the lives of people there to gather information.

PIXELBUTIK
BY DELI PICTURES
JAN RICHTER
— Every frame of a film should look good hanging above the sofa.

Red Dot: Best of the Best
→ TV, Film, Cinema & Animation: p. 116–117

Jan Richter is a classical example of someone who has advanced through the ranks. Starting as an apprentice in the graphics department, he moved to 2D and 3D animation in the motion graphics department, then became motion designer and is currently a director of motion design films.

What do you understand by good communication design?
Translating complex, often unwieldy contents into beautiful, intelligible images.

What are the qualities a successful communication designer must have?
A delight in experimenting, patience, the ability to put him- or herself into the viewer's shoes, a feeling for harmony, etc.

Why did you become a communication designer?
I like beautiful pictures.

What inspires you?
Everything around me, humour, people, the work of other designers and artists – and music!

What else would you like to learn?
… that a good design takes time.

PIXELPARK / ELEPHANT SEVEN
KATJA BORSDORF, UDO HOFFMANN, MICHAEL LEDWIG

— The difficulty lies not in finding new ideas, but in getting rid of the old ones.

Red Dot: Best of the Best
→ Mobile & Apps: p. 232-233

Red Dot
→ Online World: p. 173
→ Online World: p. 178
→ Online World: p. 186-187
→ Interface Design: p. 223

Katja Borsdorf studied multimedia/virtual reality design at the Burg Giebichenstein Art School. When her diploma thesis won the Annual Multimedia Award 2010, she attracted the attention of digital agency Elephant Seven, where she now works as art director.

Udo Hoffmann, cabinetmaker and qualified media designer, worked in advertising, as well as event and film production before beginning to design interactive games and CD-ROMs. He then moved to Pixelpark where he has headed up the design department as creative director since 1999.

Michael Ledwig was already working for a number of different agencies in Krefeld and Düsseldorf during his training as design assistant for media and communication. He has been a senior designer at Pixelpark since 2011.

What do you understand by good communication design?
Good communication design is straightforward, honest and surprising.

What are the qualities a successful communication designer must have?
Patience and passion. Patience, because only rarely do all factors that make a project successful come together in the ideal combination in everyday working life. And passion is the motor that drives one to the continuous search for innovative ideas.

What does the future of communication design look like?
Communication is increasingly turning into one-to-one communication.

Designer Portraits

PXD
— People, experience and design.

Red Dot: Best of the Best
→ Interface Design: p. 198-199

pxd is a group of professionals providing consulting services in the areas of creative and innovative UI, GUI and service design based on user observation. The group provides its clients with product planning and service strategies based on a thorough understanding of the connection between product, technology, business and users. The key to pxd's business success lies in its keen insight into unarticulated user needs, gained through specialist and systematic methods of observation and analysis.

What do you understand by good communication design?
Designers' understanding of users' problems and clients' business goal is the first step towards good communication. We think good communication design depends on the designers' sincere empathy with users and clients.

What are the qualities a successful communication designer must have?
For designers, it is very important to sympathise with the users' problems and grasp clients' demands, because designers must, in the end, satisfy both. In addition, the ability to problem-solve and learn is also important.

What does the future of communication design look like?
We expect communication design to be more comprehensive in the future. However, there are many aspects that have not yet been studied. Thus, designers today should keep working on those areas and attempt a multidisciplinary approach to design.

SCHOLZ & VOLKMER
MAURICIO FRANICEVICH GARCIA, SEBASTIAN ZIRFAS
— Think positive, man!

Red Dot: Best of the Best
→ Online World: p. 144-145

Mauricio Franicevich Garcia, born in Buenos Aires in 1979, studied graphic design at the university there and later visual communication at the Academy of Art and Design Offenbach. He has worked for a number of different agencies such as Razorfish and Armando Testa and, today, is art director at Scholz & Volkmer with a focus on digital design, print design, corporate identity, illustration and advertising.

Sebastian Zirfas, born in 1983, completed his degree in communication design at the University of Applied Sciences in Wiesbaden in 2008 and subsequently began working for Scholz & Volkmer as junior art director. Since 2011, he has been senior art director at their Berlin office in the department of interactive media, digital brand management and motion design.

What do you understand by good communication design?
It has to get the message across with as light a touch as possible. Regardless of whether it's a web app, image film, poster or guidance system. What counts is efficiency and whether it creates a thrill.

What are the qualities a successful communication designer must have?
He should be curious, be able to surprise people, work cleanly and be memorable for at least one particular trait.

With whom would you like to work?
With the manufacturer of large construction machinery or diggers. This area has great potential for staging things.

SMART MOBILE FACTORY
SABINE BRAMBACH
— Designers are thought leaders!

Red Dot
→ Mobile & Apps: p. 254

Sabine Brambach studied design in Munich as well as in San Francisco and worked for various design studios and advertising agencies in the US, Germany and India (Scholz & Friends Interactive, incorporate berlin, Please See) before joining Smart Mobile Factory in 2012 as creative director. Always driven by her desire to learn and focus on content driven design, she has developed her skills in line with trends in technology starting from corporate through web to app design.

What do you understand by good communication design?
"Don't make me think" is a classic in the literature about web design. Although the book was published in 2002, its underlying concept remains pertinent. Clearly structured content and accessibility are what matters most in times of 24/7 information overload. Employing best-in-class usability design relieves the user of having to think and makes them focus on the content. Guiding users in their actions is the key component of good communication design.

What are the qualities a good communication designer must have?
A good communication designer has to work like an actor in a theatre. As a designer you must be able to assume the different roles of the potential users of the application. Establishing an astonishing design and personal style are important, but you should never loose track of focusing on the user and creating added value for him or her.

STEREOLIZE
— presenting tomorrow.

Red Dot: Best of the Best
→ Interface Design: p. 192-193

Red Dot
→ Interface Design: p. 221

stereolize was founded in 1994 as a motion design agency. The upcoming demand for motion graphics was driven by television and soon paired with brand development. Around 2000, industry clients detected the power of motion branding and stereolize expanded into the field of corporate communication. During a project for Microsoft, the agency discovered presentation design as a business area and, as a result, developed the realtime presentation software VENTUZ. VENTUZ was built around the agency's design philosophy and later split off as a separate company. stereolize quickly specialised in the field of high-end presentations and operates in design, technological innovation and presentation consulting.

What are the qualities a successful communication designer must have?
The ability to listen thoroughly, to get to know the client's interpretation of his own aim. Then, the ability to ignore these results confidently in order to find the real key issues. Question your own ideas, change them, bring them to life until the result is what you would buy yourself and still love – not the other way round.

With whom would you like to work?
With whoever inspires us to think ahead, to cross the line and to evolve, because this is what drives us and what we love.

What inspires you?
Simplicity, beauty and the end of the known. Words like "impossible", as well as attitudes like "go on".

SUH ARCHITECTS
EULHO SUH
—To be a good architect, a good father and a good husband.

Red Dot
→ Event Design: p. 48-49

Eulho Suh received an undergraduate Bachelor of Architecture from the Rhode Island School of Design and a post-professional degree from the Harvard University Graduate School of Design in Massachusetts, USA. He then worked at Morphosis Architects in Santa Monica, California and for Kohn Pedersen Fox in New York before founding Suhdesign in Los Angeles in 2004 and Suh Architects in Seoul, Korea, in 2006. Eulho Suh has since completed a range of commercial, recreational, and residential projects, while also serving as a design consultant for various companies. He has been a visiting critic at several architecture schools, and is currently teaching at Seoul National University.

What do you understand by good communication design?
A design with impact is simple and memorable. The process required to create that simple experience may have been extremely laborious, but a clear design leaves an impression that is surprising yet obvious.

What are the qualities a successful communication designer must have?
He/she is as good as his/her team and collaborators. We seek out engineers, artists, and designers willing to go the extra mile to work with us in deciding which opportunities to pursue. We unravel the story together; the common denominator is probably a sense of adventure, hope and craftsmanship, of course.

Designer Portraits

DO HO SUH
— To be a better person.

Red Dot: Best of the Best
→ TV, Film, Cinema & Animation: p. 114-115

Do Ho Suh is renowned Korean artist whose site-specific installations and meticulously crafted sculptures question boundaries of identity and conventional notions of scale and space in both its physical and metaphorical manifestation. His works have been presented in the world's leading museums, including the Museum of Modern Art in New York, the Whitney Museum of American Art at Philip Morris in New York, the Tate Modern in London, and Serpentine Gallery in London. His recent solo exhibitions and projects include The Perfect Home at 21st Century Museum of Contemporary Art, Kanazawa, Japan, Fallen Star in Stuart Collection, University of California, San Diego, and Home within Home at Leeum – Samsung Museum of Art, Seoul. Do Ho Suh lives and works in London, New York and Seoul.

What do you understand by good communication design?
Besides life in general, I'm inspired by architectural space, clothing and food – three essential elements of the human condition.

What inspires you?
Life in general is very inspiring. To be specific, I'm inspired by architectural space, clothing and food – three essential elements of the human condition.

What does the future of communication design look like?
It will engage with every element of the viewer's sensory system through different media incorporating space, sound, movement, smell and taste, as well as atmospheric elements including light and air.

Designer Portraits

TANGOMIKE
KYUNGSEOK HAHM
— Work hard, play harder.

Red Dot: Best of the Best
→ Mobile & Apps: p. 228–229

Kyungseok Hahm received a Bachelor of Engineering from Korea University before working at Samsung Electronics Telecommunication Network. He then went back to school to study communication design at SADI (Samsung Art and Design Institute) focusing on the synergy between design and technology. In 2011, Kyungseok Hahm founded the interactive design studio VOID Creative working for clients such as Samsung Museum of Art Leeum, UNICEF, Samsung Electronics and Switzerland Tourism. Together with friends who had also studied at SADI, he founded the interactive design company Tangomike in early 2013. He works there as a designer and creative coder.

What do you understand by good communication design?
Good communication design delivers a clear message.

Which of your projects has been the biggest challenge for you so far?
The Leeum Interactive Project was a big challenge for me because the project had to solve the dilemma posed by combining ancient artefacts and new technology – two very different aspects.

Why did you become a communication designer?
I always wanted to try something new when I began studying design. Communication design was a perfect design field for me even with my engineering background.

With whom would you like to work?
Daft Punk. Music, technology and design.

TISCH13
CARSTEN RÖHR
— Using first-class ideas to draw attention to brands across all media channels.

Red Dot: Best of the Best
→ Event Design: p. 20-21

Carsten Röhr studied communication design at Akademie U5 in Munich. From 2000, he worked in the city as junior art director for Jung von Matt, then moved to d.efect as managing director in 2001. That same year, he founded tisch13 together with Heidi Bücherl. This owner-run design agency, focused on two- and three-dimensional brand communication in Munich, is characterised by its cross-media approach and its feel for new communication possibilities and trends. With its team of 30 employees, who have grown into a team of experts, it orchestrates international trade fair appearances, interactive applications and outstanding brand experiences.

What do you understand by good communication design?
Communication design must touch people and trigger emotions, but can never be narcissistic.

What are the qualities a successful communication designer must have?
He should be hungry and have a feeling for trends and styles. He should never think he had learnt everything there is to learn. Every day brings new challenges.

Which of your projects has been the biggest challenge for you so far?
The conversion of our own office. One's own projects always turn out to be the most challenging.

What inspires you?
Everything around us can be inspiring. One just has to keep one's eyes open!

Designer Portraits

ZEROS+ONES
LUCA CAPELLETTI
— Carpe diem!

Red Dot
→ Mobile & Apps: p. 260-261

Luca Capelletti, born in Cesena in 1963, obtained the technical baccalaureate from the Istituto Tecnico Industriale Statale in Forlì and went on to work as technical draughtsman. In 1986, he set off to travel the world and then worked as industrial designer, before moving to Germany in 1990 and spending all his savings on acquiring a Macintosh IIci. That was the simplest, most enduring and carefree decision of his life. Between 1990 and 1993, he worked for publishing houses and advertising agencies in Munich. In 1993, he founded zeros+ones GmbH together with Torsten Green, Michael Teltscher and Dietrich Hueck. Since then, he has worked on projects for Audi, BMW, Bayerischer Rundfunk, Deutsche Bank, E.ON and ZDF, to name but a few.

What do you understand by good communication design?
Good communication design is empathetic communication (empátheia = passion).

Which of your projects has been the biggest challenge for you so far?
Every single one, as designers are often viewed as mere surface creators (even by clients). However, the true challenge for designers remains to reduce complexity, to make things more approachable, and to communicate content and inspiration.

What does the future of communication design look like?
The flood of information will keep on growing in future. Communication design must therefore focus even more on clarity and on becoming transparent and inconspicuous.

INTERNATIONAL YEARBOOK COMMUNICATION DESIGN 2013/2014

AUGSBURG UNIVERSITY OF APPLIED SCIENCES / FALMOUTH UNIVERSITY
— They think it's all over. Well, is it really?

Red Dot: Best of the Best
→ Red Dot: Junior Award
  Editorial: p. 302-303

35 design students from the University of Applied Sciences in Augsburg, Germany and Falmouth University believe in the power of creative ideas and in them being an integral part of their training. The collaboration between Ashley Rudolph, Senior Lecturer on the BA (Hons) Graphic Design course at Falmouth University, and Prof. Stefan Bufler, leading the Identity Design study programme at the University of Applied Sciences in Augsburg, dates from a trip to England in May 2010 by members of the Augsburg Design Faculty. Since then, the cross-border exchange of Erasmus students and lecturers has become the norm for both universities, as has a joint approach to projects.

What do you understand by good communication design?
Owen Harvey: It conveys information and ideas concisely and effectively to its target audience. The viewer should be actively engaged with the information via the use of visual wit and decoration.

Why did you become a communication designer?
Henrike Großer: As a communication designer you gain insight into a tremendous variety of subjects and mindsets. That way the job stays exciting and interesting.

What kind of project would you like to realise?
Jessica Webb: The perfect project would be the one that would test your knowledge, push you to your limits and communicate your idea in a way that you have not done before, both with your peers and your audience.

Designer Portraits

SHIH-LUN CHEN, YU-RU CHO, SIAO-HUEI TANG, JIA-HONG LIN

— The integration of oriental and western cultures is our precious treasure.

Red Dot
→ Red Dot: Junior Award
　Typography: p. 368

Shih-Lun Chen, associate professor and chairman of the department of visual communication design at China University of Technology, Taiwan, and creative director at Rice Advertising, has dedicated himself to the profession and education of design for years. The international and well known design awards he received include the iF Communication Gold Award 2012, the CF Golden Bell Award (by the Executive Yuan of Taiwan), and Grand Gold Award of Magazines (in Taiwan 11th Times Advertising Awards). Jia-Hong Lin, Yu-Ru Cho and Siao-Huei Tang are graduates of the department of visual communication design at China University of Technology, Taiwan, and, in 2013, were very successful in the Taiwan Young Designers' Awards.

Why did you become a communication designer?
Long having been influenced by and highly interested in Chinese culture and global design trends, I chose the career of designer.

Which of your projects has been the biggest challenge for you so far?
Promoting the culture of Chinese characters via design.

With whom would you like to work?
I love to see how my students improve and develop when we work together on design projects.

What inspires you?
Chinese culture, especially calligraphy and the inscriptions on bone shells.

YA-CHI CHIU, LEE-WA LIN, CHENG-EN CHANG, YAN-YU HUANG, YAN-TING CHEN
— The devil is in the detail.

Red Dot: Best of the Best
→ Red Dot: Junior Award
  Illustrations: p. 314-315

Red Dot
→ Red Dot: Junior Award
  Packaging Design: p. 336

Ya-Chi Chiu, Lee-Wa Lin, Cheng-En Chang, Yan-Yu Huang and Yan-Ting Chen all studied visual communication design at Asia University in Taichung, Taiwan, and graduated or are about to graduate in 2013. They specialise in different fields and create projects ranging from graphic design to illustration and packaging design.

What developments do you currently see in your industry?
An increasing number of industries work with design. That has lead to the establishment of ever more art places and art jobs. Designers have the platform to present their work. Taiwan appreciates these creative members of society.

How do you approach new projects?
Firstly, by thinking and gathering information. Then, after absorbing and transforming it, we have a team discussion. When faced with difficulties, we clarify the opinions of the team and solve problems using the professional expertise of each team member.

What inspires you?
Text, music, movies, everything really – and everyone around us.

Which role does communication design play in our everyday life?
It is as important for us as water for the body.

HSUN-YANG CHO, TIAN-YU GUO, YING-TING LYOU, GUAN-LING LU, TAI-HSIN LIN, YU-TIAN SUN

— Our idea of design is goal-oriented and all about aesthetic balance.

Red Dot: Best of the Best
→ Red Dot: Junior Award
  Editorial: p. 308-309

Hsun-Yang Cho, Tian-Yu Guo, Ying-Ting Lyou, Guan-Ling Lu, Tai-Hsin Lin and Yu-Tian Sun are all students of visual communication design at Shu-Te University, Kaohsiung, Taiwan. They specialise in different fields of design, including sketching, structural packaging, animation, and many others. The team divides its work very carefully and works together harmoniously and efficiently.

What do you understand by good communication design?
It can convey ideas to the audience and is equipped with the aesthetics to influence people in real life.

What kind of project would you like to realise?
In addition to inventing different types of folding paper books in Taiwan, we would like to work on some projects that integrate art into design.

With whom would you like to work?
We hope to work with people who cherish the same ideals and take the same approach as us or seek interdisciplinary cooperation in order to develop more design ideas.

What does the future of communication design look like?
It will develop based on market and cultural needs and result in a more caring and problem-solving orientation.

PHILIPP DETTMER
— Understanding through design.

Red Dot: Best of the Best
→ Red Dot: Junior Award
  TV, Film, Cinema & Animation: p. 318–319

Philipp Dettmer initially studied history at the Ludwig Maximilian University in Munich, but then became increasingly interested in the visualisation of information. He switched industries and studied communication design at the design faculty of Munich University of Applied Sciences with an emphasis on infographics and visual aspects of knowledge transfer. Since graduating he has worked as a freelance information designer for various media productions while simultaneously building up a network of like-minded people who are passionately committed to imparting knowledge and education in an easy-to-understand and vivid way.

What do you understand by good communication design?
It conveys information and is, at the same time, of great aesthetic value.

With whom would you like to work?
With scientists of all disciplines, educational institutes or video production companies. My greatest dream is to make science more accessible and to educate people further. Given the right specialists, learning in Germany could be transformed and restructured in such a way that school-age children and students would learn with more enjoyment and curiosity.

What inspires you?
Books. Above all factual books about complicated scientific topics, but also children's books. They represent both ends of the spectrum – difficult to understand and readily accessible. You can easily park me in a bookshop for hours.

DONG YUEXI
— Our future is in our own hands and opportunities are available to all of us.

Red Dot
→ Red Dot: Junior Award
  Editorial: p. 344-345

Dong Yuexi, born in Beijing, China, in 1989, is a graduate student in the department of visual communication design at Central Academy of Fine Arts (CAFA), Beijing. He has received many international awards, including the Red Dot Award, Art Directors Club New York, China International Young Designers, Tencent Innovative Grand Prize, Apple Chinese College Best Experience Award and the CAFA Excellent Graduation Works First Prize. He has participated in many exhibitions, e.g. at the CAFA Art Museum, the Art Directors Club New York, the Finland Co-Core Art and Design World Conference, the Asian Art Fair and the Taipei IDA Congress, and is working as designer for the Nanjing 2014 Youth Olympic Games and the Nanjing 2013 Asian Youth Games.

Which of your projects has been the biggest challenge for you so far?
I think challenging ourselves is the most difficult; design is not just about winning over the client or others. Designers are expected to transcend themselves and fight against stubbornness, laziness and for a fluke on their mind in this process, so that they can keep moving forward, keep walking and keep creating a better future.

Why did you become a communication designer?
I like creating surprises and finding connections between different objects. As a designer specialising in visual communication, I get to deal with and reflect on many things that I've never imagined before, and then create surprises with my design.

Designer Portraits

JU-HO HAN, DA-WOON JUNG, KYUNG-CHAN AHN
— No challenge, no gain.

Red Dot
→ Red Dot: Junior Award
　Print Advertising: p.341

Ju-Ho Han, Da-Woon Jung and Kyung-Chan Ahn majored in visual design at Gachon University in Incheon, South Korea. Together, they formed a group called "The GrandSlam" which has taken part in numerous design competitions demonstrating great tenacity and passion. Not afraid to make mistakes, the group has made failure a steppingstone to success. Challenges always make their hearts beat faster.

Why did you become a communication designer?
Our constant aim is to be "caring designers" for people living in a tougher environment than we do. Although our design activities might not bring about many changes in society, we will continue to strive ..., if there is even the slightest chance of introducing small, positive changes for such people.

What does the future of communication design look like?
We will have increasing access to other people, but for a much shorter period of time. That means public attention will not last very long. Designers will therefore have to develop very innovative, influential and memorable designs that will stay in people's minds after a short time. That will lead to more visually stimulating design that will reach a greater number of people more easily and at minimal cost.

SUSANNE HARTMANN

Red Dot: Best of the Best
→ Red Dot: Junior Award
  Corporate Design: p. 298-299

Susanne Hartmann studied graphic design at hKDM Hochschule für Kunst, Design und Populäre Musik in the southern German town of Freiburg im Breisgau. After a number of internships, she went on to work as graphic designer and exhibition organiser for companies in the Basel and Freiburg area. In 2010, she decided to add a master's degree from the Masterstudio Design at the Academy of Art and Design in Basel. Her master's thesis "Morphogen – The Crystallisation of Acoustics" was based on her interest in audiovisual correlations. Today, she works as a brand designer while also teaching at the Academy of Art and Design in Basel and pursuing private projects in the area of media art.

What are the qualities a successful communication designer must have?
As generally known he/she should be a good observer, work hard and be critical. But he/she should also be aware of the fact that a wide spectrum of interests and curiosity are powerful driving forces in this profession as well, because the interface with relevant societal and scientific subjects requires careful research every single time.

With whom would you like to work?
Working with musicians whose music I like is my favourite. But also with scientists, whose research methods and outlook on the world open up new perspectives.

What inspires you?
Conversations about realities, identities, perception, music and mathematics.

Designer Portraits

MU-HUAI HSUEH, TZE-YEN JUANG, CHING-WEN CHANG, BING-RU YANG, CHENG-YANG CHEN

— When it comes to creativity, the possibilities are limitless.

Red Dot
→ Red Dot: Junior Award
  Posters: p. 364-365

Mu-Huai Hsueh, Tze-Yen Juang, Ching-Wen Chang, Bing-Ru Yang and Cheng-Yang Chen are part of a team based in the department of visual communication design at Shu-Te University, Kaohsiung, Taiwan. These five team members are responsible for the image design of the Visual Ark project, which appeared in the graduation exhibition of 2013. Mu-Huai Hsueh was in charge of the visual design, Tze-Yen Juang did the illustration design, Ching-Wen Chang was responsible for the graphic design, Bing-Ru Yang took care of the exhibition layout, and Cheng-Yang Chen handled the multimedia design.

What are the qualities a successful communication designer must have?
He or she should be good at communicating with others and be able to think carefully before taking action bravely.

Why did you become a communication designer?
Because we are passionate about design. Designing things is everything for us.

With whom would you like to work?
We are happy to work with anyone in order to increase our experience and learn from the process.

What inspires you?
Beautiful, touching and impressive things inspire us the most.

Designer Portraits

MUSTAFA KARAKAŞ
— Typography expresses more than a thousand words.

Red Dot: Junior Prize
→ Red Dot: Junior Award
  Posters: p. 294–297

Mustafa Karakaş is a designer focused on typography, editorial design and photography. Following his training as a technical design assistant, he studied mechanical engineering, as well as media communication in the design faculty of University of Applied Sciences and Arts in Dortmund. He has already been awarded a prize for his work by the Art Directors Club Germany. Beyond that, his work has been nominated for the German Design Award 2013.

What do you understand by good communication design?
Conceptual and content-related work has to be the priority. It should always attempt to highlight new approaches to solving problems. Design has to trigger feelings and emotions, make people think, be fun, attract attention and, above all, work.

Which of your projects has been the biggest challenge for you so far?
My work on "women's rights". Political and religious topics always present a particular challenge.

What inspires you?
Good work by other designers encourages me to dare and provides me with motivation and inspiration. Positive competition always helps to keep one on one's toes.

Designer Portraits

XIAO-HAN LAI, SU-HUEI CHEN, SZU-JUNG HO, YI-TING DONG, YU-ZHENG LIN, CHE-WEI HSU

— Our design philosophy is about dramatic real life.

Red Dot
→ Red Dot: Junior Award
 Editorial: p. 352–353

The project was created by a group of people who are experts in different design areas. By brainstorming and combining traditional and innovative ideas, they want to imbue their work with love and care.

What do you understand by good communication design?
Good work can communicate with audiences and touch them as well.

Which of your projects has been the biggest challenge for you so far?
The biggest challenge is to think about how to use interesting and creative ways to make people understand traditional Taiwanese culture and spirit.

Why did you become a communication designer?
Because we love design, enjoy life, and want to colour the world.

What inspires you?
All kinds of life experiences.

What does the future of communication design look like?
Technology will definitely become the communication bridge for designers.

Designer Portraits

SOL-E LEE, HEEYEON JUNG

— Hardware and Software should never be separated. Good ideas create a synergy effect by connecting product and interface.

Red Dot: Best of the Best
→ Red Dot: Junior Award
　Mobile & Apps: p. 322-323

Sol-E Lee and Heeyeon Jung are a couple of 24-year-old friends studying interaction and product design at Hanyang University in Korea. While Sol-E Lee's role is graphic design, Heeyeon Jung is responsible for product design. The Planto project was developed by the two of them in collaboration.

What do you understand by good communication design?
We think the critical thing about communication design is understanding the user and providing what he wants. That means, we are always on the lookout for what the user wants and needs. Achieving that makes design successful and clever.

Which of your projects has been the biggest challenge for you so far?
For this project, we merged our two roles. As a result, we managed to create an interactive digital device with analogue aesthetics.

Why did you become a communication designer?
Communication design is something essential that has no boundaries. We therefore want to try new things and challenge ourselves.

What else would you like to learn?
We want to learn more about interaction and product design.

Designer Portraits

SAMANTHA LEWIS
— Everyone is just making it up as they go along.

Frank Chimero

Red Dot: Best of the Best
→ Red Dot: Junior Award
  Typography: p. 312-313

Samantha Lewis graduated from Massey University in 2012 with a degree in visual communication, majoring in graphic design. During her study she became interested in designing for social change, and concentrated her final year on creating a typographic solution for adult learners with low literacy levels. She now works as a designer at Base Two in Wellington. In 2012 she received a Merit from the International Society of Typographic Designers and was a finalist in the DINZ Best Design Awards.

What do you understand by good communication design?
A feeling and energy about the content is created through great design.

Why did you become a communication designer?
I began by studying fine arts, but found that I need some limitations and boundaries to drive the work I created. After taking some time out, my love for type became more apparent as I became increasingly bored not working in a creative profession. I then went back to university to study graphic design.

What inspires you?
Learning new things, great conversations, and my physical surroundings and environments within New Zealand. Learning about wider community and political issues that can impact people's lives provides inspiration for finding a potential solution.

PO-HUA LIN, REN-WEI PAN, YUNG-CHING CHEN, SHIH-YU HUANG, SHAN-YAO YANG, LI-TING KAO

— Design is our life. We do it for our own happiness but also in order to serve others.

Red Dot
→ Red Dot: Junior Award
 Corporate Design: p. 325

Po-Hua Lin, born in Taiwan, dreamt of becoming a designer ever since he was a child. His aim is to use design in order to enhance the quality of life. Ren-Wei Pan studied design and has since been recognised for his work with a series of awards. Yung-Ching Chen, born in Taoyuan, Taiwan, in 1991, graduated from China University of Technology in the department of visual communication design. Shih-Yu Huang studied design for seven years. Shan-Yao Yang and Li-Ting Kao are passionate students of design.

What do you understand by good communication design?
Practicability.

What are the qualities a successful communication designer must have?
Humour and perseverance.

Why did you become a communication designer?
Because we are really passionate about communication design.

What inspires you?
Travelling and photography.

Where and how do you gather information on trends?
From the Internet and bookstores.

What does the future of communication design look like?
It will achieve greater recognition than it does today.

Designer Portraits

YURIY MATVEEV, SOPHIA PREUSSNER, NIKOLAS BRÜCKMANN

Red Dot: Best of the Best
→ Red Dot: Junior Award
Editorial: p. 310-311

Nikolas Brückmann, born in Rüsselsheim in 1983, and Yuriy Matveev, born in Lvov, Ukraine, in 1985, began studying visual communication in 2005 at the University of Art and Design Offenbach. Since 2007, they have worked together as freelance artists, designers and art directors, from 2012 onwards under the name sure.is.

Born in Riesa in 1985, Sophia Preußner studied art history, art education and philosophy before switching to the University of Art and Design Offenbach in 2009 to study conceptual design and illustration. Since 2011, she has been working as a freelance art director for a number of different clients and agencies and, in 2012/2013, won a Germany Scholarship.

What are the qualities a successful communication designer must have?
Nikolas Brückmann/Yuriy Matveev: Intuition and intelligence.

Why did you become a communication designer?
Sophia Preußner: As a communication designer, you keep changing perspective, but are simultaneously confronted with a type of evanescence, which one has come to grips with. One can adhere to traditional design or combine it with contemporary trends. It is possible to interpret a briefing in a highly individual manner that requires an interdisciplinary approach.

BRODIE NEL, JOSHUA THOMPSON

— Combining collaboration, execution and exploration for effective visual communication.

Red Dot: Best of the Best
→ Red Dot: Junior Award
 Illustrations: p. 316-317

Brodie Nel and Joshua Thompson recently graduated from Massey University with a degree in visual communication design majoring in illustration. They now work as freelancers creating and executing good illustration design. Inspired by design that pushes stylistic boundaries and communicates effectively with the viewer they offer a wide range of styles to satisfy any potential client's illustrative needs. Currently, they are working on editorial illustrations e.g. for the Scriptus Literary Journal and the Massive Magazine.

What do you understand by good communication design?
It is built on three key elements: form, function, and aesthetic. That's your platform for communication, without it you may as well say nothing.

What inspires you?
Hemingway said something along the lines of "if it's bad I'll hate it, if it's good I'll envy it and hate it even more". Weirdly this insecurity drives us further into the unknown. We feel the more you expose yourself to amazing design and creativity, the more you question your own.

What kind of project would you like to realise?
We would love to see our comic come to life as a series. We have mothered it from a few sketches into a comic. To see it reach maturity as a series and make its way into the world is a dream of ours.

PEI-LING OU
— Design is a language of communication.

Red Dot
→ Red Dot: Junior Award
   Posters: p. 362-363

Pei-Ling Ou is a student of visual communication art at Shu-Te University, Kaohsiung, Taiwan. She won third place in the iF concept design award 2013 and is passionate about graphic design.

What do you understand by good communication design?
Good design is simple but able to convey ideas to the audience successfully.

What are the qualities a successful communication designer must have?
He or she should be very observant, confident and persistent.

What inspires you?
Watching movies inspires my imagination the most.

What kind of project would you like to realise?
I want to work on graphic design books and similar things.

What does the future of communication design look like?
There will be more and more digital work created by and for personal tablet computers, which will eventually replace traditional non-digital print media.

JEONG HO PARK
— Stay hungry. Stay foolish.

Steve Jobs

Red Dot
→ Red Dot: Junior Award
   Editorial: p. 306-307

Jeong Ho Park, born in South Korea, studied mineral and resources engineering, graduating in 2003. As soon as he graduated, he was accepted as intern by a design studio which rapidly took him on as a full-time designer. Throughout his career, Jeong Ho Park has worked in a variety of disciplines for notable clients such as Hyundai and Samsung. He has designed promotional and marketing materials, ranging from brochures, posters, magazines, branding and publishing material to packaging. In 2011, Jeong Ho Park moved to the USA and joined the MFA programme to study graphic design with a focus on information graphics at Minneapolis College of Art and Design, where he graduated in 2013.

What inspires you?
I have always been inspired by people who are passionate and try to make things new or better. It is not important whether they are designers or not. One of my favourite online sources is TED Talk, which shares numerous amazing people's ideas, stories, and passion.

What else would you like to learn?
I am interested in combining hybrid media to allow viewers to observe data across traditional and new media. It would make visual representation of data more interactive, engaging and effective.

Why did you become a communication designer?
I am fundamentally interested in communicating using visual language.

GRAEDON PARKER
— Love the life you live, live the life you love.

Red Dot: Best of the Best
→ Red Dot: Junior Award
   Online World: p. 320-321

Graedon Parker wanted to be a designer when he was still in kindergarten. At high school, he started getting into graffiti, winning competitions and a High Achievers Scholarship to Massey University in Wellington, New Zealand. He made the move to university and, in his final year, decided to focus on a huge health problem in New Zealand seeking to communicate solutions to the general public. This gave birth to the "Education not Medication" project. Upon graduating, Graedon Parker became a freelancer working in the field of magazine editorials, layouts and identities. On the side, "Education not Medication" has branched off into a grassroots "smoothie" company called "The Organic Mechanic".

What are the qualities a successful communication designer must have?
A positive outlook on life and a knack for self-motivation in an almost psychotic sense. A clean diet with good water, sunlight and exercise is also a must if one is to throw off all of those hours spent snuggling up with a computer.

What inspires you?
Life, especially travelling through the countryside, and even navigating through traffic. It is amazing to see the diverse range of life that inhabits this planet.

What kind of project would you like to realise?
I would love to nail an educational campaign that helps people become more aware of their place in the cosmic orientation of life. To help people realise profound, simple truths and see behind the veil of the society we live in.

SUSANNE PRETTEREBNER
— Inspire! (For design brings responsibility with it.)

Red Dot: Best of the Best
→ Red Dot: Junior Award
   Editorial: p. 304-305

Susanne Pretterebner, born in the Austrian town of Klagenfurt, studied industrial design at the FH JOANNEUM – University of Applied Sciences in Graz where she graduated as designer. She went on to complete an overseas internship as product designer in Singapore and, as a lateral entrant, subsequently added master's studies in communication design with a focus on media and interaction design also in Graz. She graduated with distinction and today works as a graphic designer.

What are the qualities a successful communication designer must have?
A successful communication designer mustn't be satisfied with the first available result. Solutions aren't arrived at immediately – one's gut feeling tells one when idea and execution come together.

Why did you become a communication designer?
I came to realise during my industrial design degree course, that my true love was for communication design. It combines aesthetics, imagination and social aspects in a unique way.

What kind of project would you like to realise?
A cause close to my heart is to inform as many people as possible of the important topic of nutrition and climate protection, which I covered in my master's thesis.

BAIHAO QIU, WEIMING LAI, CHUN-YAT ZHAO

— This work follows the pattern of Taiwanese butterfly culture seeking to create touching moments.

Red Dot
→ Red Dot: Junior Award
  Illustrations: p. 374-375

Baihao Qiu, Weiming Lai and Chun-Yat Zhao are students of visual communication design at Shu-Te University in Kaohsiung, Taiwan. They fell in love with Taiwanese butterfly culture and have created different graphic design projects in order to promote it. They are specialised in both graphic design and illustration.

What do you understand by good communication design?
It can fully convey the designer's ideas to the audience or can feed its imagination.

With whom would you like to work?
We would like to work with people who care about the world and make use of the power of visual communication to help those who are in need.

What inspires you?
Anything ranging from trivial things to well-known events can inspire us. We believe good designers from different disciplines need to think outside the box in order to broaden their views.

What kind of project would you like to realise?
We would like to work on a project that can fully represent local characteristics, remodelling forgotten cultural elements.

Designer Portraits

MI-NA WEI, CHING-CHIA CHIOU
— Strive in every moment.

Red Dot: Best of the Best
→ Red Dot: Junior Award
   Packaging Design: p. 300-301

Mi-Na Wei, born in Taiwan, is a student of visual communication design at Asia University in Taichung, Taiwan. She believes design springs from human nature and culture, and that the world is full of friendship and love.
Ching-Chia Chiou, born in Taiwan, majored in visual communication design at Asia University in Taichung, Taiwan. Drawing and reading magazines since his childhood, he later became interested in design. He believes the purpose of design is to solve problems and present them in beautiful way.

How do you approach new projects?
We collect data, discuss it with team members and work on our share.

What inspires you?
Good design and unsolved problems.

What do you understand by good communication design?
Good communication design works regardless of nationality, race and language. The user and viewer will experience deep and strong recognition.

With whom would you like to work?
We would like to cooperate with people from a variety of fields, because we can learn different ideas and things from them.

Why did you become a communication designer?
Just out of curiosity.

Designer Portraits

FU-CIANG YANG, SIAN-JHEN ZENG, YAN-YI KUO, HONG-YI SHIH, YU-SHENG PAN, YU-SHU CHEN

— Cardinal Vices is the projection of human desires.

Red Dot
→ Red Dot: Junior Award
  Illustrations: p. 376-377

Fu-Ciang Yang, Sian-Jhen Zeng, Yan-Yi Kuo, Hong-Yi Shih, Yu-Sheng Pan and Yu-Shu Chen work as a team and call themselves Cardinal Vices. They love designing and care about social issues. Combining what they are good at individually they work on social problems present in Taiwanese culture.

What do you understand by good communication design?
Good communication design is simple but impressive, linking the thoughts of authors and audience.

What are the qualities a successful communication designer must have?
A good communication designer should be able to create great work with both value and emotion, which is touching and influential.

Which of your projects has been the biggest challenge for you so far?
The biggest challenge for us is how to keep a balance between designing projects and considering their market value.

What does the future of communication design look like?
We think future communication design will simultaneously appeal to different senses and will increasingly interact with audiences.

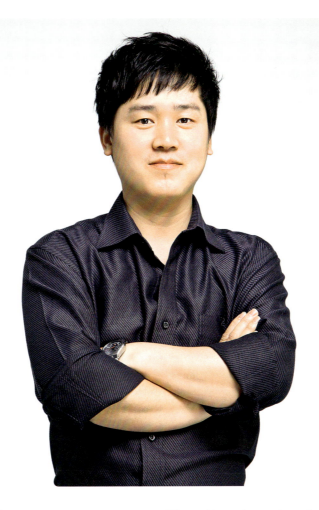

ZHANG YANGSHENG
— Designers should be good at producing spiritual resonance with their work.

Red Dot
→ Red Dot: Junior Award
  Corporate Design: p. 330-331

Zhang Yangsheng, born in Guixi City, China, in 1978, studied at Lanzhou University. After graduating from Jiangxi Normal University in 2000, he worked in the garment industry for ten years. During that time, he was awarded the National Outstanding Brand Management Division Prize. In 2011, Zhang Yangsheng returned to Lanzhou University to begin student life anew. He believes that design is not just art, and that every symbol, colour, information and architecture must be selected to maximise the brand value for a company. His approach is to understand the creation of brand popularity through business-related thinking and design methods.

What do you understand by good communication design?
Good communication design should impress the audience. Apart from innovative design thinking, it should also take into account environments, educational backgrounds, life styles and other aspects of communication objects. At the same time, good communication design should convey the positioning, cultural and value information of a brand in a suitable way, in order to obtain the audience's acceptance and arouse its empathy. Finally, it must achieve that goal through effective communication.

What are the qualities a successful communication designer must have?
A successful designer must have a wealth of first-hand emotional experience, followed by comprehensive knowledge. He has to move himself first in order to be able to move others.

INTERNATIONAL YEARBOOK COMMUNICATION DESIGN 2013/2014

VOL. 2

JURY PORTRAITS

Jury Portraits

01

RENNE ANGELVUO
FINLAND

Renne Angelvuo studied advertising, marketing and design at the Institute of Marketing in Helsinki and afterwards he studied art at the Free Art School Helsinki. Additionally, he works as a professional musician and producer. Since 1980, Renne Angelvuo has worked as an art director in the fields of advertising and design, before in 1994 he launched his first own company called PRIORITY Advertising & Design and his second one WIN WIN BRANDING in 2004. He has expertise in packaging design, industrial design, brand concepts and product innovations and is also a board member of the epda (European Packaging Design Association).

01 **THIS IN NOT CALVADOS**
Bottle

02 **The wild berry boxes**
have an innovative idea: A combination of wild bilberry with a high percentage of dark chocolate, which makes the product super healthy.

Jury Portraits

02

— GOOD DESIGN NEEDS A NEW INNOVATIVE IDEA, SIMPLE DESIGN AND GREAT EXECUTION, WHICH MANY PEOPLE LOVE.

When you think about the jury session: What will in particular stay in your mind?
I enjoyed very much such a great atmosphere in Essen during my whole stay. And, of course the jury session itself, the chance to see a lot of good design with great ideas and great execution was very interesting. Also to meet all jurors from around the world, sharing thoughts and having interesting discussions and lots of laughter, too. One more thing I had to add – the good food, wine and excellent company!

What do you think is the most important quality a designer must have to succeed?
A good designer has to have a vision and an innovative idea, he needs to think different, take risks and succeed to make a brilliant execution.

In your opinion, which feature or characteristic is most representative for Finnish design?
In my opinion in Finnish design there are three important, inseparable fundamentals: minimalism, aesthetics and functionalism. As an example Alvar Aalto's door handles: they look beautiful, feel good when touching and are long lasting, so very functional.

What is your life motto?
Innovative ideas are all you need!

Jury Portraits

01

ALI BATI
TURKEY

01 **CNN campaign**
    "Stories with the full background"

02 **WWF campaign**

Ali Batı is the most internationally-awarded art director in Turkey, winning over 100 national and international awards, including Cannes Lions, the New York Festivals, the Epica Awards, Eurobest, Golden Drum, the Crystal Apple Awards and several Effie Awards. Ali Batı's success came early on in his career. During his first year in advertising, he earned Turkey's first success at Cannes Lions, making him the youngest creative in Turkey to win an award at Cannes. In 2007, he went on to be awarded Art Director of the Year in Turkey by GMK (Turkish Society of Graphic Design).

Two years later he won two Lions, contributing to his agency ranking third on the Agency of the Year roll at the Cannes Lions International Festival of Creativity. In 2010, he was awarded two Lions, helping the agency to rank fourth in the Agency of the Year listing. He also brought three awards home from the 17th Golden Drum Advertising Festival, including Turkey's first Grand Prix. That same year, Ali Batı became the first Turkish creative to have his work published on the cover of Luerzer's Archive and was named by Luerzer's Archive as the number one art director in the world. He has worked at Rafineri, Fabrica (Italy), DDB&Co., Apple (London) and Lowe and Partners. Last year, Ali Batı gained his PhD in Graphic Design at the University of Marmara, where he previously completed his BA.

02

— GOOD DESIGN
NEEDS A GOOD IDEA.

What are the most challenging aspects of your job?
I work for different brands and on different products every day. Rather than just having challenging aspects, every brief is a totally new challenge in and of itself.

What does being a Red Dot juror for the first time mean to you?
It is a privilege to be a part of the Red Dot jury. It is a chance to be part of something that is greater than the sum of its parts, something that is really inspiring.

What is your philosophy of life?
I'll quote from Benjamin Franklin: "Either write something worth reading or do something worth writing."

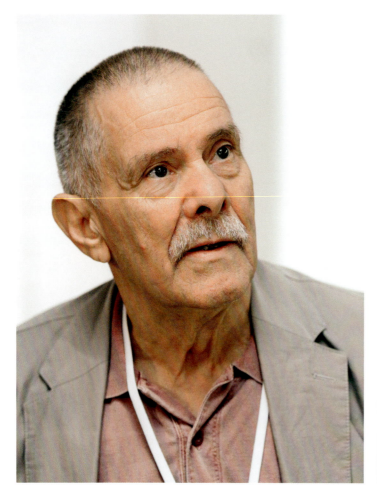

WOLFGANG BAUM
GERMANY

Wolfgang Baum studied graphic design in Munich where he is currently the managing director of the U5 academy and lecturer for visual communication. After internships in typesetting and printing, he worked for a music publisher before he became active as a freelancer for book and magazine publishers as well as advertising agencies and TV stations. From 1983 to 1990, he was president of the Federation of German Graphic Designers, and between 1986 and 1996, assistant professor for communication design at the Bavarian Academy for Advertising and Marketing (BAW) in Munich. Wolfgang Baum is a committed juror in various expert committees and as chairman of the Professional Association of German Communication Designers, Bavaria Group, among others. He works as freelance communication designer and is a member of the professional associations BDG, AGD, DT, BDW and Icograda.

Jury Portraits

With your many years of experience as a Red Dot juror, how has the competition changed in the field of communication design during the past years?
The competition has not only become more international due to the applicants, but influences also have a greater international reach and introduce more variety. Additionally, the expectations of good design have become higher in many fields, such as game design. This becomes apparent among other things by the fact that advertising agencies now take part in the competition with excellent works in many different categories.

— GOOD DESIGN NEEDS INSPIRATION, PERSUASIVE POWER, ENTHUSIASM AND THE WILLINGNESS TO TAKE RISKS.

What advice would you give to young designers?
To be straightforward, not to pretend to be someone else, to develop self-confidence without becoming presumptuous. To listen to criticism very carefully, without justifying yourself. To learn from it. To make mistakes and to learn from them. The only mistake you must not make is wanting to avoid mistakes.

What do you look for as juror, when evaluating a submission?
I want to feel something of the enthusiasm and the pride of the designer, who successfully broke rules, pushed boundaries and conquered new territory, in order to create, in his very individual way, a meticulously elaborated design that fully lives up to the task.

What is your philosophy of life?
Stand up for your opinions and views, and treat the opinions and views of others with respect and patience. As Gregor von Rezzori put it, retain serenity of the soul, even in difficult situations.

01/02

PROF. MICHEL DE BOER
NETHERLANDS

01/02 **Kai Tak**
Brand strategy, street naming concept, identity design, city furniture and public art for a new city district in Hong Kong named Kai Tak (former airport of Hong Kong). Currently in implementation.
[Design Public Creatives: by Kan & Lau, Kurt Chan and Michel de Boer]

Hoarding design for a construction site which is the first implementation of a large series of items (in progress).

03 **Selection of "Swirls"**
They are part of the Kai Tak visual behaviour.

04 **Kai Tak logotype**

Michel de Boer, born in 1954, studied at the Academy of Fine Arts and Higher Technologies in Rotterdam. In 1989, he became creative managing partner at Studio Dumbar, where he was responsible for the creative output up till 2010. From 2011, he started his independent design company: MdB Associates with liaising offices in Germany, Korea, Hong Kong and Malaysia. With more than 25 years of experience in corporate design, brand identity and graphic design, Michel de Boer has worked for clients around the world such as Apple, Allianz, Shell, Nike, Randstad, General Motors China, TNT, Woongjin as well as the Dutch and the South Korean government. He has won numerous awards, takes part in international design conferences as well as in the jury of international design competitions.

In 2005, Michel de Boer became professor at the Istituto Universitario di Architettura in Venice, Italy. From 2011, he has run a design course, Communicazione d'Impresa (corporate image), at ISIA in Urbino, Italy. Next to this he has been working to set up a design educational programme in China, to be started in 2013. He is a member of several professional organisations, and he is the co-initiator of the start-up of a new design joint venture in Shanghai.

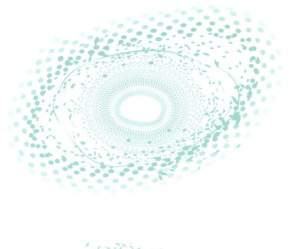

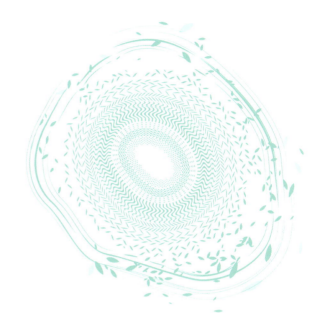

03/04

— GOOD DESIGN NEEDS A WIDER RECOGNITION IN THE WORLD AS THERE ARE STILL TOO MANY ORGANISATIONS WHO DO NOT UNDERSTAND THE VALUE OF GOOD DESIGN.

In retrospect, what do you know now that you wish you had known before pursuing your design education?
Not much. A certain lack of innocence is important to start with. At that point, uncertainty is allowed. That is important during your whole professional life. The way you handle it and the ability to redirect it is of great value.

What are some common myths about your profession?
That those extensive, usually obligatory marketing or communication reports dictate the design strategy. On the contrary: it is the creative idea that sells and which is usually strategically stronger than any report. Another is that large clients are in search of bigger agencies. However, as I have experienced in the past few years, better ideas are produced by energetic, adaptive creative teams but usually do not come from static teams within large design firms.

What are the most interesting aspects of being a Red Dot juror?
There is not only one single aspect. As usual in life, there are many things like being inspired by seeing great design solutions, debating these with fellow jury members and enjoying good wine with all jury members and the Red Dot team.

What is your philosophy of life?
To enjoy life and to push boundaries in order to make the impossible possible, in a way that works for the client, but more importantly, for the target audience and, furthermore, to charge my creative batteries.

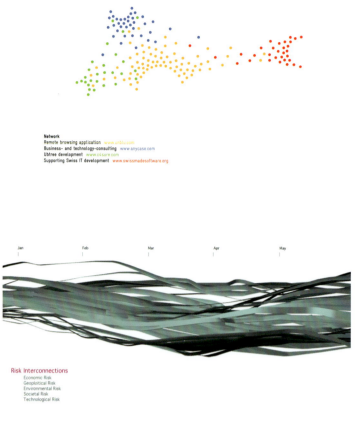

01 / 02

ALAIN LECLERC VON BONIN
SWITZERLAND

01 **Network**
    Data visualisation,
    2010

02 **Riskscape**
    Data visualisation,
    2011

03 **Atelier Pfister App**
    Interactive furniture catalogue,
    2010

Alain Leclerc von Bonin is an independent designer and art director who focuses on the realisation of communication and cultural projects. He worked with renowned agencies in Paris and London, before founding the Zurich-based studio VisualContext. Backed up by a network of agencies and specialists, the studio creates concepts and designs for corporate identities, corporate communications, websites, infographics, user interfaces, games and data visualisation.

A key approach in the works by Alain Leclerc von Bonin is to break down the boundaries between traditional and new media. He lectures on topics at the intersection of design and technology. His playful approach towards technology allows him to create efficient systems that not only make use of the technological possibilities but also appeal to the user's emotions. Many of his works have garnered prizes in international award competitions, including the Art Directors Club Switzerland, the Red Dot Design Award and the Best of Swiss Web.

Jury Portraits

03

— GOOD DESIGN
NEEDS DEDICATION.

Which dream project would you like to realise one day?
It is high time to fundamentally rethink how annual reports are presented medially. An annual report should convey an overview of the last financial year, while well-conceived data visualisations can help make a crucial difference.

Which trends have you identified when judging this year's submissions?
It is great to see that digital media have gained more maturity. Many projects make well-directed use of interaction and dynamic presentation forms in their communicative goals. Designers are increasingly discovering forms of expression that go beyond what is possible in print.

What fascinated you most in the Red Dot Award: Communication Design 2013?
Judging the submitted works and exchanging opinions about them with the other jurors was an inspiring experience.

What is your philosophy of life?
Maximum demand and modesty.

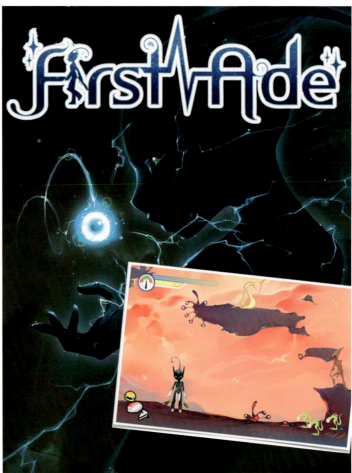

01

PROF. DR. LINDA BREITLAUCH
GERMANY

01 **First Ade**
Prototype of a serious game for kids and teenagers with type 1 diabetes, 2010 [content4med GmbH, King Baudouin Foundation, Ion Games]

02 **The "Hover Cubes" puzzle game**
in ego-perspective involves placing and removing blocks with the help of CubeGun in order to solve conundrums. The developers from the Nerdy Cat studio are seven game design students from the Mediadesign University of Applied Sciences in Düsseldorf, under the supervision of Prof. Dr. Linda Breitlauch

Prof. Dr. Linda Breitlauch initially studied business economics before she graduated in film and television scriptwriting from the Film & Television Academy (HFF) in Babelsberg, Germany. In 2008, she completed her PhD on dramatic composition in computer games. In addition to working as a project manager in the export and publishing sectors, she has been the creative producer of several film projects, has written film scripts and game concepts as well as scientific and expert articles, among other things.

In 2007, Linda Breitlauch was appointed Europe's first female professor of game design at the Mediadesign University of Applied Sciences in Düsseldorf, Germany. There, she teaches and researches with a special focus on serious/applied games, and dramatic composition. Furthermore, she works as an evaluator and is a consultant in the areas of media didactics and interactive storytelling. In 2011, she was nominated for the European Women in Games Hall of Fame award.

Jury Portraits

02

What qualities should someone have to study game design?

To study game design, you should first and foremost possess a fascination for innovation, an extraordinary way of thinking and an absolute will to design something. Talent in the fields of game mechanics, storytelling, artwork, programming, sound and project management are of course also desirable. Most important, however, is an affinity for all aspects of game development, since game designers are often the hub between the different disciplines. There are certain admission requirements for studying game design, since academic education always involves scientific reflection. Finally, it is the passion for games and everything behind the scenes that counts: discovering potential not only for the entertainment market, but also for art, culture, technology and education for yourself and for others, and helping to shape it.

— GOOD DESIGN NEEDS PERSONALITY, PASSION, CREATIVITY AND THE COURAGE TO DISCARD.

According to which criteria do you evaluate the submitted works in the Red Dot Award: Communication Design 2013?

A game – be it digital or analogue – becomes accessible primarily through its aesthetics and the so-called gameplay. The quality of the game experience is the decisive factor: How is the player involved in the world and, as a result, what messages and emotions are thus created?

The assessment criteria are manifold: graphical and music aesthetics, interface design, storytelling, level design, balancing, technology. Moreover, a good game has a new point of view, a visible innovation or even a new topic or target group.

What trends could you find during the adjudication?
The quality this year was impressively high. The innovative achievements, especially in the fields of technology, graphics and storytelling, were surprising. Many submissions dealt with topics that are still rather the exception in the game market: learning by playing, understanding by playing. This shows the wide-ranging impact that game design can already have today.

What is your philosophy of life?
Don't be put off playing just because you are afraid to score!

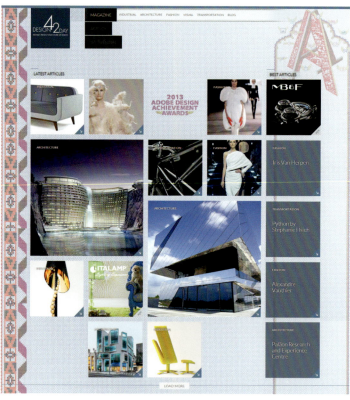

01

RICCARDO CAPUZZO
ITALY

01 **Design42Day**
is a company set up in Milan and specialised in the research, selection and promotion of design at an international scale.

Riccardo Capuzzo studied visual and web design at the Scuola Politecnica di Design in Milan. In 2004, he moved to Chicago for two years working for a company as a visual designer. Afterwards, he wanted to change the environment around him and started working in Istanbul as a freelancer. From 2006 to 2008, he was commuting between Milan and Istanbul as he used to have some clients in Milan as well. In 2008, Riccardo Capuzzo started a blog as he did not like any available magazines. He wanted to show the real good design of today. What was actually meant to be a hobby turned into a proper web magazine in 2010. The same year, Patrick Abbattista, one of his mates in kindergarten, joined the project. Within two years, the magazine became one of the most prestigious voices of the design world and a partner of Beijing Design Week, Moscow Design Week, International Talent Support, Istituto Europeo di Design, Red Dot Design Award, agIdeas, Adobe Design Achievement Awards, Electrolux Design Lab and many others.

What do you enjoy most about your career?
I have always been working hard to assure myself some range of freedom from schedules and business strategies and to plan my own path without being forced to work with incompetent people. Today I can say I succeeded in that. For me, it is the only way of working to be 100 per cent productive.

What has been or still is your personal key to success?
The variables are endless. Comfortable environment conditions, key contacts, determination are among them. But if I have to pick up just one, I would say that most of your professional success depends on how much you love what you are doing. That really makes a difference. If you are deeply passionate about what you are doing, you bend the environment conditions to your will, reaching the key contacts you need because you are determined.

What are the best ways to get a foot in the door into the world of design/companies for a young talent? In how far can Red Dot contribute to this?
A young talent should consider earth not too big, but just as big as a city, where every country is just a district. Being aware of what happens in every country, being ready to work far away, meeting design players from different countries and learn from them. It is not important to remember designers' names or when that popular chair has been designed if you don't know what is going on outside your yard. A designer should be more focused on understanding the whole picture of what is design. The Red Dot can give you an institutional and internationally recognised statement that says you are a good designer. It's a hallmark more valuable than all the MBA or design master courses. It is a remarkable facilitator in order to present your work to potential clients.

What is your life motto?
When love and skill work together, expect a masterpiece.

— GOOD DESIGN NEEDS TO GET RID OF "PR DESIGN".

01

PROF. DON RYUN CHANG
SOUTH KOREA

01 Meritz hotel

02 Korea tourism organisation

Don Ryun Chang is professor and Dean of the Graduate School of Advertising of Hongik University in Seoul, Korea where he also heads the Brand Media Evolution lab. He was CEO of Interbrand Korea and currently advises KT&G and Eeung, one of the premier new media companies in Korea. He is also a former president of the International Council of Graphic Design Associations (Icograda) and the Chief Event Director for the 2015 IDA Congress to be held in Gwangju, Korea. Don Ryun Chang has been a jury member for the Red Dot Design Award, the President's Design Award Singapore and the Australian Graphic Design Award and has worked on numerous corporate identities and place branding projects including Dynamic Korea, Korea Tourism Office, 2002 FIFA World Cup, Paju City and Incheon Airport. He lead workshops at design schools worldwide, including Parsons, RISD, Monash University in Melbourne and the IIT Mumbai and has written seven books on branding. He received numerous awards including the Special Citations from the Ministers of Culture and Commerce of Korea as well as the Meritorious Lifetime Achievement Award from the Korean Federation of Design Associations.

— GOOD DESIGN NEEDS DIVERSE AND PROACTIVE COLLABORATION.

02

How do you rate the quality of the works that you assessed?
I was very impressed with the overall quality and the diversity of the entries. In many of the selected works the designers clearly seemed to have a keen awareness of many of the pertinent socio-economic and cultural issues that have been affecting many countries over the past several years. It again confirmed the integral value of intelligent and creative designs that merge the best aspects of relevant contents with visual forms to become thought-provoking communication vehicles.

What is good design in your opinion?
Good design is the culmination of a holistic process that involves the most effective collaboration between the designer and client to collectively achieve the most effective outcome. It needs to be an active co-creation partnership between the client and designer that assesses the core project imperatives to plan, design and implement the highest degree of creativity. Good design may start with a good idea, but its life cycle is ultimately determined by the amount of necessary details that have to be infused in various stages on the path to its final completion.

Red Dot has an international jury. Can you give us an insight into the design culture of your country?
Design in Korea has been an important catalyst for the immense economic growth of the country during the last 40 years. With the strong national emphasis on education, design has been one of the most important areas of studies in many universities, which have expanded their programmes to reflect the multidisciplinary design evolution of the industry. Many of the successful companies like Samsung Electronics, Hyundai Motors and LG have achieved enormous success by planning and implementing a comprehensive design management agenda to enhance the quality and visual look of their products and customer services.

In recent years, companies in the financial sectors such as Hyundai Card and search engine firms such as Naver have attained prolific brand awareness by conducting an integrated media communication programme that is reflective of contemporary lifestyle. The current communication design field is becoming more segmented and versatile, ranging from Korean Hangul typography, editorial, corporate branding and wayfinding to new media user interface and interactive design.

What is your life motto?
To design the best life synergy.

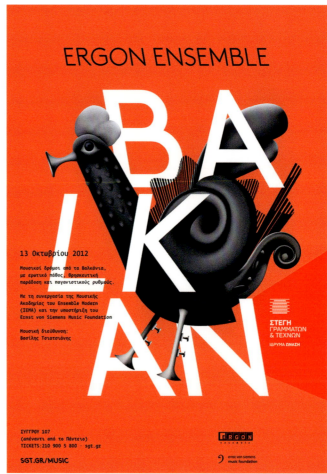

01

YIANNIS CHARALAMBOPOULOS
GREECE

01 **Onassis Cultural Centre**
The new visual identity of the OCC, Athens' new cultural space, included a new logo in which the centre's name is placed in a solid red polygon, a special font (LLBROWN) for the titles of the events and an original illustration style for the use as a creative tool in compositions.

02 **Museum of Byzantine Culture**
The new signage system for the Museum of Byzantine Culture shows subtly coloured monolithic information tablets, the outlines of which are rectangles that are "pulled" towards the direction they indicate and a set of new "mosaic" icons that were recreated in three dimensions using real mosaic stones.

03 **A couple of drops**
Packaging design for a Greek olive oil.

Yiannis Charalambopoulos, born in Thessaloniki, Greece, studied graphic design and typography in Athens and London where he completed the MA course in Typo/Graphic Studies at the London College of Communication. He is one of the founding members of Beetroot Design Agency, the Greek-based team that was awarded Red Dot: Agency of the Year 2011 and created "The Greek Monsters" exhibition after that.

Beetroot's creative mission is to discover, develop and utilise the true essence of an idea, service or product, and then grow and expand it into a strong brand that becomes recognised, appreciated and praised all around the globe. Beetroot operates and promotes collaborative work between multidisciplinary artists and designers and the team's ethos may be summarised by the phrase "I am many". Beetroot is the communication design force behind Greece's most prominent organisations, institutions, products and companies and its unconventional perspective and signature never-the-same-thing-twice work has won the team many national and international awards.

02

03

You are a member of the Red Dot jury for the first time. What kind of impressions did you get? How did you experience this year's jury session?
The Red Dot Award: Communication Design competition is one of the most important design communication platforms in the world so we expected nothing less than the outstanding level of professionalism and organisation we were offered as members of the jury. The procedures were stark, clear, efficient and fair, with special attention to the presentation of the work that was divided – very conveniently – in different categories. Meeting with designers from all over the world is one of the many important reasons for entering the Red Dot Award: Communication Design contest. It was great to see that this is also true for the judging team and we were thrilled to participate in what was a truly multinational team of designers with very diverse backgrounds and focus areas. Also – as one would expect, but it needs to be emphasised – the Red Dot Design Award administration was truly impartial and offered the judges complete freedom of choice according to their own criteria within a common and fair framework.

— GOOD DESIGN NEEDS A GOOD WORKING TEAM!

Has your approach to design changed over the years, and if so, how and why?
Our design approach is like a genetic code: it is the same but it also evolves, adapts and mutates according to its living environment in order to sustain and prosper. As we grow we become more precise and focused to a philosophy that keeps our work coherent although visually nothing we create "looks" or "feels" like anything else we did in the past or will do in the future. We are a team whose work is the result of an organic blend of different backgrounds, approaches and personalities; so, this philosophy, although it is shared by all, may be applied in many ways as well.

How would you describe Greek communication design?
Greece goes through a very interesting period of its modern history where it has to prove its contemporary worth. Among the Greeks, contemporary Greek designers are some of the first who regard this as a great opportunity to promote design creation amongst the many splendid national products and services Greece has to offer. Greek communication design is very much focused on the "idea" and the "context" as opposed to being mainly a visual affair. Most of the design outcomes are driven by a concept that can be described with a few words before even being visualised. This is quite true to an essential way of Greek thinking and the respect of the "logos" (reason, talk, speech). In this way, Greek design is almost always focused, comprehensible and "to the point".

What is your life motto?
I am many.

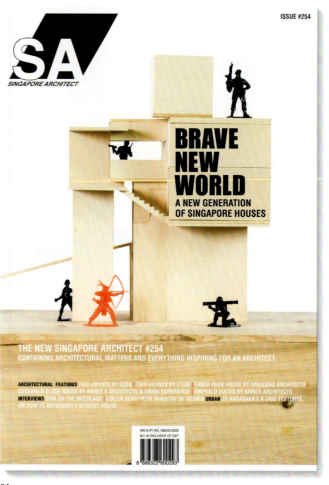

01

KELLEY CHENG
SINGAPORE

01 **Singapore Architect**
Magazine Design

02 **iSh**
Magazine Design

03 **The Dubai Mall: From Sand to Spectacles**
Book Design

Kelley Cheng, born in 1972, studied art and architecture at the National University of Singapore where she graduated with honours. As its editor and creative director, she published the award-winning design magazine "iSh" and, in 2001, was recruited by the Page One Group, where, under her leadership, hundreds of art, design and architecture books were published worldwide. Today, she runs her own publishing and design consultancy The Press Room, designing everything from books, brands, graphics, spaces, experiences, and even stage and film set design. An active educator, Kelley Cheng is an adjunct professor in visual communications at the GSA and also serves the advisory panel for the Singapore Polytechnic and the Singapore Contemporary Young Artists society, etc. and is regularly a member in international design judging panels such as the Red Dot Design Award, Nagoya-Do!, Creative Circle Award and James Dyson Award. Her projects include the Youth Olympic Games, iLight Marina Bay light art festival, Singapore Pavilion at the World Expo Yeosu 2012 and currently the exhibition and graphics for the National Art Gallery, Singapore.

— GOOD DESIGN NEEDS TO BE LOGICAL, MEANINGFUL, EMOTIVE AND, MOST OF ALL, GOOD DESIGN NEEDS TO INSPIRE.

Jury Portraits

02

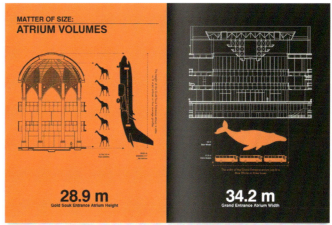

03

A typical day in the life of Kelley Cheng, what is it like?
I need my morning coffee; it is almost the only incentive for waking up in the morning ha ha! The day doesn't start until I have my coffee and a nice breakfast really wakes me up. I can skip lunch or dinner but never breakfast. It is also the time I use to plan the day, and can have complete quiet time to myself because once the day starts, I will have so many things to do, people to meet, staff to watch over and I won't have a quiet moment.

Usually I do my meetings with clients or run errands in the morning. And, by the afternoon, I'll be back at the studio and I will sit with every designer to go through their works and make adjustments and improvements. Everyday there seem to be endless problems to solve – from design issues to client issues to the practical nitty-gritties of running a design studio. And everyday there seem to be endless decisions to be made – from design decisions to business decisions. It is mentally very draining and exhausting, actually!

Like with my morning coffee, I look forward to my evening beer – either in the bar below my studio or at the comforts of my home – which really relaxes me and, again, it is a time to myself where I can have some quiet time to brainstorm for ideas or just chill out.

What inspires you?
Like most creative people, I am a keen observer of everything as everything has the possibility of inspiring me. But I get my regular creative fuel from movies, books and magazines, music, theatre; and I love watching dance and, funnily, I've come up with many great ideas for my design work while watching dance. In life, I am often inspired by compassion for the less privileged and generosity of strangers, both of which I strive to practise everyday, a little a day.

In your opinion, what is so special about the Red Dot jury session?
I've judged for many international competitions and the Red Dot jury sessions are the ones I enjoy the most and it is truly in a league of its own. Red Dot has built up a fraternity of judges and it is like an alumnus where, every time you return, you can be sure to see some old friends amongst the judges. This relationship of judges with Red Dot becomes very precious as it helps to build up a history and culture of judging for Red Dot, which I dare say no other jury sessions in the world share. This history and culture of judging has definitely given depth to the judging processes as there is a continuity and in the end, a legacy.

What is your life motto?
Be a good person first, then a good designer. Five words that I live by – strength, honour, integrity, passion and compassion.

01

MEHMET ÇIFTCI
TURKEY

01 **Migros M-Selection**
Packaging design for a new range of special mixed fruit juices, 2011.

02 **Feast**
Concept development and new design for the product line of Aegean fish recipes, 2013.

Mehmet Çiftci began his career studying communication and advertising in Reims, France. Upon graduating from school and living in France for 25 years, he had the opportunity to work in packaging design for Ulker, one of the industry's most influential brands. The invaluable experience gained from designing for Ulker inspired Mehmet Çiftci to fulfil his lifelong dream and launch his own company Paristanbul in 2003.

His professionalism in the areas of branding, packaging innovation projects and core strategic designing in the food sector lead him to successful packaging solutions and commercialisations. His brand Paristanbul is the first "Branding & Packaging Design Agency" specialised in packaging design and branding, with renowned clients such as Ulker, Pinar, Polonez, Lesaffre Group, Komili, Migros, Canderel, Café Crown, Aytac, Godiva and etc.

— GOOD DESIGN NEEDS LOVE. LOVE CREATES PASSION.

02

You are Turkish, and studied and lived in France. To what extent do those two countries have an influence on your work?
According to the "one person, one language" approach, being bicultural is one of the best qualities I could have. Integrating these two unique cultures has been a wonderful experience and I still keep both alive in my life and at Paristanbul. This absolutely has an influence upon our management of business, people and art. However, this approach is neither French nor Turkish. This is Paristanbul, which is a third way. Passion is the integrating point for both cultures, passion is the GCD, the greatest common divisor for both. Thus, passion influences me a lot.
– In business management: Turks see me as result-oriented, the French see me as practical.
– In people management: Turks see me as ethical, the French see me as empathic.
– In art management: Turks see me as rationalistic, the French see me as mystical.
In other words: I am Eastern from a Western point of view, and Western for the East.

Where and how do you gather information on trends?
I aggregate research reports from professional research companies as every agency does. A creative agency has to observe people and get a feel for the beauty and rhythm of the community around it. Talking to the owner of the corner grocery store, drinking Turkish tea with him, querying his behaviour is also essential for gathering information on local trends. I do observe him and also myself every now and then. A designer has to get to the heart of the matter. Everything can be seen in community life.

How did you experience your premiere as Red Dot juror?
Even though we depend on intangible data in our lives, our senses never mislead us. I never forget this equilibrium, which I re-experienced during the Red Dot adjudication. As a jury team, we had the same synergy and the same harmony. In this way, we made the right decisions. We also had the same synergy with the Red Dot team. I am happy to have been part of it.

What is your life motto?
Creating is daring ...

01 / 02

CATHERINE CORTI
SWITZERLAND

Catherine Corti, born in 1973, studied graphic design at the former Basel School of Design, where she received her diploma in 1997. Afterwards, she worked as graphic designer in various design agencies, including Nose AG Design Intelligence, in Zurich.

In 1999, she was a founding member of the Agency for Design and Communication, Büro4 in Zurich. Furthermore, she is a jury member of the journal Hochparterre, nominating the best websites for design and architecture in Switzerland.

01 **Anoushka Matus book**
"The light on your face warms my heart", 2004

02 **Swiss Radio and TV,**
2013

03 **Museum of Communication,**
Bern, 2004

Jury Portraits

03

— GOOD DESIGN
NEEDS A CLEAR MIND.

Which of your projects has been the greatest challenge for you?
One of our first exhibitions – the permanent exhibition "near and far" in the Museum of Communication in Bern (Switzerland) – was a project of around 1,000 sqm. There was an incredible amount of information to convey, workshops to set up and a large collection of historic objects to administer. With comparatively little experience in this area, those were very challenging 1,000 sqm.

What would you still like to learn?
At the moment I am really interested in graphic animation. I would like to sound out some options and have a more confident understanding of the technical side of it.

What was special for you about evaluating the submitted works?
Just assessing existing projects was unusual. I like looking for opportunities to develop something further and love improving works. Of course, this is also an issue during the evaluation, but one that cannot be realised.

What is your philosophy of life?
I like designing life flexibly.

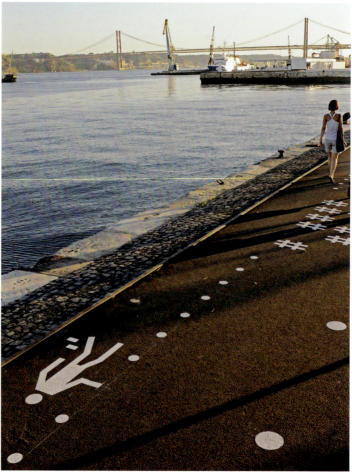

01

NUNO BOTELHO DE GUSMÃO
PORTUGAL

01 **Lisbon Bikeway –
Belém/Cais do Sodré**
Environmental,
Lisbon, Portugal,
2008–2009.

02 **REFLEX**
Exhibition in the
Assembleia da República
(Assembly of the Republic),
Lisbon, Portugal, 2011.

Nuno Botelho de Gusmão, born in Lisbon, Portugal, in 1966, studied four years of architecture and two years of fine arts at the University of Lisbon (ESBAL) working as graphic artist. He professionally develops environmental design and communication projects, mostly graphic interventions on architecture. Since 2006 he is the senior partner and founder of "P-06 Atelier – ambientes e comunicação", a national and international award-winning firm specialising in communication and environmental design on a wide range of scales. Based in Lisbon, it undertakes a variety of projects from complex, large-scale wayfinding systems, museum and exhibition design, to communication and editorial design for the printed page, with a bold, striking style. P-06 Atelier actively engages in collaborations with architects, urbanists, landscape designers and engineers, in a continuous, seamless workflow with complementing disciplines, enriching the company's scope of work and amplifying every intervention's outcomes.

02

— GOOD DESIGN NEEDS NEW IDEAS.

What are some favourite projects you've completed and why?
The environmental graphic design project Skin and the Lisbon Bikeway Belém/Cais do Sodré, are an immediate choice to me, due to the process of interdisciplinarity with architecture, landscape architecture and engineering. But I cannot leave behind Reflex, an exhibition about the Portuguese constitution and the wayfinding project for the Sacred Art Museum, because I think they express well my experimentalist approach in aesthetic terms.

Regarding internationality: in your opinion, which is the current leading country in communication design and why?
I don't see a single country leading, I do see several with different aesthetic approaches, and each one with its own features.

Which developments in graphic design could you observe in this year's jury session?
None in particular, maybe the "expected" increase in multimedia solutions could stand out, with good examples of a fine integration in the ambience.

What is your life motto?
"… and let …" (please complete using the same word on each blank space)

01

MILO HELLER
GERMANY

01 **Videoload**
Sound logo for Videoload, an online video rental shop; several spots featuring Bastian Pastewka were conceived for its launch in 2008.

Milo Heller, born in Switzerland, has lived in Hamburg since 1989, starting his professional career as a sound editor. Since 1993, he has worked as a sound designer at the Hastings Audio Network. Since 1994, he is known as a pioneer in sound branding for his development of the sound logo for AUDI and since 2010, he has worked as a freelance sound brander.

Milo Heller successfully transferred companies of various branches into new sound dimensions, with sound logos for Postbank, Aral, Vattenfall, Toshiba, Conrad and mobilcom among others and managed to build up an enormous expertise in the field of sound branding. Thus, he plays an active role in establishing Germany as a pioneer in creating and establishing sound logos.

Jury Portraits

— GOOD DESIGN NEEDS IDEAS, SKILFUL CRAFTSMANSHIP AND ABOVE ALL PERSUASIVENESS AND ASSERTIVENESS WHEN DEALING WITH CLIENTS.

How did you experience this year's adjudication?
In our team of jurors the mix was just right: we had humorous days, concentrated but not doggedly at work. For the most part, we agreed quickly after a short discussion. In general, the works from Taiwan were the most difficult ones for us to evaluate. Here, an often highly impressive imagery met with very conservative and conventional communication.

Which town is in your opinion the most interesting place for design at the moment?
Berlin, Lisbon.

What is your philosophy of life?
Who the cap fits, shall wear it.

01

JAN RIKUS HILLMANN
GERMANY

01 **RadioEins Website**
Concept and design of radioeins.de, the most visited radio website of the broadcasting company Rundfunk Berlin-Brandenburg rbb. 2012

02 **De:Bug – The Sound of Berlin iPad-App**
Overall implementation of the Cityguide iPad app "De:Bug – the sound of Berlin". Ten Berlin DJs, producers, artists, photographers and club founders show us around their city: a Berlin that constantly reinvents itself, lives for the moment and recycles and remixes its own history. 2011

03 **FontBook Universal App**
The multiply award-winning FontBook app is the most extensive atlas worldwide for typefaces. Just as with a map, fonts are can be searched for by similarity, designer, producer or year of design. 2011–2013

Jan Rikus Hillmann works on an interdisciplinary basis in the fields of concepts, user interface and interactive design. The focus of his work as a designer and art director of his studio burningbluesoul in Berlin is on interactive applications and editorial services comprising e-commerce and product websites, as well as social web applications. His special competency is in accurate media-tailored staging and communication of contents and information.

Jan Rikus Hillmann is a co-founder of the magazine "De:Bug – Elektronische Lebensaspekte", was managing designer with "it's immaterial GmbH", art director with Pixelpark in Berlin and senior designer with MetaDesign in Berlin. He holds a teaching position at the School of Design in Bern (SfGB), where he devised the interactive design degree programme. In 2004, he received the Online Grimme Prize for designing the information offer for the film "Stauffenberg" (ARD) and was honoured for the FontBook iPad app, an encyclopaedia of fonts, in 2012 with the Red Dot: Grand Prix.

02

03

What characteristics must a successful communication designer possess?
Designers should always be able to work like partners on an equal footing with their clients. To do so requires interdisciplinary understanding and a firm stance in the process of making consistent inquiries.

Taking part as a juror for the first time this year, what was particularly impressive about the Red Dot Award: Communication Design 2013?
The outstandingly professional and open-minded international jury.

— GOOD DESIGN CALLS FOR SIMPLICITY, ATTITUDE, A MOMENT OF SURPRISE, AND A BREAK WITH THE NORM.

As a communication designer and co-editor of a magazine, what future developments do you see regarding the debate about print versus online?
As a "digital native" myself, it is difficult for me to take a definite stance. On the one hand I am a proponent of open source, free information and well aware of the potential of crowd development and the sharing of knowledge, content, code and design. On the other hand I know the value of journalistically edited contents, expert evaluations and commentaries that are produced by publishing and broadcasting houses. Today, each medium, including TV, radio, newspapers, video, books, apps and magazine, has found its rightful place in the canon of the media, and each form of presentation is meaningful in the different situations.

The role adopted by publishers and broadcasters as victims of the Internet seems presumptuous when considering that it is the users who are the Internet, not the publishers, not Facebook or Google. The users are senders and receivers who make use of social services as gateways and means for their own digital identity. For the future development of content I would like to see this: the dropping of "Like" as a statement – i.e. a stronger implementation and editorial moderation of user contents when designing presentations of journalistic information. This form of citizen journalism should imply a relocation from Facebook to appropriate media sites in order to promote qualitative user opinions.

01

RAINER HIRT
GERMANY

01 **Partnership**
As a worldwide partner for premium access solutions and services, DORMA stands for integrated system solutions paired with a passion for design and architectural excellence. Developed together with DORMA, the acoustic leitmotif "Klang-Raumerlebnis" (sound space experience) reflects the core of the brand and combines the aspects of ambience, aesthetics, dynamics, emotions and accessibilit y.

02 **Corporate sound for DORMA**

Rainer Hirt, born in Überlingen, Germany, in 1979, studied communication design at Hochschule Konstanz, University of Applied Sciences. After graduating, he founded "audity" together with Michael Hoppe and Markus Reiner, an agency that specialises in audio branding, audio interaction and audio experience. Back in 2003, he had already founded the corporate sound Internet platform audio-branding.de, a well-known expert resource on the topic of sound branding.

Rainer Hirt is, among other things, the author and co-editor of the compendium "Audio-Branding". He is in charge of research projects at various universities and, in 2009, founded the first independent institution for acoustic brand communication, the Audio Branding Academy, together with Kai Bronner and Cornelius Ringe.

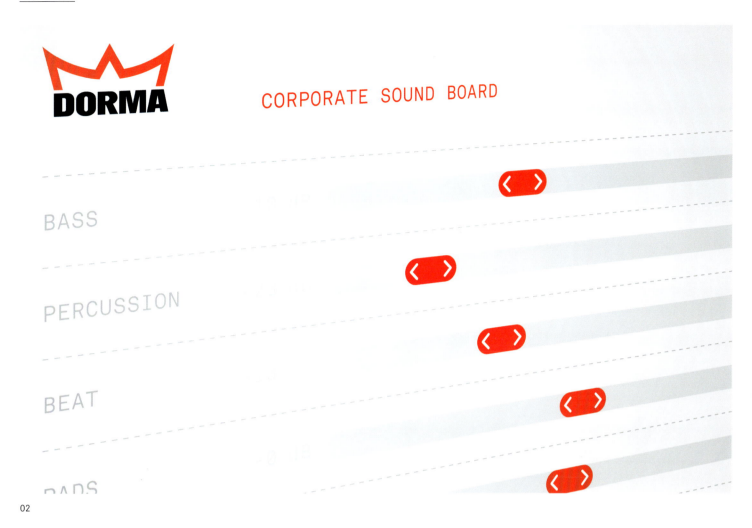

— GOOD DESIGN NEEDS COURAGE.

Why do you think it is so important today to provide a brand not only with a visual appearance but also with a sound?
Humans are multi-sensual beings who perceive the environment with all their senses. Making a brand perceivable for all senses is a logical consequence of this. Thus, the auditory channel is also just a part of the whole, but one which has been gaining considerable recognition by brand managers over the past few years.

What developments do you currently see in your industry?
There are more space-related tasks, for example in the field of museums, at the points of sale and in various man-machine interfaces (automotive, medical, etc.).

The Red Dot cosmos is not a new experience for you. What motivates you to take part in it as a juror again and again?
Every time I am fascinated anew by the entire Red Dot atmosphere! The highly professional organisation and the top-class international jury make the jury session a great experience!

What is your philosophy of life?
The power is now.

01

PROF. LAURENT LACOUR
GERMANY

Laurent Lacour studied visual communication and art at the University of Art and Design Offenbach, Germany. He is an associate of the design studio hauser lacour, based in Frankfurt/Main. hauser lacour carries out extensive, award-winning corporate design projects. He developed corporate identity programmes and ran communication projects for the Deutsche Börse Group, Munich Re, Sony, De Gruyter, Bavarian Re and Siemens. But also in the cultural sector, i.e. the corporate design for the Museum of Modern Art in Frankfurt/Main, the Kölner Philharmonie, the Frankfurter Kunstverein, the Museum of Contemporary Art in Siegen and further institutions and companies. hauser lacour developed book and magazine designs such as the current layout of the design magazine "form".

He taught visual communication as design research at the universities of Zurich, Basel, Karlsruhe and Darmstadt (Karlsruhe and Darmstadt as a visiting and substitute professor). Since April 2011, he has held a full professorship at the University of Applied Sciences in Düsseldorf, Germany.

01 **Corporate Design for the MMK Museum für Moderne Kunst Frankfurt/Main (Museum of Modern Art)**
The corporate design of the MMK Museum für Moderne Kunst Frankfurt/Main (Museum of Modern Art) is based on its triangular floor plan and the unusual architecture of the building. The triangle has been employed as a flexible design element in all media. Different artworks are layered or shown as cut-outs to reflect the collection character of the museum.

02 **Signage and media system for Fraport (Frankfurt Airport) corporate head office**
This system focuses on optimum orientation for the visitor and an accompanying media installation in the rooms, which generates a clear image transfer. Alongside the enormous media display for the entrance area, the building also houses smaller, interactive designs.

02

— GOOD DESIGN NEEDS FREEDOM AND CULTURAL EDUCATION.

Do you have role models in the field of design or outside of it?
I am inspired by people who come from design-related disciplines. Especially by artists such as David Lynch, Fischli Weiss, Olafur Eliasson and many others. I cannot exactly say if these persons are real role models for me or if they are just sources from which I draw my creative inspiration. Maybe an especially charismatic character, such as Christoph Schlingensief, who goes far beyond boundaries, thinks multi-dimensionally, is indeed a role model for me.

How do you evaluate the quality of the submissions of this year's competition?
In the category film only rarely is something realised with a new type of humour and there is still room for improvement in aesthetic quality. Looking at the other categories, I am absolutely thrilled. In the online categories especially there has been a lot of development. Maybe this is also the medium for moving images of the future.

How did you experience this year's jury process?
It is just incredibly exciting to float through this flood of inspiring and creative worlds with professional colleagues. Everyone is highly motivated. No one gets tired. Every year, I am excited to be privileged in this way, at having the opportunity to seriously learn something new through the jury process and the screening of the qualities of the submitted works.

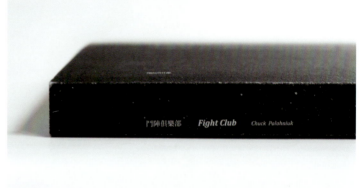

01

AARON YUNG-CHEN NIEH
TAIWAN

Aaron Yung-Chen Nieh, born in 1977, received a bachelor's degree in industrial and commercial design from the National Taiwan University of Science and Technology and afterwards studied at the Graduate School of Applied Media Arts at the National Taiwan University of Arts. The Council for Cultural Affairs selected him as a resident artist for the 18th Street Arts Center in Los Angeles, USA. With a body of works seen extensively in the music industry, publications and art-related projects, he is among the most outstanding designers of Taiwan of the past decade and his works appeal to a great public of the greater China's vast consumer society, being awarded e.g. Best Album Cover Design by Golden Melody Awards in Taiwan, Red Dot Award: Communication Design and iF communication design award in Germany, Asia Pacific Design Awards or Type Directors Club Tokyo. In 2012, Aaron Yung-Chen Nieh became a member of AGI and he is now the proprietor of the Aaron Nieh Workshop.

01 **Fight Club**
Cover design for the novel "Fight Club" by Chuck Palahniuk in the Chinese version.

02 **Yoga Lin "Fiction"**
Packaging design for the album "Fiction" by the Taiwanese singer Yoga Lin.

Jury Portraits

02

— GOOD DESIGN NEVER NEEDS TO BE REVISED.

It was your first time as a Red Dot juror. How would you describe this feeling?
I felt kind of "renewed". Everything came at me as if it was unprecedented. I, too, enjoyed the company of all the jurors from all over the world. Their points of view and cultural upbringings were something I took profound interest in. I was also amused by all those discussions on aesthetics in all those different languages. I saw quite some well-made works with very distinct conceptions behind them. This delighted me.

What kind of satisfaction do you get from your work?
Every single piece of my works was born in a very specific period of time, which can be looked upon as an embodiment of the challenge and of my self-fulfilment in that peculiar phase. If there is this something one has to celebrate for, that'll be my design. The excitement behind it reaches further than any birthday or Valentine's Day celebration.

Please give us a few characteristics necessary for every communication designer.
Take care of yourself.

What is your life motto?
Bold, detail-minded and resolved.

01/02

MALGOSIA PAWLIK-LENIARSKA
POLAND

01 **Onet.pl**
Rebranding of Onet.pl, the leading Internet portal in Poland, 2011.

02 **NEO Tools**
Rebranding of the hand tools brand NEO Tools, September 2012.

03 **Redd's**
Redd's packaging redesign, June 2013.

Malgosia Pawlik-Leniarska is managing partner of Dragon Rouge Warsaw, the first branding agency in Central and Eastern Europe which she founded in 1994. She started her marketing career at Colgate-Palmolive, where she was responsible for introducing new products into the market. As a consulting director, she managed projects for major company clients in the region such as Coca-Cola, Nestlé, Danone, Kamis, Bahlsen, Hochland, Pernod Ricard, ETI and others.

Committed to brand design education, she lectures at the Brand Strategy School and at the Academy of Fine Arts in Warsaw. Malgosia Pawlik-Leniarska is president of the Brand Design Club and board member of the epda (European Packaging Design Association). She holds an MA in cultural studies and an MBA from the International Business School and the University of Illinois.

03

— GOOD DESIGN NEEDS TO ENGAGE PEOPLE.

Please describe a typical day of work for you.
Say hi, smile, have a coffee and a quick chat on what's important today, brand channel, marketing news, project review with team, call, laugh, ideation workshop, call, mails, call, call, lunch, mails, call, call, client meeting, call, chocolate, call, short meeting with the creative director, short meeting with the client service director, say bye, mails, plan for tomorrow, article in Fast Company and … it's 9.30 p.m.

What do you enjoy most about your career?
Working with interesting people; creating an environment where talents and ideas meet every day.

Could you comment on the Polish influence in this year's Red Dot Award: Communication Design?
Still below expectations. I believe that Polish designers need to be bolder in terms of design solutions presented to clients and more confident in sending their work to such an important international competition.

What is your life motto?
If you can dream it, you can do it.

01

JACK RENWICK
SCOTLAND/
UNITED KINGDOM

01 **The Orchard**
The typographic tree ring, engraved into a concrete wall, was designed for The Orchard, a boutique property development in London's Clerkenwell, echoing the long and vibrant history of this area and the building's name. Completed in July 2013 as part of a large branding programme.

02 **METRO Newspaper Cover**
Four page newspaper cover wrap to brighten the day of UK commuters and encourage them to pass on the newspaper to help reduce the amount of waste on public transport. The edition of the free Metro was printed in 6.5 million copies across Britain, April 2010.

Jack Renwick, born in Glasgow, Scotland, studied graphic design at Duncan of Jordanstone College of Art & Design at the University of Dundee in Scotland. Today a multi-award-winning designer in London, she won her first D&AD pencil when she still was a student in 1998. Since then, she has also worked with The Partners branding and design agency as Creative Director before setting up her own agency, the Jack Renwick Studio, in 2012. She has a strong passion for ideas, enjoys working closely with her clients, getting to the heart of their problem and showing how creative thinking can be the way forward.

Jack Renwick has worked on a huge variety of projects over the past 15 years for clients including eBay, BBC, Penguin, Nokia, Royal Mail and Stella McCartney, receiving recognition from D&AD, Design Week, Benchmarks, NYF, ADC and Creative Review. Her most recent award was a second Gold Lion at Cannes. Besides acting as a jury member for different awards, she is a strong supporter of design education in the UK, is on the education board of ISTD (International Society of Typographic Designers) and the current external examiner at Duncan of Jordanstone College of Art & Design.

Jury Portraits

02

— GOOD DESIGN NEEDS
TO MAKE A DIFFERENCE.

What kind of project will always be your favourite?
One where the client has an appetite for being challenged and is willing to keep an open mind. One where there is a strong concept that runs through all the various communications of the brand and where it genuinely makes a difference to how the company is perceived and ideally where it can make a difference to how the company behaves.

Which advantages do designers have by participating in the Red Dot Award: Communication Design?
The chance to have their work acknowledged for being amongst the best in the world.

What would you do if you were a superhero?
Kick all the bad guys asses!

What is your life motto?
Never give up.

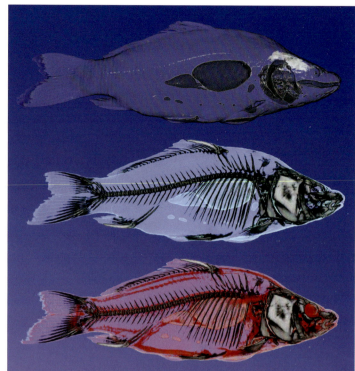

01

PROF. DR. CHRISTOF REZK-SALAMA
GERMANY

01 **Computed tomography of a carp**
Interactive visualisation, realtime Volume Graphics, 2006.

02 **Monte Carlo Volume Rendering of a female head, computer tomography angiography**
Interactive Visualisation in a virtual reality environment. GPU-based Monte-Carlo Volume Raycasting, Pacific Graphics, 2007.

Prof. Dr. Christof Rezk-Salama studied information technology at the Friedrich-Alexander University in Erlangen/Nuremberg, Germany. Subsequently, he obtained his PhD with honours in computer graphics and visualisation. After working as a design engineer in the field of research and development at Siemens Medical, he returned to studies where he completed his post-doctoral qualification at the University of Siegen in 2009. He then taught and researched as a professor and tutor at the Mediadesign University in Düsseldorf in the department of game design for several years.

In October 2012, he accepted a professorship for game development in the department of computer science at the University of Applied Sciences in Trier, Germany. Christof Rezk-Salama regularly gives lectures and workshops on the topics of computer graphics, visualisation and game development at international events, such as ACM SIGGRAPH, Eurographics and IEEE Visualisation. In the course of his career, he has received several high-level awards. He has furthermore acquired practical knowledge in different disciplines, for example medicine, geology and archaeology.

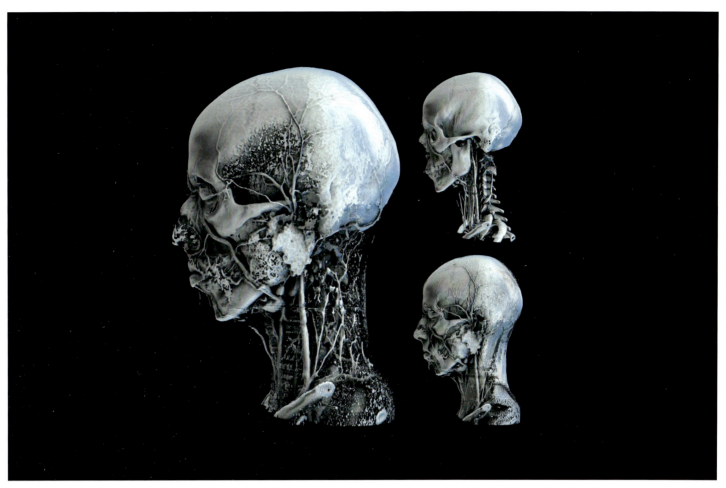

02

How will game design advance in the next few years? Can you observe certain trends?

The professional gaming industry is still relatively young and constantly changing. It is hard to anticipate what is going to happen. As with all digital media at the moment, many new marketing and distribution models are being tried, discarded or developed further. However, for me, the change the game industry is facing regarding content is much more interesting. In recent years, the film industry has experienced a similar change. Alongside the success of casual games, mobile games for use in-between times, I definitely see a trend away from "McGames" towards titles that appeal to adults in terms of the depth of the storyline and artistic ambition. Titles such as Heavy Rain, Mass Effect and Bioshock Infinite are both demanding and commercially successful. In any case, the industry will mature. I hope that more developers will have the courage to take more complex paths.

— GOOD DESIGN NEEDS THE COURAGE AND THE FREEDOM TO BREAK AWAY FROM WELL-TRODDEN PATHS.

Who would you once like to work together with? Why?

I am a huge fan of comic books. I like its visual way of storytelling, which you also very often find in games. To create interactive stories for some of the sophisticated, high-level European comic books would be very exciting. And of course it would be great to work on this together with interesting people from the European scene, such as Enki Bilal ("La Foire aux Immortels"), Jodorowsky and Beltran ("Megalex") or Barbucci and Canepa ("Sky Doll"), to name but a few. The scenarios of these works would allow one to tell interactive stories very successfully. Players could influence the game world with their decisions.

How did you experience the adjudication of the Red Dot Award: Communication Design 2013?

The days of the adjudication in Essen were really great. The many discussions with international co-jurors from a range of different fields were very inspiring and opened up new perspectives on familiar and not so familiar issues. Overall, the submitted works in our categories were of an extremely high level and the many different points of view of the jurors were helpful in reflecting and deciding on the truly best entries.

What is your philosophy of life?

"Find what you love and let it kill you!" This quotation is attributed to Charles Bukowski, but actually the source is unclear.

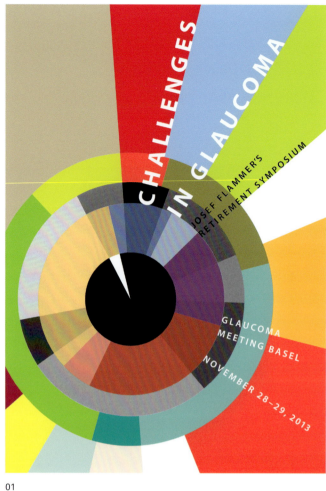

01

JEAN JACQUES SCHAFFNER
SWITZERLAND

01　Poster "Knabenkantorei" (boys' cantor's house)

02　Poster of a concert of the Collegium Musicum Basel

03　Red Dot poster "Stephen"

Jean Jacques Schaffner, born in Basel, Switzerland, in 1954, studied graphic design at the early age of 15 at Basel arts school with Adrian Frutiger, among others. Further training as a photographer and as a music film director with Leo Nadelmann, as well as his attendance of the Ecole des Beaux-Arts in Paris and study stays in San Francisco are reflected in Schaffner's great variety of skills. In 1976, together with his partner Silvana Conzelmann he founded the Designersfactory in Basel, which includes a photo studio and a department for interactive media and Internet applications. In this way, the agency offers the complete range of visual communication services.

Since 1987, Schaffner has run trainings in graphic design, CAD, typography and packaging design and has held lectures all around the world. He was president of the Pan-European Brand Design Association (PDA) from 2000 to 2003 and is also a member of many design juries.

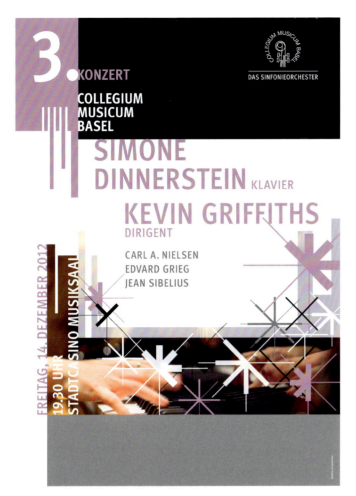

02

03

How do you approach new projects?
Before I start a new project, I always plan to not become concrete and leave all creative options and scenarios open for as long as possible. That way, I prevent self-censorship of my own ideas. Logically, it always takes a fair amount of curiosity to become fully engaged with the required task. After 40 years of professional experience, I know that one will always find a solution, even if there might also be others.

What is your philosophy of life?
Do everything with passion, otherwise don't do it at all!

— GOOD DESIGN NEEDS CURIOSITY AND UNDERSTANDING.

What were your expectations regarding the submitted works?
Each year is unique in character, depending on the submitted works. Accordingly, I never have any specific expectations in advance. However, I begin with the assumption that the participants take their work absolutely seriously. It is certain that, with more than 6,000 submissions, one can identify a kind of cross section of what is important for each designer, less in the sense of short-term trends than through the use of media and styles.

In your opinion, how do you evaluate the communicative development in the field of social media with regard to social networks, weblogs, micro-blogging etc.?
Sometimes I feel that people believe in Pandora's box or in a rags-to-riches fairytale. Social media, micro-blogging and weblogs are great tools in a media mix tailored to a specific target group. However, it is a mistake to believe that every Facebook page or every YouTube film leads to a Justin Bieber effect. We have found that there are hundreds of thousands of blogs that no one ever looks at, and that Facebook pages with just 200 followers are no real thrillers either. We always use social media in combination with other activities. Doing one thing, without neglecting the other.

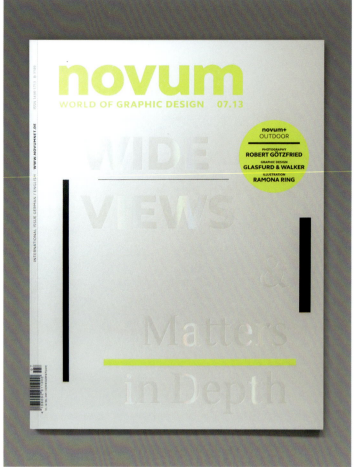

01

BETTINA SCHULZ
GERMANY

Bettina Schulz, born in Munich, Germany, in 1974, has been editor-in-chief of the international journal "novum – World of Graphic Design" since 2001. She joined the editorial staff of the magazine in 1994. Bettina Schulz also works for national and international magazines and for a range of clients in different sectors as a freelance writer and editor. She is a co-founder of the Creative Paper Conference in Munich and has already been a member of design juries on a number of occasions, e.g. for the European Design Awards, for the Best of Corporate Publishing award, for the MfG competition of the German printing and media industries federation (bvdm), the Monaco de Luxe Packaging Award and the biannual diploma awards presentation at the U5 design academy.

01 **novum 07/13**
cover design:
Johannes König,
Melville Brand Design,
Munich, Germany.

02 **novum 08/13**
cover design:
Twopoints.Net,
Barcelona, Spain.

03 **novum 10/13**
cover design:
clormann design,
Munich, Germany.

— GOOD DESIGN
FIRST AND FOREMOST
NEEDS CLIENTS
WHO APPRECIATE IT.

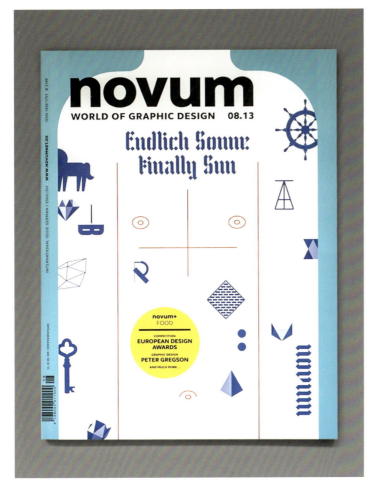

02

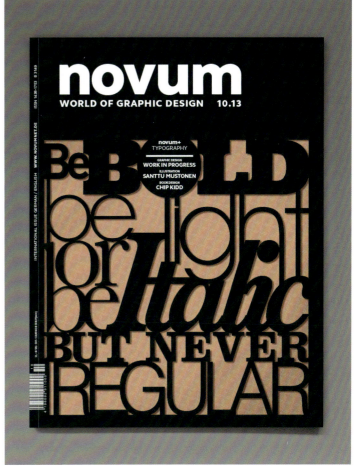

03

How do you evaluate German design by international standards?
Maybe it is better to characterise it: it is very precise, often technically of the highest level and – even if it sounds like a cliché – generally also very serious. Loosening up and being a bit cheekier would probably do us no harm, provided that the client is open to it, of course. However, Germany is without a doubt one of the leading design nations.

According to what criteria do you decide whether you will write about a work or a designer?
Here, many factors play a role, such as technical quality, whether the work is up-to-date, how innovative the approach is, etc. However, I also take into account, to some extent, where the work is coming from, since we also want to shed light on the creative scenes of countries that are very young historically and thus do not possess such high standards of education.

A view on the global design world is all the more interesting when one considers the differences. Finally, I am not alone in deciding about content – although I have learned from my many years at novum to disregard my personal taste. When working for a magazine, teamwork in this regard becomes even more important.

How did you experience this year's adjudication?
It was again very intense and focused, working in a great team, even if I personally missed the very big highlights. Nevertheless, there were many appealing projects to discover and, in its entirety, the quality of the entries again was at a high level.

What is your life motto?
I have no motto, but I have two quotations that have been hanging in my office for ages: "If you can dream it, you can do it" (Walt Disney) and "One day someone with a shovel will throw dirt over your face – so why not go the whole hog?" (Tracy Goss, corporate consultant). You can take both to heart …

01 / 02

PETER PHILIPPE WEISS
SWITZERLAND

Peter Philippe Weiss, born in 1962, works as a consultant, composer, sound artist, sound designer, producer, speaker and guest lecturer at the University of St.Gallen, the HWZ in Zurich and also as associate professor at the University of Applied Science in Offenburg. In 1994, he founded the Corporate Sound AG in Basel, one of the first professional communication agencies for acoustic brand staging, which today supports national and international clients' sound projects in the fields of sound branding and sound design for exhibitions, architecture, museums, events, electronic media and product design.

In 2009, the Corporate Sound AG was awarded a Red Dot for sound branding. Peter Philippe Weiss realises artistic sound projects – also at his own research centre for new sound visions. In 2005, for instance, he implemented an urban sound installation in the city of Basel. In 2009, he developed the sound installation "unterwelten" in cooperation with the Association of the Hard of Hearing in Basel. The same year Peter Philippe Weiss wrote the film music for the film "Manipulation".

01 **unterwelten**
City sound installation in collaboration with the Association of the Hard of Hearing Northwest Switzerland: Surprising sounds and voices came from a drain in the Freie Strasse in the centre of Basel.
www.unterwelten.ch

02 **VALSER TV**
Sound design/music for a TV spot for VALSER (CocaCola) in collaboration with the voice artist Christian Zehnder, 2012.
http://youtu.be/22zDijZhEe0

03 **MANIPULATION**
Film music for the feature film "Manipulation" with Klaus-Maria Brandauer and Sebastian Koch, 2010.
http://youtu.be/K4SMStSgwJM

03

— GOOD DESIGN NEEDS A VISION, PERSISTENCE AND AT THE SAME TIME THE OPEN-MINDEDNESS TO RECOGNISE THE POTENTIAL OF SERENDIPITY DURING THE REALISATION PROCESS AND TO INTEGRATE THESE INTO THE DESIGN.

What was special for you about evaluating the submitted works?
The dynamics and the exchange with fascinating people from all over the world. That was amazing! The adjudication took place in a professional and very well organised context and the submitted works came from a surprisingly wide quality spectrum.

What developments in design would you still like to witness?
That sound will one day establish itself as a strong and wide-ranging design dimension within the scope of multi-sensual design of media, rooms and products.

What would be your profession, if you hadn't become a designer?
Architect! I have always been enthusiastic about architecture and even as a child I drew entirely crazy houses. Even today I am fascinated by architecture and I find exciting similarities to my work, since rooms can also be created in the auditory dimension. With sound installations, I create immaterial architecture and rooms so to speak that originate inside people's heads.

What is your philosophy of life?
;-)

Index Designers

0–9

3deluxe
www.3deluxe.de
Vol. 2: 73

3st kommunikation GmbH
www.3st.de
Vol. 2: 238

A

achta design
www.achta.de
Vol. 2: 152, 394

Alt Group
www.altgroup.net
Vol. 2: 68
Vol. 1: 91, 146, 147, 407

Ammunition LLC
www.ammunitiongroup.com
Vol. 2: 214, 258

Anima Boutique Oy
www.animaboutique.fi
Vol. 2: 103

Asia University
www.asia.edu.tw
http://vcd.asia.edu.tw
Vol. 2: 300–301, 314–315, 336, 337, 348, 358, 370

AVerMedia Technologies, Inc.
www.avermedia.com
Vol. 2: 256–257

B

Babiel GmbH
www.babiel.com
Vol. 2: 165, 172

Bar Vinya Film
www.janreiff.com
Vol. 2: 127

Bassier, Bergmann & Kindler
www.bb-k.com
Vol. 2: 158

Christopher Bauder
www.christopherbauder.com
Vol. 2: 50–51

BBDO Proximity
Berlin GmbH
www.bbdoproximity.de
Vol. 2: 53, 118–119, 286–287, 288, 395, 396
Vol. 1: 310–311, 451

becc agency GmbH
www.becc-agency.de
Vol. 2: 62, 63

beierarbeit GmbH
www.beierarbeit.de
Vol. 2: 135

BiBoBox Studio
Dalian Nationalities University
www.bibobox.com
Vol. 2: 280–281, 397

BMW China
www.bmw.com.cn
Vol. 2: 63

BOROS GmbH
www.boros.de
Vol. 2: 104–105

Brigada
www.brigada.hr
Vol. 2: 37

Nikolas Brückmann
www.sure.is
Vol. 2: 310–311, 454

ATELIER BRÜCKNER
www.atelier-brueckner.com
Vol. 2: 46

Brückner Innenarchitekten
www.bruecknerinnenarchitekten.de
Vol. 2: 72

Bruketa&Žinić OM
www.bruketa-zinic.com
Vol. 2: 37
Vol. 1: 172–173, 235, 452

Leo Burnett Germany
www.leoburnett.de
Vol. 2: 78–79, 159, 222
Vol. 1: 114, 115, 253, 315, 317, 318

BVD
www.bvd.se
Vol. 2: 69
Vol. 1: 298–299

C

CaderaDesign
www.caderadesign.de
Vol. 2: 196–197, 398

Cheil Worldwide
www.cheil.com
Vol. 2: 170

Chen-Ping Chen,
Shun-Ming Yang
Asia University
www.asia.edu.tw
Vol. 2: 358

Shih-Lun Chen,
Jia-Hong Lin, Yu-Ru Cho,
Siao-Huei Tang
China University of Technology
www.cute.edu.tw
www.facebook.com/ricead
Vol. 2: 368, 441

Yu-Cheng Chen
frank4478@gmail.com
Vol. 2: 328

Chihlee Institute of Technology
www.chihlee.edu.tw
Vol. 2: 372–373

China University
of Technology
www.cute.edu.tw
Vol. 2: 368

ChineseCUBES
www.chinesecubes.com
Vol. 2: 220

Ya-Chi Chiu, Lee-Wa Lin, Cheng-En Chang, Yan-Yu Huang, Yan-Ting Chen
Asia University
http://vcd.asia.edu.tw
Vol. 2: 314–315, 336, 442

Hsun-Yang Cho, Tian-Yu Guo,
Ying-Ting Lyou, Guan-Ling Lu,
Tai-Hsin Lin, Yu-Tian Sun
Shu-Te University
Department of Visual
Communication Design
www.stu.edu.tw
www.vcd.stu.edu.tw
Vol. 2: 308–309, 443

Jin-An Chung
www.flickr.com/photos/michelle82318
Vol. 2: 366–367

Crytek
www.crytek.com
Vol. 2: 276–277, 399

Kate Cullinane
Auckland University
of Technology
kate.cullinane@gmail.com
Vol. 2: 342

CUP GmbH
www.c-u-p.de
Vol. 2: 224–225

Karen Cuthbert
www.karencuthbert.de
Vol. 2: 335

cyclos design GmbH
www.cyclos-design.de
Vol. 2: 81

D

Daedalic Entertainment
www.daedalic.de
Vol. 2: 278–279, 400

Das Büro am Draht GmbH
www.dasburo.com
Vol. 2: 184

Dell Inc.
Experience Design Group
www.dell.com
Vol. 2: 244

denkwerk GmbH
www.denkwerk.com
Vol. 2: 96–97, 215, 401

Design and Communication
www.dncbiz.com
Vol. 2: 239

designconcepts GmbH
www.designconcepts.de
Vol. 2: 153, 402

designfever
www.designfever.com
Vol. 2: 164, 251

Philipp Dettmer
www.philippdettmer.com
Vol. 2: 318–319, 444

DMC Design for Media
and Communication GmbH
www.dmcgroup.eu
Vol. 2: 126
Vol. 1: 100–101

515

Index

Dong Yuexi
dongyuexi@sina.com
Vol. 2: 344–345, 445

Dongdao Design Co., Ltd.
www.dongdao.net
Vol. 2: 83

Draftfcb
Deutschland GmbH
www.draftfcb.de
Vol. 2: 76–77, 122–123,
130–131, 252, 403
Vol. 1: 415, 436–437, 443, 457

E
e:mg
www.emg.ru
Vol. 2: 124, 125

EDA Communications, Inc.
www.edacom.co.kr
Vol. 2: 259

Eight Inc.
www.eightinc.com
Vol. 2: 22–23, 404

Evernote
www.evernote.com
Vol. 2: 255

F
Fabrique [brands,
design & interaction]
www.fabrique.nl
Vol. 2: 146–147, 181, 247, 405

Falmouth University
BA (Hons) Graphic Design
www.falmouth.ac.uk
Vol. 2: 302–303, 440

Fjord
www.fjordnet.com
Vol. 2: 272–273

Lina Louisa Fliedner
l.fliedner@gmx.net
Vol. 2: 343

FRISCHE BRISE FILM
www.frischebrise.de
Vol. 2: 100

G
g-p-u-n-k
www.gpunk.de
Vol. 2: 234–235

Gachon University
www.gachon.ac.kr
Vol. 2: 341

Gang of Berlin
www.gangofberlin.com
Vol. 2: 53, 286–287, 396

gate.11 GmbH
www.gate11.net
Vol. 2: 28

GAXWEB GmbH
www.gaxweb.com
Vol. 2: 148–149

Gessaga Hindermann GmbH
www.gessaga-hindermann.ch
Vol. 2: 42–43, 406

GfG /
Gruppe für Gestaltung
www.gfg-bremen.de
Vol. 2: 58–59

giraffentoast design gmbh
www.giraffentoast.com
Vol. 2: 52

GMK Markenberatung
www.gmk-markenberatung.de
Vol. 2: 62

gmp Architekten
von Gerkan,
Marg und Partner
www.gmp-architekten.com
Vol. 2: 44

Andreas Golde
www.andreasgolde.de
Vol. 2: 359

Lin Gong
www.lingongdesign.com
Vol. 2: 360

Thomas Granjard Design
www.t-granjard.com
Vol. 2: 129

Grass Jelly Studio
www.grassjelly.tv
Vol. 2: 106–107, 132, 407

Great Apes Ltd
www.greatapes.fi
Vol. 2: 246

Greco Design
www.grecodesign.com.br
Vol. 2: 35, 82
Vol. 1: 120–121, 356–357, 462

Caroline Grohs
caro.grohs@web.de
Vol. 2: 332–333

Anna Gruchel
anna@gruchel.com
Vol. 2: 349

GUCC GmbH
www.gucc.de
Vol. 2: 137, 289

H
Hakuhodo
www.hakuhodo.jp
Vol. 2: 176

Ju-Ho Han, Da-Woon Jung,
Kyung-Chan Ahn
Gachon University
www.gachon.ac.kr
http://blog.naver.com/
karismajuho
Vol. 2: 341, 446

Hanyang University
www.hanyang.ac.kr
Vol. 2: 322–323

HardCase Design
www.hardcase.de
Vol. 2: 86–87

Susanne Hartmann
www.morphogen.ch
Vol. 2: 298–299, 447

Hastings media music
www.mediamusic.de
Vol. 2: 291

hauser lacour
kommunikationsgestaltung gmbh
www.hauserlacour.com
Vol. 2: 163
Vol. 1: 37

Havas Worldwide
Düsseldorf
www.havasww.de
Vol. 2: 80
Vol. 1: 380–381

Prof. Klaus Hesse
www.adc-sushi.com
Vol. 2: 310–311

HID
Human Interface Design
www.human-interface.de
Vol. 2: 208–209, 408

hillus Engineering KG
www.hillus.de
Vol. 2: 134

HMI Project
www.hmi-project.com
Vol. 2: 211

hoch5 next GmbH & Co. KG
www.hoch5-next.com
Vol. 2: 266–267

Hosoya Schaefer Architects AG
www.hosoyaschaefer.com
Vol. 2: 190–191, 409

Che-Wei Hsu, Su-Huei Chen,
Yi-Ting Dong, Yu-Zheng Lin,
Xiao-Han Lai, Szu-Jung Ho
Shu-Te University
Department of Visual
Communication Design
www.stu.edu.tw
www.vcd.stu.edu.tw
Vol. 2: 352–353, 450

Lung-Kai Hsu
National Yunlin University
of Science and Technology
www.media.yuntech.edu.tw
Vol. 2: 384–385

Ming-Chieh Hsu
beyondnote@gmail.com
Vol. 2: 328

Mu-Huai Hsueh, Tze-Yen Juang,
Ching-Wen Chang, Bing-Ru Yang,
Cheng-Yang Chen
Shu-Te University
Department of Visual
Communication Design
www.stu.edu.tw
www.vcd.stu.edu.tw
Vol. 2: 364–365, 448

Scottie Chih-Chieh Huang
BIO Lab + SDAID
Chung Hua University
www.sites.google.com/
site/scottiehuang0107
Vol. 2: 138–139, 410

Index

Ya-Li Huang, Syue-Ru Chen,
Yu-Chi Chung, Yu-Shu Sun,
Tien-Yuan Ku, Chia-Hsuan Wu,
Hsiao-Ling Wu
Asia University
www.asia.edu.tw
Vol. 2: 337, 370

Yan-Yu Huang, Yan-Ting Chen,
Ya-Chi Chiu, Lee-Wa Lin,
Cheng-En Chang
Asia University
http://vcd.asia.edu.tw
Vol. 2: 314–315, 336, 442

Mareike Hundt
mareike.hundt@
folkwang-uni.de
Vol. 2: 350–351

hw.design GmbH
www.hwdesign.de
Vol. 2: 174, 175
Vol. 1: 188, 189, 342

I
Idispartners
www.idispartners.com
Vol. 2: 55
Vol. 1: 110

incorporate berlin
GmbH & Co. KG
www.incorporateberlin.de
Vol. 2: 155

Interaktionsbyrån
www.interaktionsbyran.se
Vol. 2: 202–203, 411

Interbrand
www.interbrand.com
Vol. 2: 88, 94–95, 136, 412
Vol. 1: 183, 250–251, 468

Ippolito Fleitz Group GmbH
www.ifgroup.org
Vol. 2: 32, 33, 60, 61

J
JamZoo Inc.
www.jamzoo.com.tw
Vol. 2: 248–249

jangled nerves
www.janglednerves.com
Vol. 2: 24, 25, 38

Martin Jendrusch
www.martinjendrusch.de
Vol. 2: 101

JNS communications
www.jnsdream.com
Vol. 2: 242–243, 413

Heeyeon Jung
Hanyang University
Vol. 2: 322–323, 451

Yeji Jung
yi3403@gmail.com
Vol. 2: 338

K
Mustafa Karakaş
www.mustafa-karakas.com
Vol. 2: 294–297, 449

Benjamin Kempf
www.benkem.de
Vol. 2: 100

Kia Design Center
Kia Design Team
www.kia.com
Vol. 2: 92–93, 414

Hyosin Kim
Vol. 2: 338

KINOBLAU
Büro für Kommunikationsdesign
www.kinoblau.de
Vol. 2: 128

KircherBurkhardt GmbH
www.kircher-burkhardt.com
Vol. 2: 156–157, 162, 230–231, 269, 415

KMS BLACKSPACE
www.kms-blackspace.com
Vol. 2: 26, 27, 30, 31, 110–111, 185, 416

KNSK Werbeagentur GmbH
www.knsk.de
Vol. 2: 120–121, 417

Koeweiden Postma
www.koeweidenpostma.com
Vol. 2: 54

Janet Kofler
kofler_janet@gmx.at
Vol. 2: 326

Enni Koistinen
www.behance.net/
ennikoistinen
Vol. 2: 382–383

KOKUYO FURNITURE
Co., Ltd.
www.kokuyo-furniture.co.jp
Vol. 2: 66–67, 418

KOKUYO FURNITURE
Commerce and Trading (Shanghai)
Co., Ltd.
www.kokuyo.cn/furniture
Vol. 2: 66–67, 418

Kolle Rebbe GmbH
www.kolle-rebbe.de
Vol. 2: 282–283
Vol. 1: 112, 113

komma Mannheim
University of Applied
Sciences Mannheim
www.komma-mannheim.de
Vol. 2: 356–357

krafthaus –
Das Atelier von facts
and fiction
www.factsfiction.de
Vol. 2: 36

Thomas Kühnen
www.thomaskuehnen.de
Vol. 2: 359

Hsien-Chu Kuo
www.zoozookuo.com
Vol. 2: 378–379

Yan-Yi Kuo, Hong-Yi Shih,
Yu-Sheng Pan, Yu-Shu Chen,
Fu-Ciang Yang, Sian-Jhen Zeng
Shu-Te University
Department of Visual
Communication Design
www.stu.edu.tw
www.vcd.stu.edu.tw
Vol. 2: 376–377, 462

L
Xiao-Han Lai, Su-Huei Chen,
Szu-Jung Ho, Yi-Ting Dong,
Yu-Zheng Lin, Che-Wei Hsu
Shu-Te University
Department of Visual
Communication Design
www.stu.edu.tw
www.vcd.stu.edu.tw
Vol. 2: 352–353, 450

Ilari Laitinen
www.ilarilaitinen.com
Vol. 2: 382–383

Lean Design GmbH
www.wearelean.com
Vol. 2: 129

Kyung Lee
Vol. 2: 338

Sol-E Lee
Hanyang University
solsol222222@naver.com
Vol. 2: 322–323, 451

Sookwung Lee
sookwunglee@gmail.com
Vol. 2: 369

Leeum
Samsung Museum of Art
www.leeum.org
Vol. 2: 228–229

Lenovo (Beijing) Ltd.
Innovation Design Centre
www.lenovo.com
Vol. 2: 216

Samantha Lewis
Massey University
sam.lewis.gdesign@gmail.com
Vol. 2: 312–313, 452

LG Electronics Inc.
www.lg.com
Vol. 2: 212, 213
Vol. 1: 305, 307

Jun-Kai Lin
brucelin1993@gmail.com
Vol. 2: 366–367

Po-Hua Lin, Ren-Wei Pan,
Yung-Ching Chen, Shih-Yu Huang,
Shan-Yao Yang, Li-Ting Kao
cutevcd07@gmail.com
Vol. 2: 325, 453

Christoph Lohse
www.exakteaesthetik.de
Vol. 2: 380

Lots
www.lotsdesign.com
Vol. 2: 200–201, 419

Index

Lisa Lufen
lisalufen@web.de
Vol. 2: 347

M

macio GmbH
www.macio.de
Vol. 2: 206–207

Martin et Karczinski
www.martinetkarczinski.de
Vol. 2: 150, 161

Yuriy Matveev
www.sure.is
Vol. 2: 310–311, 454

Meiré und Meiré
www.meireundmeire.de
Vol. 2: 205

melting elements gmbh
www.meltingelements.com
Vol. 2: 236–237, 421

hg merz architekten
museumsgestalter
www.hgmerz.com
Vol. 2: 24

MESO Digital Interiors GmbH
www.meso.net
Vol. 2: 205

Claudia Mikosch
cmikosch@yahoo.de
Vol. 2: 371

Ming Chuan University
www.mcu.edu.tw
Vol. 2: 386–387

BUERO PHILIPP MOELLER
www.bueropm.com
Vol. 2: 29

Momkai
www.momkai.com
Vol. 2: 142–143, 154, 194–195, 422
Vol. 1: 155

büro münzing
3d kommunikation
www.bueromuenzing.de
Vol. 2: 39

Mutabor Design GmbH
www.mutabor.de
Vol. 2: 28, 47, 177
Vol. 1: 10–23, 26–27, 34–35, 111, 117, 330–331, 396–397, 402–403, 440–441, 479

N

N!03 srl
www.ennezerotre.it
Vol. 2: 18–19, 423

Nascent Design
www.nascentdesign.com
Vol. 2: 34

National Museum of
Modern and Contemporary Art,
Korea
Design Team
www.moca.go.kr
Vol. 2: 45, 424

Brodie Nel
Massey University
seven7jt@gmail.com
Vol. 2: 316–317, 455

NHN CORP.
www.nhncorp.com
Vol. 2: 179
Vol. 1: 64, 432–433

Nikon Corporation
www.nikon.com
Vol. 2: 210

NINEFIVE
www.ninefive.kr
Vol. 2: 250, 262–263, 425

O

Moriyuki Ochiai Architects
www.moriyukiochiai.com
Vol. 2: 70–71, 426

OKIN
Zhang Yangsheng
www.okinok.com
Vol. 2: 330–331, 463

ONCE
Vol. 2: 170

Pei-Ling Ou
Shu-Te University
Department of Visual
Communication Design
www.stu.edu.tw
www.vcd.stu.edu.tw
Vol. 2: 362–363, 456

Oval Design Limited
www.ovaldesign.com.hk
Vol. 2: 56–57

P

Jeong Ho Park
www.jeonghopark.com
Vol. 2: 306–307, 457

Youngha Park
younghanyc@gmail.com
Vol. 2: 324

Graedon Parker
Massey University
www.mrgraedonparker.com
Vol. 2: 320–321, 458

Patrick Pichler
www.adronauts.com
Vol. 2: 339

pilot Hamburg GmbH & Co. KG
www.pilot.de
Vol. 2: 166

Pixelbutik by Deli Pictures
www.delipictures.de
Vol. 2: 116–117, 427

Pixelpark/Elephant Seven
www.pixelpark.com
Vol. 2: 173, 178, 186–187, 223, 232–233, 428

Susanne Pretterebner
www.susannepretterebner.com
Vol. 2: 304–305, 459

Preuss und Preuss GmbH
www.preussundpreuss.com
Vol. 2: 133

Sophia Preußner
www.sophiapreussner.de
Vol. 2: 310–311, 454

pxd, Inc.
www.pxd.co.kr
Vol. 2: 198–199, 429

Q

Baihao Qiu, Weiming Lai, Chun-Yat Zhao
Shu-Te University
Department of Visual
Communication Design
www.stu.edu.tw
www.vcd.stu.edu.tw
Vol. 2: 374–375, 460

Sven Quadflieg
www.svenquadflieg.de
Vol. 2: 346

Quadrolux – Agentur für Bewegtbild
www.quadrolux.com
Vol. 2: 99

R

Razorfish GmbH
www.razorfish.de
Vol. 2: 240

Realgestalt GmbH
www.realgestalt.de
Vol. 2: 98

Redaktion 4
www.redaktion-4.de
Vol. 2: 268

Anne-Katrin Reinl
www.anne-katrin-reinl.de
Vol. 2: 390–391

res d
design und architektur
www.resd.de
Vol. 2: 40–41

ringzwei
www.ringzwei.com
Vol. 2: 218–219

Rithma Music
Etienne Stehelin
www.lzf-lamps.com/highfidelity
Vol. 2: 290

Robinizer Design Studio
GmbH & Co. KG
www.robinizer.de
Vol. 2: 160

RTT AG
www.rtt.ag
Vol. 2: 234–235

S

salient doremus
www.salient.de
Vol. 2: 151

Samsung SNS Co., Ltd.
www.samsungsns.com
Vol. 2: 245

SapientNitro
www.sapient.com
Vol. 2: 204, 241, 264

SCHMIDHUBER
www.schmidhuber.de
Vol. 2: 26, 30

Schober Design
www.schoberdesign.com
Vol. 2: 102

Index

Scholz & Volkmer GmbH
www.s-v.de
Vol. 2: 144–145, 169, 182–183, 430

Ricarda Schweigler
www.ricardaschweigler.com
Vol. 2: 354–355

SEK & GREY Finland
www.sek.fi
Vol. 2: 246

Shao Shu Wen, Zeng Yi Chun,
Lin Jia Yan, Lin Meng Pei, Yu Kun Ho
Asia University
http://vcd.asia.edu.tw
Vol. 2: 348

Shu-Te University
Department of Visual
Communication Design
www.stu.edu.tw
www.vcd.stu.edu.tw
Vol. 2: 308–309, 352–353, 362–363,
364–365, 372–373, 374–375,
376–377

Jennifer Laura Signon
jennifer.signon@live.de
Vol. 2: 381

simple GmbH
www.simple.de
Vol. 2: 64–65

Smart Mobile Factory GmbH
www.smartmobilefactory.com
Vol. 2: 254, 431

Logan Smith
Massey University
www.smiddysstudio.com
Vol. 2: 340

stereolize. GmbH
www.stereolize.com
Vol. 2: 192–193, 221, 432

Steuer
Marketing & Kommunikation GmbH
www.agentur-steuer.de
Vol. 2: 171

Suh Architects
www.suharchitects.com
Vol. 2: 48–49, 433

Do Ho Suh
www.lehmannmaupin.com/artists/
do-ho-suh
Vol. 2: 114–115, 434

Dawang Sun
College of Design and Innovation
Tongji University
www.sundawang.com
Vol. 2: 329, 361

Sungkyunkwan University
www.skku.edu
Vol. 2: 334

SYZYGY Deutschland GmbH
www.syzygy.de
Vol. 2: 168

T
Tangomike
www.tangomike.kr
Vol. 2: 228–229, 435

The Clockworks Innovate
www.theclockworks.co.kr
Vol. 2: 271

thjnk
www.thjnk.de
Vol. 2: 116–117

Joshua Thompson
Massey University
seven7jt@gmail.com
Vol. 2: 316–317, 455

tisch13 GmbH
www.tisch13.com
Vol. 2: 20–21, 436

tremoniamedia
Filmproduktion GmbH
www.tremoniamedia.de
Vol. 2: 101

Trizz
www.trizz.tv
Vol. 2: 104–105

U
UDS
Vol. 2: 66–67, 418

Universal Everything
www.universaleverything.com
Vol. 2: 92–93, 414

University of Applied Sciences
Augsburg
Fachwerkstatt Identity Design
http://brandidentity.hs-augsburg.de
Vol. 2: 302–303, 440

University of Art
and Design Offenbach
www.hfg-offenbach.de
Vol. 2: 310–311

update software AG
www.update.com
Vol. 2: 265

urbn; interaction
www.urbn.de
Vol. 2: 270

V
velvet mediendesign GmbH
www.velvet.de
Vol. 2: 108–109

Volut
www.volut.de
Vol. 2: 327

VRPE GmbH
www.vrpe.de
Vol. 2: 47

W
Büro für Gestaltung
Wangler & Abele
www.bfgest.de
Vol. 2: 84–85

Wolfgang Warzilek
www.adronauts.com
Vol. 2: 339

Mi-Na Wei, Ching-Chia Chiou
Asia University
www.asia.edu.tw
Vol. 2: 300–301, 461

Nadine Weiberg
www.nadineweiberg.de
www.kaeferkunde.de
Vol. 2: 388–389

White Studio
www.whitestudio.pt
Vol. 2: 89

WHITEvoid interactive art & design
www.whitevoid.com
Vol. 2: 50–51

wysiwyg* software design gmbh
www.wysiwyg.de
Vol. 2: 253

Y
Fu-Ciang Yang,
Sian-Jhen Zeng, Yan-Yi Kuo,
Hong-Yi Shih, Yu-Sheng Pan,
Yu-Shu Chen
Shu-Te University
Department of Visual
Communication Design
www.stu.edu.tw
www.vcd.stu.edu.tw
Vol. 2: 376–377, 462

YellowBlack
www.yellowblack.fi
Vol. 2: 103
Vol. 1: 195

Z
ZEITSPRUNG
COMMERCIAL GmbH
www.zeitsprung-commercial.de
Vol. 2: 104–105

zeros+ones GmbH
www.zeros.ones.de
Vol. 2: 260–261, 437

Zhang Yangsheng
OKIN
www.okinok.com
Vol. 2: 330–331, 463

Ziba Munich
www.ziba-munich.com
Vol. 2: 217
Vol. 1: 89

Zum Kuckuck /
Büro für digitale Medien
www.zumkuckuck.com
Vol. 2: 167, 180

Index Clients/ Universities

0–9
9292
www.9292.nl/en
Vol. 2: 247

A
ABEDESIGN
www.abedesign.org.br
Vol. 2: 35

adidas AG
World of Sports
www.adidas-group.com
Vol. 2: 64–65

Aegon
www.aegon.com
Vol. 2: 142–143, 194–195

AIA Korea
www.aia.co.kr
Vol. 2: 164

AIRBUS Operations GmbH
www.airbus.com
Vol. 2: 47

Airport Authority Hong Kong
www.hongkongairport.com
Vol. 2: 56–57

Akademie der Künste Berlin
www.adk.de
Vol. 2: 44

Allianz
www.allianz.de
www.allianz.com
www.projectm-online.com
Vol. 2: 160, 269
Vol. 1: 189

ames GmbH
www.amesdesign.de
Vol. 2: 152

Amnesty International
www.amnesty-frankfurt.de
Vol. 2: 78–79

Municipality of Amsterdam
www.amsterdam.nl
Vol. 2: 54

Arco
www.arco.nl
Vol. 2: 146–147

Armstrong DLW GmbH
www.armstrong.eu
Vol. 2: 33

Art Directors Club für Deutschland (ADC) e.V.
www.adc.de
Vol. 2: 310–311

Asia University
www.asia.edu.tw
Vol. 2: 300–301, 314–315, 336, 337, 348, 358, 370

Auckland University of Technology
www.aut.ac.nz
Vol. 2: 342

AUDI AG
www.audi.com
Vol. 2: 8–15, 20–21, 26, 27, 110–111, 184, 185, 240, 241

Audi Tradition – Museum Mobile
www.audi.com
Vol. 2: 108–109

AUER – Die Bausoftware GmbH
Part of the NEMETSCHEK GROUP
www.bausoftware.at
Vol. 2: 224–225

Autostadt GmbH
www.autostadt.de
Vol. 2: 190–191

AVerMedia Technologies, Inc.
www.avermedia.com
Vol. 2: 256–257

B
Babiel GmbH
www.babiel.com
Vol. 2: 165

Beiersdorf AG
www.beiersdorf.com
Vol. 2: 122–123
Vol. 1: 126–127, 292

Bergfürst AG
www.bergfuerst.com
Vol. 2: 98

Bin Music
www.bin-music.com
Vol. 2: 132

BMW China
www.bmw.com.cn
Vol. 2: 63

BMW Group
www.bmwgroup.com
Vol. 2: 28, 62, 205, 291
Vol. 1: 204–205, 297

Bonnier R&D
www.bonnier.com
Vol. 2: 258

BSH Bosch und Siemens Hausgeräte GmbH
www.bshg.com
Vol. 2: 30

BUND Bund für Umwelt und Naturschutz Deutschland Landesverband Berlin e.V.
www.bund.net
www.treeconcert.de
Vol. 2: 53, 286–287

Bundesministerium der Finanzen
www.bundesfinanzministerium.de
Vol. 2: 173, 223

Bundesverband der Obstverschlussbrenner e.V.
www.obstbrenner.com
www.echterobstbrand.de
Vol. 2: 153

C
Calligaris spa
www.calligaris.it
Vol. 2: 34

Canvasco GmbH
www.canvasco.de
Vol. 2: 155

Center for Medical Informatics
Seoul National University Bundang Hospital
www.snubh.org
Vol. 2: 198–199

China Central Academy of Fine Arts
www.cafa.edu.cn
Vol. 2: 344–345

ChineseCUBES
www.chinesecubes.com
Vol. 2: 220

Chung Hua University
www.chu.edu.tw
Vol. 2: 138–139

Cineplex Deutschland GmbH & Co. KG
www.cineplex.de
Vol. 2: 137, 289

CIRCLE – PRIVATE HEALTH CLUB
www.circle-munich.de
Vol. 2: 72

Crytek
www.crytek.com
Vol. 2: 276–277

D
Daedalic Entertainment
www.daedalic.de
Vol. 2: 278–279

Daimler AG
www.daimler.com
Vol. 2: 25, 118–119, 182–183, 288

Daishin Securities
www.daishin.co.kr
Vol. 2: 262–263

DeguDent GmbH
www.dentsply.com
Vol. 2: 128

Dell Inc.
www.dell.com
Vol. 2: 244

denkwerk GmbH
www.denkwerk.com
Vol. 2: 96–97, 215

Deutscher Bundestag
www.bundestag.de
Vol. 2: 172

Deutsches Schauspielhaus in Hamburg
www.schauspielhaus.de
Vol. 2: 116–117

Discovery Communications Deutschland GmbH & Co. KG
www.dmax.de
Vol. 2: 126

Dongduk Women's University
www.dongduk.ac.kr
Vol. 2: 338

Drändle
www.draendle7030.com
Vol. 2: 161

DRYKORN Modevertriebs GmbH & Co. KG
www.drykorn.com
Vol. 2: 180

Düsseldorfer Schauspielhaus
www.duesseldorfer-schauspielhaus.de
Vol. 2: 346

Index

E

E.ON Vertrieb Deutschland GmbH
www.eon.com
Vol. 2: 260–261

eastar air
www.eastarjet.com
Vol. 2: 334

eckball.de
www.eckball.de
Vol. 2: 135

energiekonsens
www.energiekonsens.de
Vol. 2: 58–59

Esporão S.A.
www.esporao.com
Vol. 2: 89

Evernote
www.evernote.com
Vol. 2: 255

Evonik Industries AG
www.evonik.com
Vol. 2: 120–121, 268

Ewha Womans University
www.ewha.ac.kr
Vol. 2: 369

Exzellenzcluster TOPOI
www.topoi.org
Vol. 2: 40–41

F

Falmouth University
www.falmouth.ac.uk
Vol. 2: 302–303

FH JOANNEUM –
University of Applied Sciences
www.fh-joanneum.at
Vol. 2: 304–305, 354–355

FHNW
Academy of Art and Design Basel
www.fhnw.ch/hgk
Vol. 2: 298–299

Fiat Group Automobiles Germany AG
www.fiat.com
Vol. 2: 159, 222

fiftyfifty
www.fiftyfifty-galerie.de
Vol. 2: 80
Vol. 1: 380–381

Fisher & Paykel Appliances
www.fisherpaykel.co.nz
Vol. 2: 68
Vol. 1: 91

Folkwang University of the Arts
www.folkwang-uni.de
Vol. 2: 350–351

Fondazione Pirelli
www.fondazionepirelli.org
Vol. 2: 18–19

FOVEA
www.fovea.eu
www.kaeferkunde.de
Vol. 2: 388–389

Franz Schneider Brakel GmbH
www.fsb.de
Vol. 2: 151

Fresenius Medical Care AG & Co. KGaA
www.fmc-ag.com
Vol. 2: 175

Froli
Kunststoffwerk GmbH & Co. KG
www.froli.com
Vol. 2: 171

G

Gachon University
www.gachon.ac.kr
Vol. 2: 341

Gaggenau Hausgeräte GmbH
www.gaggenau.com
Vol. 2: 208–209

Die Gestalten Verlag GmbH & Co. KG
www.gestalten.com
Vol. 2: 177
Vol. 1: 34–35, 330–331, 396–397

Glyptotheque HAZU
www.gliptoteka.mdc.hr
Vol. 2: 37

gmp Architekten
von Gerkan, Marg und Partner
www.gmp-architekten.com
Vol. 2: 44

Thomas Granjard Design
www.t-granjard.com
Vol. 2: 129

Gruner + Jahr AG & Co. KG
www.geo.de
Vol. 2: 282–283
Vol. 1: 112

H

Hansei University
www.hansei.ac.kr
Vol. 2: 338

Hanyang University
www.hanyang.ac.kr
Vol. 2: 322–323

Harvard Medical School
www.hms.harvard.edu
Vol. 2: 272–273

hillus Engineering KG
www.hillus.de
Vol. 2: 134

HOAS
Foundation for Student Housing in the Helsinki Region
www.hoaslab.fi
Vol. 2: 382–383

hoch5 next GmbH & Co. KG
www.hoch5-next.com
Vol. 2: 266–267

HOERBIGER Holding AG
www.hoerbiger.com
Vol. 2: 148–149

HOFFMANN UND CAMPE
Corporate Publishing
www.hocacp.de
Vol. 2: 160, 268

hw.design GmbH
www.hwdesign.de
Vol. 2: 174
Vol. 1: 342

Hyundai Department Store Co., Ltd.
www.ehyundai.com
Vol. 2: 55
Vol. 1: 110

Hyundai Motor Company
www.hyundai.com
Vol. 2: 50–51

Hyundai Motor Group
www.hyundai.com
Vol. 2: 48–49, 92–93, 114–115

I

IN.D Institute of Design Düsseldorf
www.ingd-dus.de
Vol. 2: 332–333, 347, 381

Innocean Worldwide
www.innocean.com
Vol. 2: 50–51

Intel
www.intel.com
Vol. 2: 214

IWC Schaffhausen
www.iwc.com
Vol. 2: 218–219

J

Janoschka Holding GmbH
www.janoschka.com
Vol. 2: 32

K

Kerkhoff Cost Engineering GmbH
www.kerkhoff-consulting.com
Vol. 2: 101

KfW Stiftung
www.kfw-stiftung.de
Vol. 2: 168

Kia Motors Corporation
www.kia.com
Vol. 2: 239, 242–243

KircherBurkhardt GmbH
www.kircher-burkhardt.com
Vol. 2: 162

KOKUYO FURNITURE Co., Ltd.
www.kokuyo-furniture.co.jp
Vol. 2: 66–67

Korean Bible University
www.bible.ac.kr
Vol. 2: 338

Kose Corporation
www.kose.co.jp
Vol. 2: 176

Kyobo Life Insurance Co., Ltd.
www.kyobo.co.kr
Vol. 2: 259

L

A. Lange & Söhne
Lange Uhren GmbH
www.alange-soehne.com
Vol. 2: 144–145

Regional Council Of Lapland
www.onlyinlapland.com
Vol. 2: 246

Leeum
Samsung Museum of Art
www.leeum.org
Vol. 2: 228–229

Lenovo (Beijing) Ltd.
www.lenovo.com
Vol. 2: 216

Index

LG Electronics Inc.
www.lg.com
Vol. 2: 212, 213
Vol. 1: 305, 307

Luxottica Retail
www.luxottica.com
Vol. 2: 204

LZF LAMPS
www.lzf-lamps.com
www.lzf-lamps.com/highfidelity
Vol. 2: 290
Vol. 1: 162–163

M
Mahou
www.mahou-sanmiguel.com
Vol. 2: 94–95

Maquet GmbH OR Integration
www.maquet.com
Vol. 2: 196–197

Massey University
www.massey.ac.nz
Vol. 2: 312–313, 316–317, 320–321, 340

Melitta SystemService
GmbH & Co. KG
www.melittasystemservice.de
Vol. 2: 206–207

Mercedes-Benz Vertrieb
Deutschland
www.mercedes-benz.de
Vol. 2: 232–233

Ming Chuan University
www.mcu.edu.tw
Vol. 2: 386–387

MuKK GmbH
www.mukk.de
Vol. 2: 81

N
National Museum of Modern and Contemporary Art, Korea
www.moca.go.kr
Vol. 2: 45
Vol. 1: 68–69

National Taiwan Normal University
www2.ntnu.edu.tw
www.art.ntnu.edu.tw
Vol. 2: 368
Vol. 1: 410

National Yunlin University of Science and Technology
www.yuntech.edu.tw
Vol. 2: 366–367, 384–385

NHN CORP.
www.nhncorp.com
Vol. 2: 179
Vol. 1: 64, 432–433

Nike Inc.
www.nike.com
Vol. 2: 22–23

Nikon Corporation
www.nikon.com
Vol. 2: 210

not guilty Management GmbH
www.notguilty.ch
Vol. 2: 61

O
Adam Opel AG
www.opel.com
Vol. 2: 234–235

Otto Bock HealthCare GmbH
www.ottobock.com
Vol. 2: 166

P
Pantech
www.pantech.com
Vol. 2: 250

Philharmoniker Hamburg
www.philharmoniker-hamburg.de
Vol. 2: 76–77, 130–131, 252
Vol. 1: 415, 436–437, 443

Dr. Ing. h.c. F. Porsche AG
www.porsche.com
Vol. 2: 24, 158

Porsche Design Gesellschaft mbH
www.porsche-design.com
Vol. 2: 102

Q
Qualcomm
www.qualcomm.com
Vol. 2: 136

R
Raukamp & Raukamp GbR
www.cityshopperapp.com
Vol. 2: 254

Repsol
www.repsol.com
Vol. 2: 88

ronwit
920desu@i.softbank.jp
Vol. 2: 70–71

Russian fitness-aerobics Federation
www.fitness-aerobics.ru
Vol. 2: 124, 125

S
Sampo Group
www.sampo.com
Vol. 2: 103
Vol. 1: 195

Samsung Electronics Co., Ltd.
www.samsung.com
Vol. 2: 251

Samsung Life Insurance
www.samsunglife.com
Vol. 2: 170

Samsung SNS Co., Ltd.
www.samsungsns.com
Vol. 2: 245

Scholz & Volkmer GmbH
www.s-v.de
Vol. 2: 169

School for Design Ravensburg
www.sfg-ravensburg.de
Vol. 2: 326, 371

SeaAra
www.seaara.kr
Vol. 2: 324

SEBRAE-MG
www.sebraemg.com.br
Vol. 2: 82

serien.lighting
www.serien.com
Vol. 2: 163

Shu-Te University
www.stu.edu.tw
Vol. 2: 308–309, 352–353, 362–363, 364–365, 372–373, 374–375, 376–377

Siemens-Electrogeräte GmbH
www.siemens-home.com
Vol. 2: 31

Sino-Finnish Centre
Tongji University
www.sinofinnishcentre.org
Vol. 2: 329

ŠKODA AUTO a.s.
www.skoda-auto.com
Vol. 2: 38

SportCast
Vol. 2: 248–249

Staatliche Museen zu Berlin
Stiftung Preußischer Kulturbesitz
www.smb.museum
www.hv.spk-berlin.de
Vol. 2: 40–41

Staatliches Bauamt München 2
www.stbam2.bayern.de
Vol. 2: 84–85

Stadtwerke Essen AG
www.stadtwerke-essen.de
Vol. 2: 86–87

Star Alliance Services GmbH
www.staralliance.com
Vol. 2: 264

stereolize. GmbH
www.stereolize.com
Vol. 2: 221

Stiftung Unternehmen Wald
www.wald.de
Vol. 2: 178, 186–187

stilhaus AG
www.stilhaus.ch
Vol. 2: 42–43

STILL GmbH
www.still.de
Vol. 2: 236–237

Stockholmsmässan AB
www.formex.se
Vol. 2: 69

Sungkyunkwan University
www.skku.edu
Vol. 2: 334

Sympatex Technologies GmbH
www.sympatex.com
Vol. 2: 29

SYZYGY Deutschland GmbH
www.syzygy.de
Vol. 2: 73

T
Taipei City Government
Department of Cultural Affairs
www.culture.gov.tw
Vol. 2: 106–107

Telstra
www.telstra.com.au
Vol. 2: 192–193

The Clockworks Innovate
www.theclockworks.co.kr
Vol. 2: 271

Index

Tianjin Art Museum
www.tjbwg.com
Vol. 2: 83

Tiroler Landesmuseen
www.tiroler-landesmuseum.at
Vol. 2: 39

Tongji University
www.tongji.edu.cn
Vol. 2: 329, 361

Topstar GmbH
www.wagner-architecture.de
Vol. 2: 150

TÜV Rheinland AG
www.tuv.com
Vol. 2: 100

U

Unfors RaySafe
www.raysafe.com
Vol. 2: 200–201

University of Applied Sciences Augsburg
www.hs-augsburg.de
Vol. 2: 302–303

University of Applied Sciences Bielefeld
www.fh-bielefeld.de
Vol. 2: 335

University of Applied Sciences Düsseldorf
www.fh-duesseldorf.de
Vol. 2: 390–391

University of Applied Sciences Mannheim
www.hs-mannheim.de
Vol. 2: 356–357

University of Applied Sciences Würzburg-Schweinfurt
www.fhws.de
Vol. 2: 327

University of Applied Sciences and Arts Dortmund
www.fh-dortmund.de
Vol. 2: 294–297

University of Luxembourg
www.uni.lu
Vol. 2: 36

update software AG
www.update.com
Vol. 2: 265

urbn; interaction
www.urbn.de
Vol. 2: 270

V

Vallourec & Mannesmann Tubes
www.vmtubes.com
Vol. 2: 99

Viktor&Rolf
www.viktor-rolf.com
Vol. 2: 181

Vodafone Group Services Deutschland
www.vodafone.de
Vol. 2: 217

Volkswagen AG
www.volkswagen.de
Vol. 2: 156–157, 230–231, 238

Volvo Car Corporation
www.volvocars.com
Vol. 2: 202–203

VS Vereinigte Spezialmöbelfabriken GmbH & Co. KG
www.vs-moebel.com
Vol. 2: 167

W

Wagner System GmbH
www.wagner-system.de
Vol. 2: 127

WakuWaku
www.waku-waku.eu
Vol. 2: 60

Weber Maschinenbau GmbH
www.weberweb.com
Vol. 2: 211

Wuhan Art Museum
www.wuhanam.com
Vol. 2: 361

wysiwyg* software design gmbh
www.wysiwyg.de
Vol. 2: 253

Y

Yuan Ze University Department of Information Communication
www.infocom.yzu.edu.tw
Vol. 2: 328

Z

Zander & Partner GmbH
www.zander-partner.de
Vol. 2: 52

Aktiengesellschaft Zoologischer Garten Köln
www.koelnerzoo.de
Vol. 2: 133

Zoologischer Garten Rostock gGmbH
www.zoo-rostock.de
Vol. 2: 46

Zumtobel Lighting GmbH
www.zumtobelgroup.com
www.zumtobel.com
Vol. 2: 104–105

reddot design award

Red Dot Design Award
the qualification platform for the best in design and business worldwide

The Red Dot Design Award is one of the largest and most prestigious design competitions in the world today – with more than 15,000 entries from more than 70 nations. Divided into three disciplines, Red Dot Award: Product Design, Red Dot Award: Communication Design and Red Dot Award: Design Concept, this annual competition gives designers, agencies and companies from a diverse range of industries the opportunity to have their latest works and products assessed and adjudicated by an independent expert jury. Among innovations emerging worldwide in areas such as furniture, lamps, automobiles, jewellery, fashion and accessories, life science and consumer electronics, as well as corporate and brand identity, packaging, advertising, posters, book publications, event design, games, apps, sound and virtual design, the Red Dot Design Award identifies the most outstanding design achievements of each year. As a qualification platform for state-of-the-art design achievements, it thus not only provides orientation in a market that is becoming increasingly complex, but also creates and advances differentiation: products, works and concepts that are awarded a Red Dot rank among the best in their field. This sought-after quality label for design excellence allows the award-winning works to stand out from the myriad of competitors and thus contributes to a company's or a brand's success in the global market.

Red Dot – World of Design

Proud winners

The history of the competition dates back to 1954, when the Haus Industrieform in Essen, Germany, selected products with exemplary design for an exhibition. The strict assessment criteria adopted at the time laid the foundation for today's consistent guideline of only awarding designs of exceptional achievement. The Red Dot Design Award has thus become one of the most important trend barometers of our time, with a jury whose infallible strength of judgement continues to set standards, as the award winners belong to the top class of international design.

The Red Dot Design Award acquired a high international reputation thanks to its initiator, the design expert and CEO Prof. Dr. Peter Zec. Under his leadership, the competition was given a new name and a new face in 1991 – the basis for a quality seal that can be communicated internationally and for which designers and companies from all around the world have competed ever since.

Red Dot Award: Communication Design

In 1993, the Wettbewerb für Produktdesign (Product Design Competition) was complemented by the Deutscher Preis für Kommunikationsdesign (German Prize for Communication Design). Known since 2001 as the Red Dot Award: Communication Design, it has become one of the major, internationally recognised competitions in the industry today. It comprises all the relevant fields in contemporary communication design, subdivided into 21 categories: Corporate Design & Identity, Brand Design & Identity, Annual Reports, Packaging Design, Print Advertising, Editorial & Corporate Publishing, Magazines & Daily Press, Typography, Illustrations, Posters, Event Design, Information Design & Public Space, Online Communication, Online Advertising, Game Design, Interface Design, TV, Film, Cinema & Animation, Corporate Films, Sound Design & Sound Branding, Mobile & Apps as well as Social Media.

The entries are selected following strict criteria. Only those that meet the high requirements with regards to innovative achievement and quality of design receive an award. The winners are selected by an international jury. The jury is committed to absolute impartiality. With its high competence and judgement it guarantees the competition's extraordinary quality and contributes to its excellent reputation.

Since 2011, the award ceremony of the Red Dot Award: Communication Design has been held in the creative hub of Berlin, amidst the stylish background of the Konzerthaus. On 19 and 20 October 2013, the award-winning design achievements will be presented to the general public as part of the exhibition "Design on Stage", held in the Umspannwerk Alexanderplatz in Berlin. Afterwards, a selection of the best works will be shown in the Museum für Kommunikation in Berlin, before a special exhibition of the awardwinnig works will be on display in the Red Dot Design Museum in Essen.

Red Dot – World of Design

Red Dot Gala in the Konzerthaus Berlin

Red Dot – World of Design

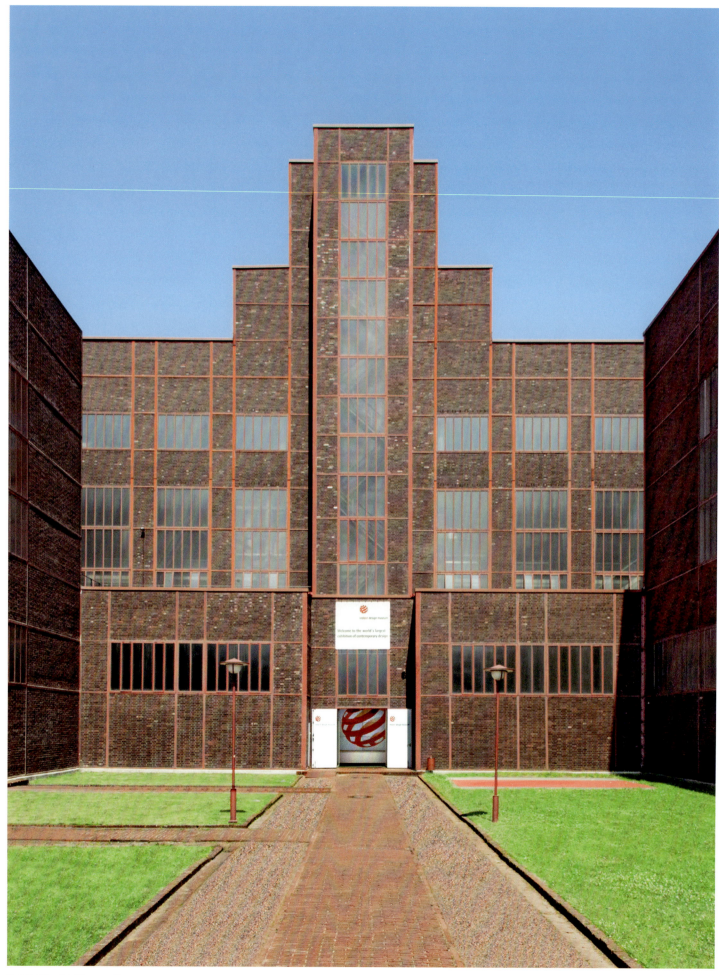

Red Dot Design Museum Essen

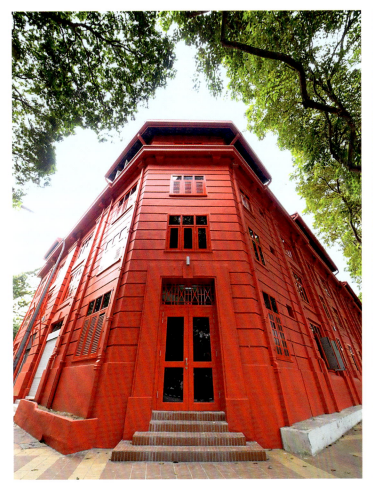

Red Dot Design Museum Singapore

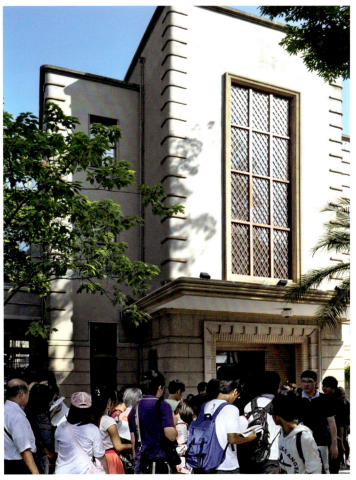

Red Dot Design Museum Taipei

Red Dot Design Museum
a fascinating exhibition forum at three venues worldwide

With its approximately 2,000 exhibits, the Red Dot Design Museum in Essen is considered the largest exhibition of contemporary design worldwide, attracting over 180,000 visitors each year. The products awarded a Red Dot are presented in the former boiler house of the Zeche Zollverein, which was redesigned by Lord Norman Foster into a unique presentation and communication forum. The crowd puller at the UNESCO World Heritage Site offers a wide range of opportunities for presenting the selected design innovations originating from all around the world.

Following the Red Dot Design Museums in Essen and Singapore, a third venue was inaugurated in August this year, the Red Dot Design Museum Taipei. Just like its two predecessors – in particular the Red Dot Design Museum in Singapore, which is the main attraction of Red Dot Traffic, a building painted in bright red that acts as a creative centre and is domiciled in the former police district of the city – the new Red Dot Design Museum Taipei also marks a consistent continuation of the concept of presenting current design developments in a place steeped in tradition. Housed in the Songshan Tobacco Factory, this historically significant industrial building is part of the Songshan Cultural and Creative Park, a historic site of 6.6 hectares located in Taipei's central Xinyi District. Together, these three venues offer a wide range of opportunities, making the activities of the Red Dot Design Award accessible to a wide audience on a global scale and presenting a forum for the best in design and business worldwide.

Red Dot – World of Design

Red Dot Online

Red Dot Services
design portal, global design directory, app, online store and edition

Red Dot 21

www.red-dot.org is a pivotal communication tool of Red Dot and one of the most interesting and most frequently visited industry forums in the world. As well as carrying information about the varied activities of the competitions and the museums, the website presents all Red Dot winners to the general public and features up-to-date news, trends and highlights from the international design scene. www.red-dot.org thus serves as a worldwide research tool and a source of inspiration for both, design experts and specialists as well as design enthusiasts.

Red Dot 21
Red Dot 21 is a new and exciting platform for those who are involved with or interested in design. On www.red-dot-21.com designers, agencies and manufacturers present themselves and their design prowess. This global design directory channels Red Dot's expertise in the fields of product design and communication design, by bringing together both areas. The result is a directory that presents outstanding products and their makers, as well as their accompanying means of communication and the best in communication design in general. Everything is linked together, thus offering a perfect presentation space for those involved in the creation of outstanding design, while giving consumers, journalists and project planers a great tool for research and discovery.

Red Dot App

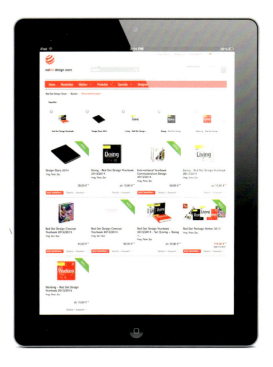

Red Dot Design Store

Red Dot App

The Red Dot App features more than a thousand design and lifestyle products, as well as communication design works and projects, backed up by extensive information on the designers and manufacturers. The app makes it possible to leisurely browse through the high-quality, Red Dot award-winning products and, via the "Next Store" function, find out quickly and easily where to purchase them. Furthermore, all works that have been awarded in the Red Dot Award: Communication Design category are linked to a GPS map so that clients can inform themselves via the "Next Design Office" button if there is a Red Dot award-winning designer in their area and where exactly the closest award-winning design is located. In addition, the Red Dot App helps design enthusiasts stay up-to-date with all kinds of news from the world of design.

Red Dot Design Store

Various products that have won a Red Dot are featured on www.red-dot-store.org. The store allows those interested in design to leisurely browse and directly order their favourite products around the clock without having to contact manufacturers or visit retail shops. The products are categorised in an easy-to-find manner, presenting a quick overview of all design products available and allowing store visitors to find them quickly again and even compare products with each other directly. The menu sections "New items", "Books", "Specials" and "Designers" round off this extensive offer by providing users with interesting and all relevant information on all subjects of design, including background information on the designers.

Red Dot Edition

The yearbooks of the Red Dot Design Award document the latest developments and trends in the industry. For many years now, they have been widely regarded as international reference works for outstanding design. The on-site publishing house, Red Dot Edition, is a specialist publisher dedicated entirely to the topic of design. So far, a total of around 150 titles have been published by Red Dot Edition. In addition to the yearbooks on the competition, the publisher's range includes sociological and economic analyses on the topic of design, compilations of the industry's "who's who" and the annual bestseller, the Design Diary.

Imprint

Editor
Peter Zec

Project and editorial management
Dijana Milentijević

Project assistance
Theresa Falkenberg
Jennifer Bürling
Sophie Angerer
Carrie Lim

Contributing writers
Kirsten Müller (supervision), Essen
Bettina Derksen, Simmern
Bettina Laustroer, Rosenheim
Karin Kirch, Essen
Martin Przegendza
Red Dot: Agency of the Year
Achim Zolke
Red Dot: Client of the Year
Burkhard Jacob

Editorial board
Kristina Alexandra Halilovic
Verena Lissek
Martin Przegendza
Marie-Christine Sassenberg
Achim Zolke
Jörg Zumkley

Proofreading
Klaus Dimmler (supervision), Essen
Mareike Ahlborn, Essen
Jörg Arnke, Essen
Dawn Michelle d'Atri, Kirchhundem
Karin Kirch, Essen
Regina Schier, Essen

Translation
Heike Bors, Tokyo, Japan
Stanislaw Eberlein, Tokyo, Japan
Bill Kings, Wuppertal
Cathleen Poehler, Montreal, Canada
Jan Stachel-Williamson, Christchurch, New Zealand
Philippa Watts, Exeter, Great Britain

Photographs
Michael Dannemann, Düsseldorf
Vol.1, page 6

Mutabor Design GmbH, Hamburg
Vol. 1, page 12

Nora Mittelbach-Schober, Graz, Austria
Vol. 2, page 304, 305

Heinrich Zimmermann, New York, USA,
and Kyung-Ho Peter Sun, Frankfurt am Main
Vol. 2, page 454

Benno Kraehahn, Berlin
Vol. 1, page 485

Peter Nierhoff, Cologne
Vol. 2, page 466–513

João Silveira Ramos, Lisbon, Portugal
Vol. 2, page 490

João Morgado, Lisbon/Porto, Portugal
Vol. 2, page 491

Jan-Paul Kupser, Berlin
Vol. 2, page 525

Kathrin Heller, Berlin
Vol. 2, page 526-527

Design
Gruschka Kramer
Visuelle Kommunikation, Wuppertal
Lena Gruschka, Johannes Kramer

Production and lithography
tarcom GmbH, Gelsenkirchen
Bernd Reinkens (Production Management)
Gregor Baals (DTP, Image Editing)
Jonas Mühlenweg (DTP, Image Editing)

Printing
Dr. Cantz'sche Druckerei Medien GmbH,
Ostfildern

Bookbindery
CPI Moravia Books s.r.o.
Pohořelice, Czech Republic

Multimedia Special (DVD)
Gruschka Kramer
Visuelle Kommunikation, Wuppertal
Lena Gruschka, Johannes Kramer, Hans Nölle

Publisher + worldwide distribution
Red Dot Edition
Gelsenkirchener Straße 181
45309 Essen
Germany
Phone +49 201 81418-22
Fax +49 201 81418-10
E-mail edition@red-dot.de
www.red-dot.org
www.red-dot-store.org

**International Yearbook
Communication Design 2013/2014**
ISBN: 978-3-89939-150-3

© 2013/2014 Red Dot GmbH & Co. KG
Produced and printed in Germany.
Bound in Czech Republic.

Bibliographic information published
by the Deutsche Nationalbibliothek
The Deutsche Nationalbibliothek lists this
publication in the Deutsche Nationalbibliografie; detailed bibliographic data are
available in the Internet at http://dnb.ddb.de

The Red Dot Award: Communication Design is
the continuation of the "German Prize for
Communication Design". The International
Yearbook Communication Design is the
continuation of the "red dot communication
design yearbook".

All rights reserved, especially those
of translation. No liability is accepted for
the completeness of the information.